Excellent argument: the violence has major impact on the people. The violence is not simply caused by Muslim-Christian hostility, but more by power-grabbing, authoritarianism, and economic injustice by those in power. They try to blame it on religious hostility, but it is more caused by political and economic concentration of power, denial of rights of others, and greed for power and money. Therefore the solution needs to be justice, checks and balances, and transparency. I recommend that the proposal that Christian and Muslim people should unite together in pushing for justice and checks and balances and transparency. The concluding chapter says that. It's a major idea and should be highlighted and dramatized for publication.

Professor Glen H. Stassen
Lewis B. Smedes Professor of Christian Ethics
Fuller Theological Seminary, Pasadena, California

Sunday Agang's work focuses on analyzing the impact of violence on the gospel vis-à-vis the role of Christian theology and Christology, particularly the Sermon on the Mount, in Northern Nigeria. He argues that violence is a moral problem that challenges the core of the nature, presence and power of the gospel in any environment. Thus he uses a number of reflections from scholars in the global north, especially Jürgen Moltmann and Walter Wink (and their interpreters) to revisit the politics of Jesus and the theology of nonviolence as articulated by the great practitioners: Leo Tolstoy, M. Gandhi, Dorothy Day, Martin Luther King Jr., and Desmond Tutu. Moltmann's interpretation of Jesus and the reign of God provide him with a pathway for articulating a Christian response to violence while Wink's analysis of power (naming, engaging and unmasking of power in the New Testament) enables him to analyze the ethics of power in Northern Nigeria. His study begs the question how much transformative potential could be embedded in a single privileged discourse. Should we not combine all the discourses as cameos in the quest for a viable solution?

The Late Professor Ogbu Uke Kalu
Former Henry Winters Luce Professor of World Christianity and Missions
McCormick Theological Seminary, Chicago

Sunday Agang has written a book that is not only very well researched, balanced, insightful, and well written, but has produced a work that is rare in doctoral dissertation—it is courageous, humane, and deeply moving. It is broader in scope than most reports on ethnic, political, and religious violence emanating from Nigeria. The basic thesis is that ethnic, political, and religious violence has affected Christian perspective and values and therefore has hampered efforts towards just peacemaking. It urges us to think more deeply about the nature of violence and its extent, which has left Nigeria as a "crippled giant." Far from bringing a new era of peace and prosperity, the end of British rule opened the gates to chaotic violence. This book explores the dynamics of this chaos, and what a genuinely Christian theology and praxis can do for Christians as they seek to ameliorate the situation. It is not only a fine academic study, but also a study that could make a contribution to justice and peace making.

Professor Colin Brown
Senior Professor of Systematic Theology
Fuller Theological Seminary, Pasadena, California

The Impact of Ethnic, Political, and Religious Violence on Northern Nigeria, and a Theological Reflection on Its Healing

Sunday Bobai Agang

Langham

MONOGRAPHS

Copyright © 2011 by Sunday Bobai Agang

Published 2011 by Langham Monographs
an imprint of Langham Creative Projects

Langham Partnership
PO Box 296, Carlisle, Cumbria, CA3 9WZ
www.langham.org

ISBN 978-1-907713-15-6

Langham Monographs

British Library Cataloguing in Publication Data

Agang, Sunday Bobai.
The impact of ethnic, political, and religious violence on
Northern Nigeria, and a theological reflection on its
healing.
1. Violence--Nigeria, Northern. 2. Violence--Religious
aspects--Christianity. 3. Ethnic conflict--Nigeria,
Northern. 4. Ethnic conflict--Religious aspects. 5. Church
and social problems--Nigeria, Northern. 6. Conflict
management--Nigeria, Northern. 7. Conflict management--
Religious aspects--Christianity.
I. Title
261.8'33'096695-dc23

ISBN-13: 9781907713156

Cover & Book Design: projectluz.com

Contents

Acknowledgments

There is no study that has been done by a single individual. Writing is communal not individualistic. I am therefore indebted to many people who have contributed significantly to my success. The evidence of their contribution, support and encouragement is the production of this work.

I am grateful to my late uncle, Elisha Agang, who sent me to school when I was eighteen years old because my parents did not have the resources to send me when I reached school age—six. Enduring thanks to Elder Takai Shamang and his family; they gave me a loan in 1998 to complete the amount I needed for the deposit for a Masters of Divinity degree at Eastern Baptist Theological Seminary. I thank Mrs. Nancy Moffitt and Pastor Valerie Garron for financially contributing to my studies at Fuller Theological Seminary. I am also very grateful to the Christian International Scholarship Foundation (CISF) and John Stott Ministries (JSM) for scholarships that enabled me to complete the doctoral program at The Center for Advanced Theological Studies (CATS), School of Theology, Fuller Theological Seminary without any hindrance.

I deeply appreciate the support of every member of my family. Sarah, my beloved wife, and our children, Nancy, Esther, Kent, and Dorcas, gave me all the extraordinary support and encouragement I needed throughout the seven years of separation from them in pursuit of my Masters (two-and-a-half years) and Ph. D (four-and-a-half years). They are great a gift to me. I thank them for persevering with me in this arduous journey. They have been very gracious and patient with me even when they had to endure the repeated trauma of the United States Consulate in Nigeria denying them visa issuance four consecutive times.

I am grateful to Dr. Richard Gorsuch at the Fuller School of Psychology who helped me in the process of preparing the field questionnaire. I thank Alhaji Balarabe Haruna Esq., who helped me with the administration of the questions in Kano and Jigawa.

I am deeply grateful to my mentors and dissertation committee. Dr. Ronald Sider, who taught me Theological Foundations, became my mentor at Eastern Baptist Theological Seminary and thereafter recommended me to Dr. Glen H. Stassen for my PhD program in Theology and Public Policy within the confines of Christian Ethics and Systematic Theology. I thank Dr. Glen Stassen and Dr. Colin Brown who served as my mentors, primary and minor respectively, at the Center for Advanced Theological Studies, School of Theology Fuller Theological Seminary. Their careful reading of the manuscript and their invaluable recommendation has given this work the clarity and form I had hoped for. Through the encouragement of Dr. Stassen as my mentor, father, friend, and brother, I was able to finish my doctoral work within four-and-a-half years. Again, through his recommendation, Fuller Theological Seminary gave me full scholarship in my first year, Fall 2002 to Spring 2003, and JSM gave me scholarship for three-and-a-half years, Fall 2003 to Spring 2007.

I am extremely grateful to Andrea Hunter, my editor. Her professional editing has given my work the shape that I had envisioned.

I thank all those whom God has used to provide all that I needed, particularly Grace Fellowship Community Church, San Francisco; and Birchwood Presbyterian Church, Bellingham. Grace Fellowship Community Church provided funds for my scholarship as well as for my ministry to widows, orphans, and the needy in Nigeria. In Bellingham, Tim and Karen and their friends also provided the kind of community that I needed to face my difficult journey. I am truly grateful to all my friends in San Francisco, Bellingham, Pasadena, and on the East Coast.

My appreciation would be incomplete if I failed to mention my dear mother, Talatu B. Agang. I am deeply grateful to her for all she did to single-handedly take care of nine children: my eight siblings and me, and how she continues to inspire and bless me with her love and faith.

Finally I thank my Creator, Lord, and Redeemer, Jesus Christ who fulfilled his promise to me: ". . . You are my chosen servant. . . . So do not fear, for I am with you; do not be dismayed; for I am your God. I will strengthen you and help you; I will uphold you with my righteous right hand" (Isaiah 41:9–10).

Abstract

This book seeks to challenge established thinking about the causes of violence in Northern Nigeria and explores immediate and long-term effects of that violence through reflection, study, and survey research.

The first section reflects on how a few unscrupulous elite manipulate ethnicity, religion, and politic to their advantage and thereby create animosity, which often ruins efforts of peacemakers to bring justice to and sew love between warring groups. By exposing the deadly ideas violence feeds on—"good guys" versus "bad guys," "Pax Romana," "manifest destiny," "infidel," and so on—I maintain that violence is neither necessary nor normal.

Some scholars naively tend to focus only on either the political or religious implications of violence in Northern Nigeria. In contrast, I have shown the underpinning link between ethnic, political, and religious violence and how it is related to the distorting influences of Christian-Muslim theologies and ethics. Secondly, research usually focuses on the victims and their grievances and less on the perpetuators of violence. I explore both, and end by asking: "How are victims and perpetrators evading the teachings (ways) of Jesus?"

Section two analyzes the impact of violence on the gospel in Northern Nigeria vis-à-vis Christian theology and Christology, particularly the Sermon on the Mount. I argue that violence is a moral problem that challenges the core of the nature, presence, and power of the gospel in any environment. Jürgen Moltmann's interpretation of Jesus and the reign of God provides me with a pathway for articulating a Christian response to violence, while Walter Wink's analysis of power (naming, engaging, and

xiv

The Impact of Ethnic, Political, and Religious Violence on
Northern Nigeria, and a Theological Reflection on Its Healing

unmasking of power in the New Testament) enables me to dissect the ethics of power in Northern Nigeria.

Finally, I look at the politics of Jesus and the theology of nonviolence as articulated by the great practitioners: Leo Tolstoy, M. Gandhi, Dorothy Day, Martin Luther King Jr., and Desmond Tutu. Thus, begging the questions: How much transformative potential could be embedded in a single privileged discourse with only one of them? Should we not combine all the discourses as cameos in the quest for a viable solution?

The Final Conclusion

Violence is continually implemented and encouraged by a brood of corrupt elite who stand in the place of their colonial masters and exploit the poor and frustrated youth for their individual interests. In the past, our elite struggled for the interest of one Northern region. But now violence has created crippling ethnic, political, and religious divides.

The elite acquired resources that they utilize to perpetuate their hold on economic power and political control to the detriment of their rivals and the poor masses. They neglect the causes of the orphans, the widows, and the poor and the rights of the marginalized. Thus the region is bent over and cannot straighten up at all.

But is there any hope? Yes! In such a situation, the components which are urgently needed are economic justice and honesty and legal and institutional restraint on greed. These measures if instituted and practiced will undoubtedly produce fruits that bring praises to God whom both Christians and non-Christians claim to worship. Violence has kept us bound for too long. The task for a just or egalitarian Northern Nigeria is the task of every Nigerian living in Northern Nigeria.

I bring an important element that is always absent when students of Northern Nigeria's situation are discussing the phenomenon of violence: theology. I believe that the solution of the problem of violence in Nigeria is to have a deep emphasis on justice, which is well grounded in the character of God. I therefore propose and stress the significance of having biblical perspectives and values.

Violence heightens fear in the life of its victims and perpetuators. In the Movie *The Amazing Grace,* Mrs. Wilberforce told her husband that people who fear lack compassion; and that they can only regain compassion when they cease to be afraid. Similarly, I recognize that in Northern Nigeria the poor masses, the elite, and the rich are afraid. The elite and the rich are afraid of losing economic and political power, therefore they often tend to lack compassion. Ethnic, political, and religious violence, youth unemployment, the HIV/AIDS pandemic, and a host of other diseases that are claiming the lives of people in the Northern region have all created a situation wherein even the poor masses are afraid. As such, they too have lost compassion, resulting in witchcraft accusation and the resultant killing of innocent victims. Therefore the rich, the elite, and the poor can only rediscover compassion when they stop being afraid.

Thus, I argue that new affections for God, for justice, for checks and balances, for accountability, and for a free press and an independent judiciary are the key to new morals and lasting political and economic reformation as well as social and theological transformation. Biblical perspective and values will undoubtedly make the justice in our society fashionable. Biblical perspectives and values give rise to genuine "affection" for spiritual maturity; this breaks the power of pride and greed and fear and leads to transformed morals which in turn leads to the political welfare of the nation.

It is vitally important to raise the profile of investigative journalism in Northern Nigeria. In other words, the media needs to provide the public with timely and accurate information on the affairs of government, business, and special interests. An honorable media with journalistic integrity will shape the climate of democratic debate and help in the establishment and maintenance of good governance.

I also recognize that "No true Christian politicians can endure in battling injustice unless his/her heart is aflame with new spiritual affections, or passions." In other words, as Wilberforce once said, "Mere knowledge is

xvi

The Impact of Ethnic, Political, and Religious Violence on
Northern Nigeria, and a Theological Reflection on Its Healing

confessedly too weak. The affections alone remain to supply the deficiency."[1]
This is the key to public and political morality. "If . . . a principle of true
Religion [the Spirit-given new affections] should . . . gain ground, there is
no estimating the effects on public morals, and the consequent influence
on our political welfare."[2]

Political reflection will enable our politicians and elite to make a
"journey from self-centeredness, achievement-centeredness, and political-
centeredness to God-centeredness. It is only this God-centeredness that
will become the driving force of our legislators perseverance not only to
pass laws that would bring benefits to society, but also that will eradicate
the activities of society (corruption) that are offensive to God."[3]

Finally, given that the Muslim and non-Muslim poor in Northern
Nigeria are the most impacted by violence, they need each other. The
Christians should make every effort to work with the poor Muslims in
the North who are also suffering the same oppression, exploitation, and
domination by their elite and the rich. This realization has helped my ministry, GAWON Foundation, to model a new approach to the question of
poverty and its resultant consequences: violence. The GAWON Foundation
focuses on reversing the social, economic, and spiritual conditions of the
people of Northern Nigeria by creating communities of sound economic
and spiritual vision—a community where both Christians and Muslim
can live together as brothers and sisters; a community where religious
freedom and economic justice are guaranteed. GAWON Foundation is a
non-governmental organization that is based in Southern Kaduna, Nigeria.
One of the objectives of GAWON Foundation is building bridges between
Muslims and Christians. Thus GAWON Foundation seeks to eradicate
poverty and illiteracy among Christian and Muslim widows, orphans, and
the less privileged people in Northern Nigeria.

Because of violence the Northern region is polarized. GAWON
Foundation realizes that in order to heal and mend broken relationships

---

1. William Wilberforce, *A Practical View of Christianity*, ed., Kevin Charles Belmonte
(Peabody, Mass., Hendrickson Publishers, 1996), 51.
2. Wilberforce, *A Practical View of Christianity*, 211.
3. Wilberforce, *A Practical View of Christianity*, 16, 17.

and the fragmentation of our society, we need to move out of our comfort zones to meet and embrace the different other. Thus the Foundation gives revolving loans to the widows in groups that tend to metamorphose into a community. This grouping is based on the economic and business interests of each member. The members of each group comprise Muslim and Christian widows and orphans. In such an arrangement, the Muslim and the Christian widows work together. Consequently, they are not only economically empowered but also spirituality invigorated. The Christian widows learn to forgive their Muslim counterparts through working with them and getting to see them not only as victims of the same structure of injustice but also as human beings created in the image of a good and compassionate God.

Introduction

Ethnic, religious, and political violence have radically contributed to the changing face of our culture, religion, and politics. These challenges have impacted the realms that are arguably Nigeria's most important and powerful realms: religion, politics, and ethnicity. The shape and form of the impact have largely remained understudied. This is why people seem not to see the impact of violence on the general lifestyle of the Nigerian peoples.

In my several years of studying this matter, I have since discovered the triadic connection of ethnic, social, political, and religious violence on the Nigerian people. On December 27, 2005 I was told of an event in one of the Local Government Areas (LGA) of Kaduna State. In a village of Jaba LGA, three people were buried alive in a dried well. They were alleged to be members of a secret cult and thus were responsible for the deaths of their family members. When a woman who was married in the community reported the case to the police the villagers denied having knowledge of such incidence. The woman was thoroughly beaten and her marriage was ended. But she was able to show where the three men were buried alive. The well was dug, and they found the three corpses. The killers were Christians, and the victims were also Christians. But why were they killed without mercy? One of the reasons was that fear of death overwhelmed the villagers, and the only way to ward off the death was to kill the alleged perpetrators. Second, violence, both ethnic and religious, has taught our people how to mercilessly kill. In fighting back at the Muslims, who usually attack non-Muslims, our youths and ex-soldiers have been forced to respond to the violence meted against them. Consequently, today, violence

2

The Impact of Ethnic, Political, and Religious Violence on
Northern Nigeria, and a Theological Reflection on Its Healing

has become part and parcel of our daily morality. We are witnessing an era of dysfunctional-deflective violence in most Christian communities in Nigeria today.

Ethnic, political, and religious violence has affected the way we do theologizing in Nigeria. By and large, Africa has faced many theological and ethical challenges. But some of the challenges are more devastating than others. Two of the challenges that have overshadowed the rest are the crises of moral values and ethical perspectives. These crises are not unrelated to a theological method that was so intense and reactionary in the heydays of African countries' independence in the late 1950s and early 1960s.[1] That theological phenomenon led to the creation of violence. The plain fact is that our theology began with a reaction to Western Imperialism on the one hand and African traditional religion/Islam on the other. This approach to theology did a lot more harm than good. It prevented our theologians from actually doing theological reflection that benefits the continent. It

---

1. Recent reflection on African Christianity often identify a "Christological crisis,"
with various explanations for why African believers struggle to appropriate Jesus Christ
authentically. African Christians allegedly need to perceive and respond to Jesus in ways
that are meaningful and relevant to their own mentality and experience. For example, in
1963 missionary John V. Taylor spoke where Christ is conversing with the soul of Africa.
Elaborating on the significance of Christianity being perceived in Africa as a "white man's
religion," Taylor pinpointed the heart of the problem in a most penetrating way:
> Chris has been presented as answer to the questions a white man would ask, the
> solution to the needs that Western man would feel, the Savior of the world of the
> European world-view, the object of adoration and prayer of historic Christendom.
> But if Christ were to appear as the answer to the questions that Africans are asking,
> what would he look like? If he came into the world of African cosmology to redeem
> Man as Africans understand him, would he be recognizable to the rest of the
> Church Universal? And if Africa offered him the praises and petitions of her total,
> uninhibited humanity, would they be acceptable?"
> More recently Anselme Sanon, citing Ernest Sambou, emphasizes that "in most
> African countries, the prime theological urgency consists in discovering the true face
> of Jesus Christ, that Christians may have the living experience of that face, in depth
> and according to their own genius."
> On the other hand, Christological confidence abounds in the perceptions
> of Jesus Christ "through African eyes," as operative among indigenous believers
> ever since Christianity arrived on the continent. The concept of looking at Jesus
> through African eyes can be seen, quite literally, in the iconography of the Coptic
> Orthodox Church in Ethiopia, where the "Ethiopianism" of the figures is established
> through the use of very prominent eyes. In the early twentieth century a non-literate
> South African prophet, Isaiah lamaNazaretha, gained renown as the founder of an
> independent church, the Ibandla lamaNazaretha" (Stinton, 2000, 4).

impaired dialogue with the global community and other faiths. It critiques society without equally critiquing itself. Consequently, "The land is full of bloodshed and the city is full of violence" (Ezek. 7:33). Sadly, the Christian community lacks the antibodies to resist the temptation to overreact to the Muslims onslaught. As a result, the Christian community has been lured into violence towards its own. Like in the days of Prophet Ezekiel, God is wondering, "Must they also fill the land with violence and continually provoke me to anger?" (Ezek. 8:17).

In history, the debate on the best approach to premeditated violence and war has resulted in two historic conclusions—*just war* and *pacifism*. In this book, I have decided to go beyond the two arguments to a third conclusion—*just peacemaking*. This third theory has enabled its practitioners to bring fresh understanding of Jesus' concept of "turning the other cheek." For example, Walter Wink has argued that based on the social and cultural context of Jesus' day the meaning is far from being passivity; rather it is activity. Christians in Nigeria have assumed that what the phrase "turn the other cheek" implies is passivity. This assumption has led to the revolt that is today been witnessed whenever there is a violent attack by the Muslims. It has become obvious that we have no message for the Muslims than fighting back. That conclusion itself is part of the larger impact of the incessant violence in this country. The present work intends to attend to the need to see the open door of ministry in the midst of chaotic relationship between the two missionary faiths: Islam and Christianity.

This book is divided into eight chapters. The first five chapters reflect on how a few unscrupulous elite manipulate ethnicity, religion, and politic to their advantage and thereby create animosity, which often ruins efforts of peacemakers to bring justice to and sew love between warring groups.

The last two chapters analyze the impact of violence on the gospel in Northern Nigeria vis-à-vis Christian theology and Christology, particularly the Sermon on the Mount. I argue that violence is a moral problem that challenges the core of the nature, presence, and power of the gospel in any environment. Jürgen Moltmann's interpretation of Jesus and the reign of God provides me with a pathway for articulating a Christian response to violence, while Walter Wink's analysis of power (naming, engaging, and unmasking of power in the New Testament) enables me to dissect the ethics of power in Northern Nigeria.

Finally, I look at the politics of Jesus and the theology of nonviolence as articulated by the great practitioners: Leo Tolstoy, M. Gandhi, Dorothy Day, Martin Luther King Jr., and Desmond Tutu. Thus, begging the questions: How much transformative potential could be embedded in a single privileged discourse with only one of them? Should we not combine all the discourses as cameos in the quest for a viable solution?

CHAPTER 1

Understanding the Impact of Ethnic, Political, and Religious Violence on Nigeria

Abstract

The primary objective of this chapter is to attempt a review of Nigeria's historical background of ethnic, political, and religious violence. In this first part, I examine the sociohistorical and socioeconomic, as well as the socioreligious and sociopolitical contexts of Northern Nigeria. I link this to the British indirect rule in Northern Nigeria by explicitly and implicitly pointing out that far from bringing a new era of peace, social transformation, economic reform, and moral prosperity, the end of British rule opened the gates to continuing corruption and violence. I also argue that Nigerian elite and leaders cannot completely blame the British for their problems. Thus, chapters 1–4 weigh in on the general socioeconomic, sociopolitical, and socioreligious dynamics of violence in Northern Nigeria. This part seeks to bring to the forefront the impact of violence on moral and ethical perspectives and values since the demise of British rule in Nigeria as well as since the inception of Nigeria's independence.

Introduction

> *As fish are caught in a cruel net,*
> *or birds are taken in a snare,*
> *so men [and women] are trapped by evil times*
> *that fall unexpectedly upon them.*

—Ecclesiastes 9:12

Violence and wars are evil times that fall upon humans. They are not unexpected because they are human-made: however, they do snare and trap their perpetrators and victims. As Glen Stassen observes about the Gulf War, "The war had a major impact on many people's values and perceptions."[1] This statement is not only true of the Gulf War but of any other war or violence that happens anywhere on our planet earth. So in order to understand the misery perpetrated by violence or war, we need to analyze the short- and long-term theological and ethical ramifications of such actions.

For more than four decades, Nigeria—Africa's most populous nation—has been trapped in a spiral cobweb of violence. Christian and Muslim relationships have soured.[2] What used to be seen as ethnic and political violence under the auspices of regional politics, power struggles, and competition has now translated into religious violence. In short, greed for political power welled up in each of the three regions struggling to capture more political clout and control of the economic resources of the country, resulting in the politics of numbers, which seeks to use the highest number of voters by using demagogic divisiveness. As each of the country's three major regions—the North, the Southeast, and the Southwest—have vied to capture more political clout and control of the country's economic resources, the country's two main religious communities—Islam and Christianity—have been drawn into this politics of numbers. Therefore, as Jan Boer points out, "The fear of losing out to Christianity has made Islam even more

---

1. Glen H. Stassen, *Just Peacemaking: Transforming Initiatives* (Louisville, Kentucky: Westminster John Knox Press, 1992), 236.
2. Jan H. Boer, *Nigeria's Decade of Blood, 1980–2002* (Belleville, Ontario, Canada: Essence Publishing, 2003), 35.

nervous, for it stakes its claim on the basis of an alleged continued majority. Increasing nervousness spells greater volatility."[3] Implicitly, the politics of numbers is a time bomb. It is very explosive in nature. Perhaps, this is one of the reasons why Christians in the Middle-Belt of Nigeria have been the target of Islamic onslaught, resulting in violent attacks and counterattacks.

The impact of these attacks and counterattacks in Northern Nigeria has remained largely unexamined. I recognize that there have been studies conducted on the sociological, ideological, political, religious, and cultural levels, but the theological and ethical questions that violence raises in Northern Nigeria still remain largely unexplored.

Undoubtedly, people are aware that ethnic, political, and religious violence has had negative impacts on Nigerians. However, their analyses of the issues involved tend to be one-sided. Dr. Toyin Falola notes, "The institutionalization of religious violence and the aggressive competition for dominance by Islam and Christianity continue to have a negative impact on the Nigeria[n] nation."[4] That means, according to Falola, the bulk of the problem of violence in Nigeria arises from religious conflict. If that is the assumption, I argue that it ignores the fact that violence is a multifaceted issue. Perhaps this is why like many other authors on the subject, Falola did not delineate how that negative impact also impedes Christians' grasp of the way (or the teaching) of Jesus in the region. Rather he concentrated his analysis on the causes of the crisis and the secular ideologies that propel the crisis. Generally, most authors are concerned about the sociohistorical and sociopolitical development of the issues of violence in Nigeria.

In summary, because theologians and ethicists in Nigeria have paid little or no attention to the ethical impact of violence on society, many crucial questions have remained largely unanswered. In particular questions such as the following:

(1) In view of the ethnic, political, and religious violence, which have infested our society since independence, what shape is Christian ethics taking in Northern Nigeria?

---

3. Boer, *Nigeria's Decade of Blood*, 35.
4. Toyin Falola, *Violence in Nigeria: The Crisis of Religious Politics and Secular Ideologies* (Rochester: University of Rochester Press, 1998), 1.

(2) What attitudes and opinions have Nigerians generally formed about violence and how do such attitudes influence our Christian ethics and morality? In what way have other global events contributed to what is going on in Nigeria?

(3) Is there any underpinning connection between ethnic, political, and religious violence?

(4) In essence, given this context of ethnic, political, and religious violence, in what way do Nigerian Christians perceive the way of Jesus?

The above questions to be explored in this research will help me to argue, with precision, how violence issues are profoundly ethnic, political, and religious. They will allow me to show that violence, like war, deeply affects people's worldview. War, which is a conventional violence, causes people to lose perspectives and values, especially, those perspectives and values that are transcultural. Love, justice, and compassion are transcultural (social) values: they are experienced in both Muslim and Christian communities.

Finally, ignoring the analysis of the moral and ethical impact of violence can obscure the larger, explicit, and implicit meanings of Africa's ethical, political, and social dilemmas. Therefore, my primary task is to carefully examine the thesis that religious, ethnic, and political violence impacts people's moral and ethical values and perspectives. In this vein, I attempt to paint a picture of a form of Christian morality and ethics that explores the following question: How does the way of Jesus speak to the present-day violence occurring in Northern Nigeria? Is it a form of ethics that encourages the creation of a nonviolent community amongst those of Christian and Islamic faiths? Does it preach and teach inclusive (or exclusive) ethics, where society is given a roadmap to a participatory, pluralist, and democratic community?

Violence is one of the issues of critical concern to the African church in the twenty-first century. Violent destruction is a double destruction because it impacts people's moral perspectives and ethical values, and thereby influences the type of resulting community (exclusive or inclusive) in which each individual lives. This premise suggests the question: "How do the ethical teachings of Jesus' Sermon on the Mount speak to the transformation needed in order for there to be a peaceful environment in which both Muslims and Christians can co-exist in Northern Nigeria and the country at large?" Margot Kässmann observed, "We live in a world where the image of violence permeates all sectors of life."[5] Thus if we do not pay attention to the way ethnic, political, and religious violence work against God's kingdom ethics in Nigeria, it will hinder the articulation of the larger context of Nigeria's social, political, and religious traditions. Hence the goal of this research is to cause Nigerians to start thinking deeply about violence itself. What is it? How does it affect our thinking? Where does it come from? What does it turn us into? I pertinently believe that examining violence within a Northern Nigerian context will allow my readers grasp the full story of the impact of religious, ethnic, and political violence on its victims, behind-the-scene manipulators, and perpetrators. In particular, it will encourage the Church and society to work toward a nonviolent country.[6]

1.1 The Social Context of Violence in Nigeria

The causes of violence are always very complex. Students of the phenomenon of violence in Nigeria theorize that political violence started in the country immediately after the country's independence in 1960. Perhaps that does not imply that prior to that development there were no incidences of violence in Nigeria. Rather historical events in Nigeria demonstrate that ethnic—and perhaps religious—violence has occurred ever since the inception of Nigeria as a nation state. However, the political violence that ensued after independence, more than anything, shattered the hope of a free society shared by our democratic founding fathers. This situation is well illustrated by Dele Sobowale's article in one of the national newspapers *Sunday Vanguard*, February 19, 1995. Sobowale stated:

---

5. Margot Kässmann, *Overcoming Violence: The Challenge to the Churches in All Places* (Geneva: WCC Publications, 1998), vii, viii.
6. Reinhold Niebuhr, *The World Crisis and American Responsibility*, ed. by Erwest W. Leferer (New York: Association Press, 1958), 37.

10

The Impact of Ethnic, Political, and Religious Violence on
Northern Nigeria, and a Theological Reflection on Its Healing

For some reasons perhaps deeply rooted in patriotism (however
misplaced), hope or faith in the black man's ability to rule
himself, youthful exuberance and a great deal of ignorance,
Macaulay, Zik, Imoudu, Awolowo, Sarduna, Enahoro, etc.,
went to town demanding that the British must go. Nigerians
sang for joy. We should have wept in self-pity.[7]

In part, Sobowale seems to suggest that Nigeria's democratic founding
fathers made a blunder by assuming that Nigerians were mature enough
to take care of their own administrative and political affairs. That is to say,
they miscalculated the signs of the time. If that is the inner logic of his
argument, I would contend that the problem was far from miscalculation.
Rather, Macaulay, Zik, Awolowo, Imoudu, Sarduna, Enahoro, among others, were visionary and optimistic people who meant well for the country.
However, the regional struggle of Yoruba, Igbo, and Hausa-Fulani ethnic
groups for political domination and vying for the control of more land
and taxpayers largely caused Nigeria's political stagnation. In retrospect, the
history of Nigeria's wars or violence has been the history of various shifts
between ethnic, political, and religious violence.

The historical situation of the violence Northern Nigerians are facing is
a testament to the truth that we live in the midst of a world where every
sphere of life is permeated with violence.[8] Nigerian and expatriate authors
alike have written much on the subject of violence in Nigeria. Several
influential studies have attempted to trace the causes of the violence. In his
seminal work, *Violence in Nigeria,* Falola points out how Nigeria has been
ensnared by religious violence and secular ideologies ever since independence. Consequently, as Falola reminds us, "Militancy is expressed not only
in physical violence but also in strong words."[9]

---

7. Jan H. Boer, *Nigeria's Decade of Blood, 1980–2002* (Belleville, Ontario, Canada: Essence
Publishing, 2003), 1.
8. Kässmann, *Overcoming Violence*, vii.
9. Falola, *Violence in Nigeria*, 17.

Falola's analysis demonstrates that there are ideologies that control the two major religious communities—Islam and Christianity—in Nigeria. Falola contends,

> Politicized versions of Islam and Christianity are expressions of the increasingly militant character of religion in Nigeria and elsewhere. While they [Christianity and Islam] may not be similar, they do have several features in common: they adopt the rhetoric and language of liberation from an oppressive state, they envision a new kind of society, and they seek to base values in interpersonal relationships on religious principles. Religion thus fulfills a role of political opposition where the performance of secular authorities has been shoddy and disappointing.[10]

To recapitulate, Falola's argument shows that religion—whether Islam or Christianity—tends to become militant in nature in Nigeria. But why is that the case? Boer identifies two factors that are critical to Nigeria's religious situation: corruption and the relationship between Christianity and Islam. Boer observes, "Both religions have to affect changes in attitude toward each other."[11] However, Boer is not categorically clear as to whether or not these two problems have any link to the impact of ethnic, religious, and political violence. His focus is on corruption and the relationships of the two religious bodies. He does not link the corruption and relationship issues he examined to the theological impact of violence in Northern Nigeria.

All in all, it seems it is not enough to reduce the problem to corruption and relationship without pointing us to the larger picture of the whole social and political drama of Nigeria. If we look at the triadic structure of Nigeria, we will be convinced that the problem as a whole outweighs the two problems of corruption and the relationship between Islam and Christianity. The Northern, Southwestern, and Southeastern regions of the country have engaged in the politics of exclusion. This phenomenon has

---

10. Falola, *Violence in Nigeria*, 14.
11. Boer, *Nigeria's Decades of Violence*, 14–15.

ruined and delayed Nigeria's sociopolitical and socioeconomic development. Eghosa E. Osaghae and a host of other students of Nigeria's violence
have suggested that part of the problem is the legacy of the colonial masters.
Osaghae's work shows how Nigeria got wedged in with the legacy of the
colonial masters. He states,

> In the absence of strong indigenous capital, the state assumed
> the role of entrepreneur and "control" of commanding heights
> of the economy at independence. This placed it in a position to
> alter radically the inherited structure of the Nigerian economy
> as was done in some other newly independent African
> states (Tanzania for example). But rather than establishing a
> productive base, the federal government continued with the
> extractive policies of the colonial regime and the externalization
> of the economy.[12]

In simpler terms, Nigeria had every opportunity to achieve greatness in
the world economy but let that opportunity slip from its fingertips. This
was largely due to regional and intra-regional rivalry and competition—the
three geographical regions became arenas of the politics of exclusion. That
is to say, the leaders of these three regions sacrificed national interests for
the sake of narrow regional interests. A.B. Akinyemi and his associates illustrate this by citing M. Okpara's profound statement, which was reported
in *Nigeria Outlook*:[13]

> We hold the view that the two worst threats to Nigerian unity
> are (1) the practice of regionalism . . . . and (2) the fact that
> the most important principle of federation (namely, that there
> should not be any one state so much greater than the rest
> combined that it can bend the will of the federal government),

---

12. Eghosa E. Osaghae, *Nigeria Since Independence: Crippled Giant* (Indiana: Indiana
University Press, 1998), 48.
13. M. Okpara, *Nigeria Outlook*, Enugu 14 October 1965, 5.

has broken. Until these two threats are removed, they labor in vain who labor for Nigerian unity and solidarity.[14]

Post-independence regional interests created deep socioeconomic and sociopolitical crises in Nigeria, resulting in economic stagnations as well as political conflicts. These political conflicts left the country in a bad economic state in that Nigeria became what Osaghae called a "crippled giant." What each region sought was the ability to bend the federal government to dance to its tune. Therefore I contend that this was beyond the relationship between Islam and Christianity contrary to what some authors would have us believe.[15]

Nigeria missed its opportunity to be Africa's economic and political giant because it failed to recognize, as Peter Storey points out, "the giants of history are those who have put high principles not only in words but also in action."[16] Although Storey is not specific as to what constitutes "high principles," I believe that righteousness, justice, and the fear of the Lord are high principles that sustain and maintain any government. It is these principles that prompt and inspire the rich, the elite, and the representative of the masses to make decisions on behalf of their needy citizens with righteousness, justice, and love. No doubt, righteousness, justice, and love are the realistic alternatives to violence in Northern Nigeria. It is only when the elite strictly observe these high moral values that "the poorest of the poor will find pastures, and the needy will lie down in safety."[17]

The lack of these high principles has both short-term and long-term consequences best illustrated in the work of Karl Maier. Maier asserts,

> Ethnic and political violence continued to spiral beyond anyone's control. As many as 10,000 people have been killed in ethnic, political, and religious violence since Obasanjo took

---

14. A. B. Akinyemi P.D. Cole and Walter Ofonagoro, eds., *Readings in Federalism* (Lagos: Nigerian Institute of International Affairs, 1979), 193.
15. Boer, *Nigeria's Decade of Violence*, 35.
16. Peter Storey, *With God in the Crucible: Preaching Costly Discipleship* (Nashville: Abingdon Press, 2002), 31.
17. Isaiah 14:30.

14

The Impact of Ethnic, Political, and Religious Violence on
Northern Nigeria, and a Theological Reflection on Its Healing

office [on May 29, 1999], by far the worst death toll since the civil war. Nigeria is drifting again, with the state taking on the look of that elephant staggering toward the abyss.[18]

Some Nigerians have also expressed their disappointment with the situation. U.J. Thomas-Ogboji laments, "Nigeria, the comatose giant of Africa, may go down in history as the biggest country ever to go directly from colonial subjugation to complete collapse, without an intervening period of successful self-rule. So much promise, so much waste; such a disappointment, and such a shame makes (sic) you sick."[19]

1.2 An Analysis of the Causes of Violence

The whole world knows that violence has invaded humanity. Africa knows what it means to live under the snare of violence. I argue that political, ethnic, and religious violence have overflowed all Africa's channels like floodwaters, have run over all its banks and swept on into "the giant of Africa,"—Nigeria—swirling over it, passing through it and reaching up to the neck. Violence's outspread wing now covers the breadth and length of the Nigerian nation. Consequently, Nigeria and perhaps the rest of Africa devise strategies, but they are thwarted; government officials propose a plan, but it does not stand.

Paul Gifford has done a superb analysis of the situation that I have just described above. Gifford points out three major shifts in perception in Africa. First, he tells us what transpired in the heyday of Africa's countries' independence in the 1960s. The reigning theory then was modernization. It was presumed that "Third World countries would swiftly be transformed into participative, pluralist, and democratic regimes. [The belief was that] the state and the ruling elite would be the primary agents of political and economic development and the principal bearers of modernization."[20]

---

18. Karl Maier, *This House has Fallen: Nigeria in Crisis* (London: Penguin, 2002), 296.
19. *African News Weekly*, 26 May, 1995, 6, cited by George B. N. Ayittey in *Africa in Chaos* (New York: St. Martin's Griffin, 1998, 1999), 5.
20. Paul Gifford, *African Christianity: Its Public Role* (Indianapolis: Indiana University Press, 1998), 2.

However, political forces at work both within and outside of Africa shattered this hope before it could come to fruition. Therefore by the 1970s it was obvious that this theory was "a bad idea" because it was not working; that is. Africans ran out of patience and discarded the theory.

The next option after the modernization effort failed was the *dependency* theory. Gifford states,

> Modernization theory was superseded (at least on the left) by dependency theory, already well established in Latin America in the 1950s. The *dependencistas* [italics mine] reversed many of the assumptions of modernization theory: they saw metropolitan influence as pernicious, not beneficent; foreign investment as masking even greater financial outflow; modernizing elite as essentially parasitic, servicing their own and foreign interests, not that of their people; and world trade as perpetuating structures of underdevelopment, not removing them. Dependency theory was even more evanescent than modernization theory.[21]

Dependence on the West was tantamount to continuous colonization. Africa did not want to be colonized a second time. As such the idea of dependency theory was abandoned. But why was the theory *really* abandoned? First, because Africans suddenly realized that the West and North America were not about to let Africa have an economic breakthrough since they were benefiting from the African countries' economic situation. Second, African countries could not develop if they continued to rely on the economic crumbs coming from the West and North America. In short, the real issue was that Euro-American countries were primarily concerned about their own economic interests and less about Africa's interests. In hindsight, this was during the Cold War between the West and the East. Japan and other Asian countries were already presenting political, military, and economic challenges to the West and North America. Japan, particularly, was already

---

21. Gifford, *African Christianity*, 2.

The Impact of Ethnic, Political, and Religious Violence on
Northern Nigeria, and a Theological Reflection on Its Healing

16

becoming an economic threat to the United States. The inner logic therefore was that if Africa remained underdeveloped, African countries would not present an economic threat to the Euro-American countries.[22]

Finally, Gifford tells of how by the 1980s there was a third move—away from modernization and dependency to the theory of "the new realism." This theory held that at independence power had been given to the wrong people, or "the bad guys." The proponents of this theory (the "new realists") argued that Africa's corrupt elite and their self-serving policies bore overwhelming responsibility for the disaster in Africa. It appears the new realists were equally sure about the required remedy—"structural adjustment" became the predominant theory in the mid-1990s. I must point out, however, that this view was spearheaded and promoted by international financial institutions—primarily the World Bank and the International Monetary Fund (IMF)—and American policy-oriented academics.[23] Hence, today, countries in Africa that benefited from these international "messiahs" (IMF and World Bank) know very well that their "projects" in Africa did not achieve the desired positive result. IMF and World Bank loans have catapulted Nigeria and a host of other African countries into debt.[24]

The Jubilee 2000 made an eight-point argument that drives home the fact that the whole exercise was dubious and deceitful. In fact, it is an understatement to say that it was dubious and deceitful. The report

---

22. They saw dependency theory as a continued legacy of colonialism. The historic causes of third world debt as introduced in a working chapter from the development organization, the *Southern Center*, summarizes how the developing countries' debt is partly the result of the unjust transfer to them of the debts of the colonizing States: "The history of third world debt is the history of a massive siphoning-off by international finances of the resources of the most deprived peoples. This process is designed to perpetuate itself thanks to a diabolical mechanism whereby debt replicates itself on an ever greater scale, a cycle that can be broken only by canceling the debt" (http://www.globalissues.org/ TradeRelated/Debt/Causes.asp), 2.
23. Gifford, *African Christianity*, 2.
24. Majority world countries believe that the West and North America are not genuinely interested in their economic interests. Rather Euro-American countries are often interested in their personal economic interest, resulting in majority world's debt becoming a major obstacle to human development. "Many other problems have arisen because of the enormous debt that third world countries owe to rich countries. Debt has impeded sustainable human development, security and political or economic stability" (http://www. globalissues.org/TradeRelated/Debt/Causes.asp), 1.

shows that "a lot of the borrowed money went to western-backed dictators, resulting in little benefit for most people." It demonstrates that the poverty line has skyrocketed. Therefore, Africa—and indeed most of the world—struggles to manage the limited economic resources that are often left after debt servicing is made year in and year out. Youth unemployment, hunger, frustration, and hopelessness are the order of the day; these elicit a chain reaction that trickle down to ethnic, political, and religious violence in Nigeria. Michael Barratt Brown aptly states, "The argument goes that poverty leads to violence and IMF and World Bank cuts in government spending led to poverty."[25]

Yes, "the poor have suffered the most as a result of the harsh conditions of structural adjustment."[26] The International Monetary Fund and World Bank loans were nothing but corruption and exploitation at their highest level. Brown asked a very significant question: "How can you expect poor countries that have soft currencies (values which can fluctuate) to pay back loans in hard currencies?"[27] Brown points out how these countries have been forced "to cut back on important spending such as health education in order to help repay loans. This has created a downward spiral and further poverty."[28]

Poverty facilitates violence in Nigeria. Worst of all, it elicits destructive attacks and counter-attacks, which increasingly leave the country economically and socially devastated. Poverty creates hopelessness, and hopelessness begets violence. As John Ferguson tells us, "[V]iolence tends to provoke counter-violence, as indeed the Black Panthers found; indeed it tends to escalate, as the sorry story of events in Nigeria in the second half of the 1960s may serve to remind us."[29] Roger MacGinty and John Darby also observe, "The continued political violence in some sectors of society as

25. M. B. Brown, *Africa's Choices After Thirty Years of the World Bank* (Westview Press, 1997), 102.
26. Brown, *Africa's Choices After Thirty Years of the World Bank*, 102.
27. Brown, *Africa's Choices After Thirty Years of the World Bank*, 102.
28. Brown, *Africa's Choices After Thirty Years of the World Bank*, 102.
29. J. Ferguson, *Politics of Love* (James Carke & Co., 2000), 106.

The Impact of Ethnic, Political, and Religious Violence on
Northern Nigeria, and a Theological Reflection on Its Healing

18

well as an increase in corruption patterns, are undermining safety, security, governance, and democracy at large."[30]

In summary, my main point is that Nigeria is a country that deserves our attention because of its place in the world. This research is conducted at a critical time in Nigeria's history. For as Bola Ige notes, "The resilience, the wonderfulness, the energy—Nigeria can be compared favorably with the United States of America. I put it crudely sometimes if you know how to package shit; you can sell it in Nigeria. I want this country to be the first black superpower." Bashir Kurfi also puts it thus, "The only difference between South Africa and Nigeria is that here you have a group of blacks who don't make up ten percent of the population but control the economy, while the majority are poor." These two quotes show that there are expectations and realities in Nigeria that facilitate violence. Therefore, there is the need to put a human face to the violence in Nigeria. We need a clear understanding of what violence produces in Northern Nigeria and how that impacts its victims and its perpetrators.

Studying the misery violence produces can enable us to ascertain those who are behind the scenes manipulating the violence in Northern Nigeria with the sole aim of undermining economic, social, and political development.

The point is that political forces ruin efforts of peacemakers to create a situation of justice and love between warring groups. In Northern Nigeria these political forces make the country unprofitable to its citizenry. In other words, Nigerians are put to shame because of a few unscrupulous elite, who bring neither help nor advantage, but only shame and disgrace. Ironically, these classes of elite send money to Swiss banks without asking why Switzerland is a peace-loving country. They fail to remember, as Richard J. Maybury reminds us, "Little Switzerland occupied the most dangerous location in the world—the exact center of Europe—entirely surrounded by enemies, but stayed out of both World Wars and stayed free."[31]

---

30. R. M. Ginty, J. Darby, *Contemporary Peace Making: Conflicts, Violence and Peace Processes* (Palgrave, 2003), 132.
31. Richard J. Maybury, *World War I: The Rest of the Story and How it Affects You Today: 1870 to 1935* (Placerville, CA: Bluestocking Press, 2003), 110.

Isaiah, the prophet, maintains, "The Lord is the source of strength to those who turn back the battle at the gate."[32] Switzerland is a living testimonial to this verse today—it has always been a neutral country in Europe and has never been harmed by any of the superpowers. Isaiah reminds us that God makes "justice the measuring line and righteousness the plumb line" of human relationships.[33] When people do not want to be confronted with the truth nor be transformed by it, what they bring to themselves and to their country or communities is shame and disgrace.[34]

This analysis is intended to contribute to the efforts toward finding a lasting solution to the political instability of the country. In fact, the world beyond Nigeria needs this research because it enables humans to grasp the fact that violence is unnecessary.

The world wants us to believe violence is a way of life. This is illustrated by the wave of violent messages we receive year in and year out. Gerald A. Arbuckle points out the global situation of violence. He asserts,

> Last century humankind witnessed violence to an extent never seen before—an estimated 130 million killed. At the beginning of the new violence, ethnic cleansing, famine, domestic violence, workplace abuse, cyberspace violence, intercultural violence, and accepting violence as normal.[35]

I argue that violence is not necessary or normal by exposing the salient deadly ideas—"good guys versus bad guys", "*Pax Romana*", "manifest destiny", "interests", "love of political power" and so on—that tend to facilitate violence or even civil wars in Nigeria, Africa, and the world at large. I believe that it is only the ethics of Jesus, which emphasizes the fear of the Lord, compassion, love, justice, and righteousness can guarantee a participative, pluralist, and democratic community in Northern Nigeria. Until Nigerians freely and actively participate in a community that pursues

---

32. Isaiah 28:6.
33. Isaiah 28:17.
34. Isaiah 30:5.
35. See G. A. Arbuckle, *Violence, Society and the Church* (Collegeville, Minn.: Liturgical Press, 2004), xii.

The Impact of Ethnic, Political, and Religious Violence on
Northern Nigeria, and a Theological Reflection on Its Healing

20

peace, justice, and righteousness, they will not break free from the cycle of violence.

1.3 An Alternative Approach to the Issue of Violence in Northern Nigeria

"The whole of economics can be reduced to a single sentence. . . . The art of economics consists in looking not merely at the immediate but at the longer effects of any act or policy; it consists in tracing the consequences of that policy not merely for one group but for all groups."[36]

As Henry Hazlitt claims above, I attempt to look not merely at the immediate but also the long-term effects of violence and trace the consequences of violence on the Nigerian people. I paint a picture of violence different than the one currently accepted in Nigeria. Nigerians need to grasp the fact that violence is destructive and devastating—we can begin by examining the underlying assumptions that facilitate the problems of violence in our society. I also emphasize the hidden structural violence that is rooted in systemic imbalance of power that affords greater access to power and resources for some groups at the neglect and/or expense of others.

Ethnic, political, and religious violence are intrinsically connected and therefore the impact is deeper than we tend to think. Since this is an interdisciplinary study two things are important to point out:

(1) I have observed that when looking at violence scholars often tend to focus only on either the political or religious implication. I think such dichotomy is not necessary because violence encompasses ethnic, political, and religious issues. Therefore, I show the underpinning link between the ethnic, political, and religious violence and end product of distorted Christian/Muslim ethics in Northern Nigeria.

(2) The research carried out on violence in Nigeria usually focuses on the victims rather than the perpetrators of violence. My research looks at both groups. Who are the victims and what are their grievances or prejudices? Who are the perpetrators and what are their prejudices and grievances? How are victims and perpetrators evading the ways of Jesus? I

---

36. Henry Hazlitt, *Economics in one Lesson* (New York: Crown Publishing Group, 1979), 17.

make use of the wisdom and insights of biblical and theological ethicists, critical social theorists, and theorists of validating Christian ethics. This study employs and makes use of field and library research sources.

Finally, my task is not just to trace the connecting dots of the events that lead to violence but also to analyze how violence shapes its victims' moral and ethical perspectives and values.

CHAPTER 2

Rethinking Ethnic, Political, and Religious Violence on Nigeria

Abstract

The primary aim of this chapter is to attempt an analysis of the conceptual perspective and dimension of ethnic, political, and religious in Nigeria. In other words, the primary objective of this chapter is to attempt to clarify the concept of violence by way of definition. I propose a definition of the concept of violence as it relates to ethnic, political, and religious violence in Nigeria. This helps me avoid the mistakes of some earlier works, which have tended to be one-dimensional and narrow.

1. Toward an Analysis of the Concept of Violence

Violence is variously defined. It often results in loss—loss of life, property, hope, dignity, access to basic human services (such as education and medical care), peace, justice, and loss of moral perspective. Often a perpetrator—in the case of Nigeria, the political/religious/economic elite—uses violent force on the citizenry or certain ethnic or religious groups among the citizenry. A dialectic of violence ensues: Violence perpetrated, violence responded to and reflected back, violence infused and suffusing the belief, action, culture, and national identity. Violence is not just measured by external actions and results—collateral damage—that which is visibly destructive, but also by the absence of those things which are individually and societally nurturing and "good."

1.1 Defining Violence

Some vocabularies have become so embedded in the English language that we often do not care to define them. We assume that they are very clear to everyone. But in most cases this is an unsubstantiated assumption. In an epoch when violence has become part of everyday life, such an assumption can be extremely dangerous. For this reason I must define what I mean by the term *violence*. The task is a daunting one; the term *violence*, according to Gerald A. Arbuckle, does not have a clear-cut definition. This is because violence is an idea that means different things to different societies and groups. Nevertheless, Arbuckle believes that violence refers to the act of "force or violation. Violence means every action or lack of action of persons or cultures (including customs, institutions, structures) that are insensitive to and oppressive to human persons who have been created according to the divine image and likeness."[1] In this sense the definition of violence covers a whole spectrum of issues such as "physical, emotional, verbal, theological, cognitive, sexual, visual, institutional, structural, economic, political, social, and ecological."[2]

Arbuckle's definition implies that violence involves acts and behaviors that are detrimental to humans' and creation's flourishing. Arbuckle further points out that violence is not all the time wrong or "negative." He argues,

> "Violence is not about damaging or destroying things. It is about abusing people. The tragedy is that it lowers their self-esteem, self-confidence; they experience it as sense of powerlessness and subjugation. Violence crushes the spirit of people and makes them submissive to violators for their purpose."[3]

---

1. Arbuckle, *Violence, Society, and the Church*, xii.
2. Arbuckle, *Violence, Society, and the Church*, xii.
3. Richard Horsley, *Jesus and the Spiral of Violence: Popular Jewish Resistance in Roman*

Arbuckle makes two shifts in perspective in this argument. First, he establishes that violence is not about killing. Second, he shifts from defining violence to explaining the effect of violence. Later I will argue that violence includes killing. For now I shall turn to other definitions of violence.

Richard Horsley contends, "The question of violence does not begin with the individual agent. For violence is often structured into the social-historical situation in which the individual lives."[4] Horsley demonstrates that violence has a vicious cycle that can only be broken by the recovery of the love of God the Father, which Jesus represented. Following the analysis of Dom Helder Camara, Horsley notes three stages of violence.

The first stage is injustice or structural violence. Horsley points out that in many contemporary neocolonial situations the ruling groups of the subject society cooperate with First World governments, banks, or giant international corporations in fostering and benefiting from exploitation of their countries and people. These neocolonial alliances maintain in power the political regimes—often military rule—and economic structures that further their own interests. Such "internal colonialism" thus creates a situation of structural violence for the indigenous people.

The second stage, the reaction against injustice or structural violence, is protest and resistance. Horsley maintains that in the past resistance typical of traditional peasantries was to avoid as much as possible any dealings with their rulers and exploiters. This was a form of nonviolent resistance.[5]

The third stage involves the established holders of power. They use force to subject the ruled to their illegal and unjust treatment. Horsley writes, "What I am realizing is that traditional organized religion can be used to advantage in repression. The victims of injustice can be continually reminded that any misfortune is due to their own sinfulness."[6] Horsley's conception is largely about popular structural violence. In this case, violence is fundamentally a reaction against the powers that be. In his words, it is "typical reaction to injustice or structural violence."[7] However, what seems

---

Palestine (Minneapolis: Fortress Press, 1993), ix.

4. Horsley, *Jesus and the Spiral of Violence*, ix.

5. Horsley, *Jesus and the Spiral of Violence*, 25.

6. Horsley, *Jesus and the Spiral of Violence*, 25.

7. Horsley, *Jesus and the Spiral of Violence*, 25.

26

The Impact of Ethnic, Political, and Religious Violence on
Northern Nigeria, and a Theological Reflection on Its Healing

to be lacking in Horsley's conception of violence are situations in which different religious groups are either at each others' throats or the group that claims to be in the majority is inclined to persecute the one in the minority. Perhaps such situations are indirect reactions to the powers that be. But it is possible that the powers that be manipulate religious rhetoric to achieve their goal of holding onto their hegemony against their subjects' will.

In scripture we have examples of revolts against injustice and structural violence. To borrow Horsley's analysis, the Bible is not only full of examples of all kinds of revolt but ironically reveals the fact that those who have suffered injustice tend to become violent against each other. That is to say, even when they have been delivered from the injustice they have suffered they are not mercifully disposed toward their fellow men and women. For instance, in Exodus we see the Hebrews under severe hard labor. But gradually the individuals (Moses), groups (The Hebrew midwives) and the subject people revolt against the powers that be (Ex. 5:9; 7–11).[8]

Ironically, the individuals who have suffered injustice become impatient with their fellow men and women (Ex. 2:13). Solomon's internal security system was already repressive enough. That was why, as Horsley tell us, after his death the Israelite elders protested their "heavy yoke" and "hard service" to Solomon's son and supposed successor. Rather than listening to their expressed concern, Rehoboam and his young and youthfully exuberant advisers responded with plans to intensify the repression (1 Kings 12:1–14), resulting in the division of Israel into Northern and Southern Kingdoms. Nevertheless, even in the newly independent kingdom of (Northern) Israel the spiral of violence repeated itself.[9] This phenomenon is interesting because it shows the vicious cycle of violence: people are continually slaves to different masters. They get their colonial masters off their backs only for their own cousins to take the place of their oppressive imperial regimes.

Others have undertaken the task of explaining what the term *violence* means. R.E.O. White's article "Violence" points out that "violence is a symptom of what is happening in society." The basis of his conclusion comes from Genesis 6:11, which states that "the earth was corrupt in God's

8. Horsley, *Jesus and the Spiral of Violence*, 26–7.
9. Horsley, *Jesus and the Spiral of Violence*, 27.

sight, and filled with violence."[10] This is a significant insight because it buttresses the fact that violence is the smoke not the fire itself.

The Bible is rife with violence. In Genesis text the fire that triggered violence in the world was corruption. In the same vein, Ezekiel 7:23 gives corruption as the underlying reason for violence; more specifically Ezekiel 45:9 demonstrates that princes [politicians] who are corrupt are often involved in committing acts of violence to the poor in society. For instance corrupt men and women violently seek to get ahead of their fellow brothers and sisters in society. Sometimes it can even happen within a family. Absalom sought to be ahead of his father David. Absalom stole the heart of the people of Israel who went to his father David with their complaints. He promised them that he would give them better justice if only they will elect him as their representative.[11]

Micah, the Prophet, also categorically points out that those who are corrupt become wealthy through the use of violent means. In other words, they become rich by violently taking what belongs to others. "The rich seize houses by violence and fields of the impoverished 'because it is in their power,'" thereby becoming "full of violence" [obsessed with violence] (Mic. 2:2; 6:12).

Amos unravels the core of the problem also. He says great houses are stored with treasures taken by violence (Amos 3:10). According to White, "Eccl. 5:8 expresses the realistic view of the candid observer of society: 'if you see in a province [region] the poor oppressed and justice and right violently taken away do not be amazed. . . . The high official is watched by a higher official.'"[12] This shows that a network of corrupt officials who destroy their economy and plunge their people into unnecessary socioeconomic, political, and religious crises causes violence.

These crises result in perpetual unemployment, frustration, desperation, and destitution in the midst of God's natural plenty. White maintains that violence is often coupled with plunder and deception, resulting in two

---

10. Walter A. Elwell, *Evangelical Dictionary of Theology* (Grand Rapids: Baker Books House, 1984), 1142.
11. 2 Samuel 15:1–6.
12. Elwell, *Evangelical Dictionary of Theology*, 1142.

The Impact of Ethnic, Political, and Religious Violence on
Northern Nigeria, and a Theological Reflection on Its Healing

28

types of stealing: material and spiritual. He notes that in Habakkuk 2:8 this thought is significantly extended not only to warning those guilty of shedding the blood of their fellow men and women, but also those who are doing "violence to the earth, to cities, and all who dwell therein."[13] But have these definitions really exhausted the possible definitions of violence? Whether or not they have not is not the problem. What is important is to try to analyze the misery violence brings to its victims and how that tends to have a distorting influence on their perceptions, perspectives and values. In his article, "Violence," Yusufu Turaki gives a biblical definition and delineation of *violence*. Turaki defines the term as:

> [The calculated] use of force to injure or wrong a person or a group of persons. A person or a group of persons to inflict uses force: a wrong; an injury; an injustice; an act of cruelty; or an unrighteous act. A person who exercises such force can be variously termed as: violent; violator; oppressor; insulter; striker; maltreater; despiteful; injurious; fighter; quarrelsome; persecutor.[14]

Although many definitions of violence exist, in this study I am using the term to refer to an outburst of anger against something someone values; therefore he or she protects it from being devalued or demeaned. I am aware that not every kind of anger leads to violent destruction.

I believe that anger must reach a certain degree before it becomes dangerous: *burning anger*. This kind of anger is seen in humans as well as in God. But it is only God who can control anger, which reaches a burning level.

In Exodus God is recorded as saying, "I have seen these people and they are a stiff-necked people. Now leave me alone so that my anger may burn

---

13. Elwell, *Evangelical Dictionary of Theology*, 1142.

14. In an email attachment sent to me on Nov. 25, 2006, Yusufu Turaki further explains that "The practices of *tribalism, colonialism, sexism, religious bigotry* have historically inflicted untold *violence, wrongs, oppression, and sufferings* upon the humans. *Violence/wrong* is perpetrated against individuals or a group, which is inherently *evil, immoral* and *unethical*. . . . It is wrong to inflict *violence* upon an innocent human being. It is an act of injustice to the well-being of a human being."

against them and that I may destroy them" (Ex. 32:9–10). In the same chapter Moses is also recorded as getting to this level of anger when he saw the golden calf that Aaron had fashioned for the people in his absence. Moses' anger burned and he could not help but destroy the calf in the fire. Of course anger in itself is not a bad thing. It is what we do with it that makes it dangerous. Mark 3 says Jesus got angry, and surely that is true when he turns over the tables and chases the moneychangers out of the temple; Jesus does not command we not get angry but focuses on what we do with it.

The abusive use of anger has never ceased to bring destruction. In September 2005 a Danish Newspaper published a series of 12 cartoons (later republished in German, French, and Norwegian newspapers), which Muslims claimed caricatured Prophet Muhammad. The cartoon demeaned their holy prophet, whom they valued dearly. Consequently, the Muslims strongly reacted to the newspaper because Islam forbids depictions of the Prophet. An Associated Press writer, Zeima Karam, writes,

> Thousands of Muslims rampaged Sunday in Beirut, setting fire to the Danish Embassy, burning Danish flags and lobbing stones at a Maronite Catholic Church as violent protests over caricatures of the Prophet Muhammad spread from neighboring Syria. . . . Protesters also took to the streets by the thousands elsewhere in the Muslim world, a day after demonstrations in Syria charged security barriers outside the Danish and Norwegian embassies in Damascus and sent the buildings up in flames.[15]

This was a candid example of an outburst of anger that burned its perceived enemy. It would be one thing if some Muslims got angry, another if they then resorted to violence. The plain truth is that the Muslims did not just get angry. Rather, they resorted to violence as well. On February 3, 2006, a *Wall Street Journal* reporter writes,

---

15. *The Associated Press*, Feb. 5, 2006, 1.

Muslim outrage over a series of cartoons originally published in a
Danish newspaper, including one image depicting the prophet
Muhammad with a turban shaped like a bomb, continued to
escalate yesterday. Palestinian gunmen threatened foreigners
in Gaza. Pakistan protesters chanted "Death to France" after
French newspapers joined others around Europe in reprinting
the cartoons. Boycotts of Danish goods have persisted.[16]

These newspapers were exercising their right to freedom of speech, to the
detriment of Islamic values. As such it elicited a violent reaction from both
extremists and moderate Muslims. Anger reached a burning degree that
resulted in the burning of flags and embassies and threatening foreigners'
lives in the Muslim world. In Nigeria it led to the torching of 41 churches
and the murders of over 158 people, particularly in the Northern city of
Maiduguri and the Southeastern city of Enugu. This situation reveals one
thing: violence is a complex concept.

In summary, violence can best be defined by its characteristics, forms,
defenders, God's feelings, and impact. I was blown away by the fact that
many Bible dictionary entries I have consulted do not include the word
violence. They do define *war*. I suppose we can use the definition of war in
the place of violence because war in itself is another form of violence. Of
course, not all violence involves war; but every war is an example of violence.

The idea of war as *holy* can translate to violence. Yet the users of this
concept today often fail to grasp the fact that the concept of a *holy war* is
a double-edged sword. This is best illustrated in the Old Testament. J.W.
Wevers writes, "The concept of the Holy War, declared, led, and won by
Yahweh himself, governs Old Testament military thinking."[17] Wevers shows
how this concept originated "in Israel and reached its greatest influence
during the period of the judges." It meant God's declared intent. However,
as Israel continued to corrupt their faith, "the concept was overshadowed

---

16. *Wall Street Journal*, Feb. 3, 2006, A6.
17. J. W. Wevers "War, Method of" In Buttrick George Arthur, edit., *The Interpreter's Dictionary of the Bible*, Vol. 4, (New York: Abingdon Press, 1962), 796–7.

in the monarchy by considerations of political expediency."[18] As such, the prophets, while supporting the holy war ideology, thought of war primarily as the judgment of God against rebellious Israel or against the haughty Gentile nations. That is, the holy war idea is not only for God's people to use against others but also to remind them that the sword can turn against them when their moral life runs counter to the concept they claim to support.[19]

Those who specialize in manipulating the situation or funding the actual war or violence always have monetary value attached to it. They tend to see the violence or war as a means for financial gain. Wevers' article makes this underpinning connection very clear. According to Wevers, "The regular words for 'war' in the Bible are Heb. *hâmâs* and Greek, *polemos*," both literally mean "strengthen"; by extension it also means "wealth," either economic or military, therefore "army" (cf. the English word "force"). Wevers' article shows that wars (violence) are fought for political and economic reasons. But religious rhetoric is usually employed as a pretext to obscure these ulterior motives. This might partly explain why Jesus, while willing to cite the Old Testament—particularly the wisdom of the Prophets—did not quote passages that reference war. This does not suggest, however, that Jesus was not aware or interested in the political and economic violence of his day. Rather, it means that his teaching was strongly directed toward peace and peacemaking. He believed, as G.H.C. McGregor noted, "The Kingdom of God needs no force to establish or maintain it." Hence, "the peacemaker is blessed (Matt. 5:9), and the enemy is to be met with love and good deeds instead of hate and violence (Matt. 5:43–44; Luke 6:27, 35)." That is to say, "the ethic of Jesus is the antithesis of the warlike mood, and if universally accepted, would create an ethos in which war was impossible."[20]

Glen Stassen and David Gushee (*Kingdom Ethics*, 2003) and a host of other just-peacemaking ethicists remind us that the ways of Jesus demonstrate that God is about a community of Christ's disciples who enter

---

18. Wevers, *The Interpreter's Dictionary*, 797.
19. Wevers, *The Interpreter's Dictionary*, 797.
20. G.H.C. Mcgregor, *The New Testament Basis of Pacifism* (New York: Abingdon, 1953), 801.

into God's business of delivering people from violence into a community that creates hope not only for the present generation but also for future generations. In short, violence is identified with economic power: money and power. In order to grasp this sense one needs to understand some of the salient dimensions of violence.

1.2 The Dimensions of Violence

Violence consists of various dimensions. Scholars have identified several of these obvious dimensions of violence. Nelson-Pallmeyer approaches the subject of violence from the vantage point of *the spiral of violence*. In response to those who thought that liberation theology was dangerous and therefore saw it as a threat, liberation theologians largely articulated this perspective of violence: the spiral of violence. Among them, Horsley pointed out three dimensions of the spiral of violence.

TABLE 1
THE SPIRAL OF VIOLENCE
(Distilled from Liberation Theology)

Dimension 1 ⊃ leads to	Dimension 2 ⊃ leads to	Dimension 3 ⊃ leads to
Denying humans created in God's image access to food, education, medicine and basic necessities. Dehumanizing them and treating them as objects and not people.	A nonviolent or violent outcry against "Dimension 1." Protest, demonstration, unionization. The lack of subjective influence results in a violence born out of desperation.	The lethal violence of military forces aligned with the state and with foreign or domestic economic elites, and the terror and torture practices of paramilitary groups and death squads associated with them.

(1) Violence is characterized by oppression, hunger, and poverty. For example,

Children who die of hunger or who are stunted by malnutrition are victims of violence. So too are people whose ill health, illiteracy, and death are linked to economic inequalities or concentrated land-ownership, whatever directly or indirectly prevent them from receiving medical care, attending school, or receiving adequate nourishment. This expansive definition links violence to social injustice and moves beyond traditional meanings that focus too narrowly on guns and warfare.[21]

(2) The second dimension of violence is characterized by rebellion. People living in poverty or misery or in the midst of other oppressive situations sometimes strike out violently against those they hold responsible for their misery. This type of violence is a response to and predictable outcome of the first type of violence enumerated. People who protest against the first form of violence may do so nonviolently. They may demonstrate, petition, unionize, strike, vote, and boycott. Peaceful protests, however, are often met with repressive violence—the third form of violence listed below. The apparent absence of redress through nonviolent means can lead to rebellion that is often the result of desperation and not design. It is considered an option of last resort.[22]

(3) The third dimension of violence by elite forces' repressive use of power against those who protest or rebel. This includes the lethal violence of military forces aligned with the state and with foreign or domestic economic elite, and the terror and torture practices of paramilitary groups and death squads associated with them."[23]

From his treatment of liberation theology, Nelson-Pallmeyer further points out five critical shifts in understanding the meaning of violence. He focuses on "oppression (violence 1), and rebellion (2), and repression (3)," then adds "the categories of dysfunctional deflective violence (4) and spiritual violence/violent use against others that doesn't challenge unjust

---

21. Jack Nelson-Pallmeyer, *Is Religion Killing Us?: Violence in the Bible and the Quran* (Harrisburg: Trinity Press International, 2003), 21.
22. Nelson-Pallmeyer, *Is Religion Killing Us?*, 21–22.
23. Nelson-Pallmeyer, *Is Religion Killing Us?*, 22.

34

The Impact of Ethnic, Political, and Religious Violence on
Northern Nigeria, and a Theological Reflection on Its Healing

systems (5)."[24] The fourth dimension (dysfunctional deflective violence) that
he adds is very helpful because it provides a way of critiquing the witchcraft
accusation that is going on in Christian communities of Northern Nigeria.
I argue that the murdering of innocent children and adults in the name
of a secret cult or society is the clearest example of dysfunctional deflective violence.

2. Summary

Human beings characterize violence potential to be brutal, aggressive,
furious, and injurious. That is, the violence this chapter is discussing is
referring to what I term an illegal exercise of physical force with the intent
of harming or destroying human life or property. I am attempting to trace
three sources where this kind of violence resides—religion, ethnicity, and
politics. I am carefully arguing that religious violence is an upshot of religious corruption and arrogance. Religious arrogance impinges on people's
ability to repent and forgive each other reciprocally and mutually. Violence
in its ethnic form is personified as land and chieftaincy disputes between
so-called settler and host communities in Northern Nigeria. Violence in
its political form leads to social manipulation, political intimidation, and
obsession with the love of money and wild living. Political violence leads to
irrational use of economic, social, and political power and control.

Violence is a finished product of human distortion of facts and figures
to cover up the sin of injustice. This cover-up or deception is what Walter
Wink calls the "myth of redemptive violence" in Western society. By this,
Wink implies that it is taken for granted that violence is in the interest of
society. Hence it is necessary for a society's continued existence. According
to Arbuckle, violence is redemptive in the sense that it is believed to restore
"society to a state of peace and justice. Television, cartoons, comic strips all
reinforce this belief."[25] Those whom violence enables to maintain the status
quo—the rich and the powerful—tend to present violence as something

---

24. Nelson-Pallmeyer, *Is Religion Killing Us?*, 23.
25. Arbuckle, *Violence, Power and the Church*, 18.

that solves conflicts; they tend to argue that even the threat alone of violence is able to stop aggressors—the more power one has the more effective the threat.[26]

No wonder violence is stripping Northern Nigeria of its social, political, and economic potential. This is partly because the violence in Northern Nigeria is especially driven by economic power, which institutionalizes corruption. Corruption mixed with ethnic, political, and religious arrogance leads to lack of spiritual and moral roots. Christian and Muslim politicians alike squander public wealth in wild living without public repentance or accountability. They prefer luxury to the detriment of serving the interests of the poor. They are so obsessed with the idea of wild living that they steal money to make beds of iron, thirteen feet long and six feet wide.[27] Ethnic groups kill weaker groups without repentance. Religious people justify killing those they claim do not belong and are thus out of favor with God.

These activities feed on political, religious, and ethnic arrogance and corruption. So I attempt to develop a hermeneutics of repentance that takes Jesus' teaching in the Sermon on the Mount seriously. I realize that human beings can only celebrate each other's existence when there is genuine repentance and forgiveness. Continuing in arrogance and lack of public accountability, the rich continue to squander our wealth in wild living and poverty catches up with us (Luke 15:11–24). Our ethnic groups and religious communities ought to realize that as long as their locus of control is arrogance, they are dead and lost until they repent of their wickedness against each other (Luke 15:32).

3. Conclusion

Violence deeply impacts society; it breeds insecurity, never arriving at truth, justice, or equilibrium, but always reproducing endless

---

26. Walter Wink, *Engaging the Powers: Discernment and Resistance in a World of Domination* (Philadelphia: Fortress, 1992), 13, as cited by Arbuckle, *Violence, Power and the Church*, 17.
27. Numbers 3:11.

counterviolence. Those who manipulate situations for their lethal interests largely cause violence.

Additionally, violence affects people personally and socially and leads them to raise many unresolved questions about life, morality, and faith. Violence in Nigeria fundamentally takes three dimensions: ethnic, political, and religious. This interaction is subtle. Hence it is usually hard to recognize and trace the comprehensive nature of interconnections when doing analysis of any violent phenomenon.

Therefore a key step to ridding our society of violence is to name the injustice that breeds violence. Stassen and Gushee rightly point out, in Matthew 5:39 "Jesus named the vicious cycle as violent or revengeful retaliation. Such revengeful retaliation leads to more killing."[28] The sad story of the Northern region of Nigeria buttresses this truth, as I shall further show in the pages that follow.

---

28. Stassen and Gushee, *Kingdom Ethics*, 198.

CHAPTER 3

Understanding the Triadic Connections of Ethnic, Religious, and Political Violence in Northern Nigeria

The primary concern of this chapter is an examination of the triadic connection of ethnic, political, and religious violence in Nigeria. The chapter argues that violence is a complex system, structure and institution, which feeds on multifaceted categories like ethnicity, politic, and religion. These dimensions that give nuances to violence are mutually connected and therefore the impact is deeper than we tend to realize.

That is why I believe that we cannot understand the encompassing gravity of the negative impact of violence unless we are willing to trace its linkages. Thus by virtue of the fact that I am looking at the impact of religious, ethnic, and political violence, I am arguing that Nigeria's violence is not limited to ethno-religious dimensions as most studies have shown. I also recognize that I have to understand the triadic nature of violence—ethnics, political, religious—in Nigeria so as to have the capability to assess its impacts (positive or negative) on our society:

(1) Ethnically, Nigeria is a nation of many ethnic groups with over 250 ethnic groups on record. Some studies even postulate that Nigeria has more than 500 ethnic groups. Some of these ethnic groups could stand as independent nations. The social dynamic of these ethnic groups is very interesting. The significance of grasping their social dynamic cannot be overstressed.

(2) Politically, Nigeria is a nation which is divided between three major ethnic groups: Yoruba, Igbo, and Hausa/Fulani.

(3) Religiously, Nigeria encompasses three major religions: African Indigenous Religion (here after call AIR), Christianity, and Islam. Each of these three religions has its perspectives and values that are in most cases at variance with the rest. But now Islam and Christianity have eclipsed AIR, while subtly influencing them both. Nigeria is very religious. As such the issue of religion cannot be taken lightly.

Violence embeds every fabric of life, which includes religion. Today, more than ever, the world is religiously conscious. The trouble with Nigeria, however, is that ethnicity and politics are ingrained in the religious stance. So whatever impacts one, impacts the rest even more profoundly.

The contemporary wave of violence that has engulfed Northern Nigeria and the nation at large has led to the question of (1) whether religion in its own right is the source of violence, or (2) whether the mixture of religion and politics is the reason for violence.

Nigerians have no monopoly over this concern. It is a concern that has become a global question; since 9/11 this question has occupied our global psyche. Charles Kimball asked it in the United States, "Is religion the problem?" In Nigeria Matthew Hassan Kukah and Iheanyi Enwerem and a host of other students of trends in Nigeria are asking this same question. I shall attempt to push the question further by asking, if religion causes violence in the world, whose religion causes violence? Is it only Christianity and Islam, or are other religious communities largely involved? If we had a choice of a society in which to live, which one would we prefer, a society without religion or one with religion? The point is that the sort of questions scholars ask about the phenomenon of violence in Nigeria often overshadow the triadic connection of ethnic, political, and religious violence as well as hinder these investigators' ability to grasp the depth of the impact of violence in our society.

The issue at stake is a combination of power and control. But it is not just any power. It is economic power and political monopoly. Men and women will always find ways to fight for economic power and political control, even without religion. By the term "power" I mean the capacity of an individual or a group to influence others either negatively or positively. By the word "control" I mean authoritarian control: the capacity of an individual or group to shape and dominate others against their God-intended potential. Hence we are constantly dealing with issues of power and control.[1] People who are obsessed with the desire for economic power and political monopoly can use different variables to reach this goal. In Nigeria these variables include, but are not limited to, ethnicity, politics, and religion.

Thus I argue that the corruption of religion, ethnicity, and politics is not only the problem. But the problem also includes the commercialization of religion. Put simply, the pursuit of money and power are the reasons for our moral, socioeconomic, and socioreligious ills in Nigeria. Some religious leaders see their leadership as a means to financial profit; some politicians see politics not only as a means to financial gain but also as a means to political and economic domination of resources that keep them secured.

This understanding provides me with a way of engaging in the debate of whether religion is the cause of violence. Hence, I begin with what I think are the issues at stake: economic power and political monopoly.

1. The Issues at Stake

The struggle for individual and regional economic power and political control of the country has inhibited the development of the country and the Northern region in particular. Nigeria gained independence from the British on October 1, 1960. It was not long after that when the country plunged itself into ethnic-cum regional rivalries, culminating in two of the regions, Northern and Southwestern, pitting themselves against the Southeastern region. Consequently, the country was engulfed by a civil

---

1. Power and control are not necessarily bad. But their negative use to inhibit human progress is what is lethal. One of the sources of violence is the struggle for economic and political control. The situation is characterized by intimidation, recrimination, and corruption. Therefore, decreasing violence in Nigeria will necessitate checks and balances against domination by concentrated power, and an ethic of power sharing and compromise over against an ethic of authoritarian control.

The Impact of Ethnic, Political, and Religious Violence on
Northern Nigeria, and a Theological Reflection on Its Healing

40

war, which lingered from 1966 to 1970.[2] The civil war was spurred by ethnic, political, and religious agendas. At the time the religious motif was concealed. But, as Jesus teaches us, "There is nothing concealed that will not be disclosed, or hidden that will not be known" (Luke 12:2).

Over the last two decades Nigerians have witnessed a paradigm shift in the issue at stake from regionalism and ethnicity to religion and politics. The matter of religious and political violence has preoccupied Nigeria's major news headlines as well as some prominent international media institutions. Books and articles and newspaper headlines include titles like, *A Dangerous Awakening: The Politicization of Religion in Nigeria; The Politicization Religion in Modern Nigeria: The Emergence and Politics of The Christian Association of Nigeria (CAN); Religion, Politics and Power in Northern Nigeria;* and *Nigeria's Decades of Blood.* A website maintained by Ontario Consultants on Religious Tolerance has this title: "Religious Motivated Killings in Nigeria—FEB 2000." The same website has an article titled, "Religious-Based Civil Unrest and Warfare." What has attracted such attention is connected to the series of bloody confrontations between the two major religious groups—Muslims and Christians. These violent confrontations have had a deep impact on much of the population living in the Northern region and the country at large. The violent phenomenon has led to the bloody murder of innocent victims and the destruction of businesses and properties worth millions of U.S. dollars, or billions of Naira (the Nigerian monetary currency).

These disturbing situations of violence are symptoms of systemic injustice in Northern Nigeria. As Karl Maier has correctly pointed out in a citation credited to Shehu Usman Dan Fodio: "A kingdom can endure with unbelief, but it cannot endure with injustice."[3] The situation reveals that the struggle for economic power and political monopoly has given rise to economic, political, and social injustice, resulting in desperation and uncertainty. Maier captured the sense of desperation that the situation of religious violence has generated in Nigeria. In his work, Maier seeks to identify the desperation and the sources of resilience. He realizes that the

---

2. Karl Maier, *This House has Fallen* (Colorado: Westview Press, 2000), xx.
3. Maier, *This House is Fallen*, 142.

problem of violence hinges on many factors. Among them is "the addition of ethnicity and power politics to the religious frenzy."[4] In other words, it is the combination of religion with other factors that has led to the lethal nature of religion. These factors include, but are not limited to, politics and economics.

Thus the bottom line of the issues at stake is money and power, which generally corrupt people's perspectives and values. However, religion has often been used as a scapegoat. The elite tend to hide under the cloak of religion, not only to camouflage their struggle for economic power and political control, but also to garner support from the poor innocent masses. It is against this background that they corrupt religion for their economic and political interests.

The situation is similar to Kimball's discussion of why religion often becomes evil. Kimball identifies causes of the lethal nature of religion. He tries to answer the question, "Is religion itself a problem?" his answer is "No . . . and yes." Kimball says "No" because, "[W]ithin the religious traditions that have stood the test of time, one finds the life-affirming faith that has sustained and provided meaning for millions over the centuries."[5] He says "Yes" because "At the same time, we can identify the corrupt influences that lead toward evil and violence in all religious traditions."[6]

Kimball is specifically referring to the corruption of religion. In that case, Kimball shares my concern with political, religious, and economic corruption. These three phases of corruption are the major sources of violence. Basically, Kimball argues that when people find themselves in a situation wherein somebody is doing their thinking for them, their religion will likely become extremely dangerous.[7] Kimball links this corruption to authoritarianism. In other words, the kind of corruption that Kimball is identifying is authoritarianism. In that case, it applies directly to the problem in Nigeria. This is in addition to economic corruption, which is what

---

4. Maier, *This House is Fallen*, 142.
5. Charles Kimball, *When Religion Becomes Evil* (New York: HarperSanFrancisco, 2002), 5.
6. Kimball, *When Religion Becomes Evil*, 5.
7. Kimball, *When Religion Becomes Evil*, 72.

I mean when speaking of corruption in this chapter. According to Kimball two factors are responsible for the lethal nature of religion:

(1) Corruption of religion is the issue at stake, not religion itself.

(2) When people abdicate their responsibility to reflect on their situation, and let other people who they think are wise, understanding and respected do their thinking for them, they are easily misled to dance to the tune of the tradition of men rather than the truth of God.

Although Kimball is talking about authoritarianism and I am focusing on economic corruption, authoritarianism and economic corruption are two sides of the same coin. However, I am gently critical of Kimball for implying that the solution is for us to think for ourselves. While correct, this is individualistic. I think the solution also needs a community, which encourages an enabling environment for checks and balances against concentration of power, a free press, auditing procedures, an independent judicial system, and an economic system that restrains the few from amassing huge wealth of their own. I do not believe just urging people to think for themselves is going to build in checks and balances against the greedy amassing huge economic power. It is therefore crucial to understand one of the key assumptions that are creating a conducive environment for the perpetration of violence in Northern Nigeria.

1.1 An Analysis of the Assumption

The assumption is that religion and politics are two separate spheres. In Nigeria the debate about whether or not religion is the problem has been asked and answered in another way by Matthew Hassan Kukah. The question is whether the mixture of religion and politics is the source of violence in Nigeria. If it is, can religion and politics really be separated? Kukah's argues that religion and politics cannot be separated. He asserts, "[F]or most of human history, politics, and religion have gone hand in hand."[8] His primary concern is to expound an inseparable relationship between religion and politics. His book is a significant contribution to the debate "about the

---

8. Matthew Hassan Kukah, *Religion, Politics and Power in Northern Nigeria* (Ibadan, Owerri, Kaduna and Lagos: Spectrum Books Limited, 1993), vii.

separation of religion from politics."[9] Kukah's conclusion is that religion and politics in the African context and in many ancient and contemporary contexts cannot be separated.[10] This is very helpful because at least Kukah resonates with my argument that two of the three variables of violence are inseparable. Therefore his conclusion should be carried further to the question of whether or not religion is the cause of violence.

Religion, politics, and ethnicity are intrinsically connected by, but not limited to, economic issues. This is why I believe that the question of whether religion is the threat and source of violence in Nigeria is an important one. I would, however, caution that it must be handled with care so that it does not lead to throwing away other crucial variables affecting and triggering violence—such as economic corruption, which results in religious, ethnic, and regional politics.

I therefore attempt to combine Kukah, Maier, and Kimball's insights critically to argue that the causes as well as the impact of violence permeate but are not limited to ethnic, political, and religious spheres, which are part and parcel of the "same concrete human person." For the benefit of hindsight, religion in the current political development of Nigeria has assumed a special role. Iheanyi M. Enwerem captures three issues related to the reality by narrating an incident in the 1978 presidential election in Nigeria. Enwerem relates that in the presidential campaigns of 1978 both Obafemi Awolowo, from the Unity Party of Nigeria (UPN), and Shehu Shagari from the National Party of Nigeria (NPN), were presidential aspirants. The two politicians who were vying for the presidential election launched a campaign in Sokoto State, one of the predominantly Muslim states in Northern Nigeria.

On the one hand, Awolowo was enthusiastically received in Sokoto. "Everywhere he went, he raised his hand with his traditional 'v' (victory) sign to acknowledge the cheers of admirers."[11] Awolowo was deceived by the overwhelming and enthusiastic reception that the crowd gave him.

---

9. Kukah, *Religion, Politics and Power in Northern Nigeria*, vii.
10. Kukah, *Religion, Politics and Power in Northern Nigeria*, vii.
11. Iheanyi Enwerem, *A Dangerous Awakening: The Politicization of Religion in Nigeria* (unpublished dissertation, IFRA-Ibadan, 1995), 1.

The Impact of Ethnic, Political, and Religious Violence on
Northern Nigeria, and a Theological Reflection on Its Healing

44

Thus Awolowo concluded that he was going to win the election not only in Sokoto but also throughout the Northern region as a whole because Sokoto is the Islamic cultural center of the North.

On the other hand, Shehu Shagari, himself a Muslim from Sokoto, did not receive nearly as much enthusiasm as his southwestern counterpart had received. Shagari, however, immediately realized that Awolowo's visit had had impact on the psyche of his people. So determined to undermine whatever impact Owolowo's visit had made, Shagari "adopted a mood of greetings that was intended to reach the core of the people's most treasured experience, their religion. He acknowledged the cheers from his audience by simply raising a single finger."[12] This singular act did the magic it was intended to do because it clearly showed the people that the two men were different. As Enwerem explains, "Awolowo's gesture signified two gods while Shagari's signified unity, destiny, one god, Allah." So they refused to vote for Awolowo and instead voted for Shagari.

From this narrative Enwerem drew the following conclusions as a rein-forcement of his major argument that religion has become the way of life: first, "we see how the religious phenomenon had become a divisive force in political practice and a decisive source of the potential which religion has as a tool for mass appeal and mobilization. [Also], we see how religion was being manipulated by politicians to serve their political interests."[13] These conclusions are accurate. Nonetheless they do, to some extent, obscure the other side of the coin—the ethnic and economic outlook. Awolowo was from the Christian Southwest region of Nigeria. But more than that, he was from the ethnic tribe Yoruba, which is not only one of the major ethnic tribes in the Southwestern region but also has actually been involved in rivalry with the Hausa-Fulani since Nigeria's independence. Shagari, how-ever, was from the Northern region. Above all, he was a son of the Sokoto soil and a Hausa-Fulani Muslim. Blood is thicker than water.

Finally, Shagari was, by virtue of his Islamic tradition, expected to use his political position to promote Islam in the country while Awolowo was a Christian. Thus, all these factors have played into the success of Shagari.

---

12. Enwerem, *A Dangerous Awakening*, 1.
13. Enwerem, *A Dangerous Awakening*, 1–2.

It is not a single sphere—religion—that gave Shagari success. Rather, it is a combination of several factors. One of the factors is that the Yoruba and Hausa-Fulani have been vying for political monopoly of the country since its independence from Britain. They are two of the three major ethnic groups in Nigeria who have been engaged in a localized form of the Cold War. Hence, those old and new grievances and concerns played into the election. Enwerem's inner contention is that the problem with Nigeria is religion. In *Dangerous Awakening: The Politicization of Religion in Nigeria*, 1995, which is his revised dissertation, Enwerem suggested, "while our indigenous religions are accommodationist, Islam and Christianity are exclusivist. This characteristic of Islam and Christianity lies at the center of the competition, struggle and tension between these two faiths in Nigeria."[14]

It must be noted that the above charge does not in any way dismiss the significance of Enwerem's work, which is twofold: first, to elucidate a process of sociopolitical transformation; and, second, to understand the relationship between religion and practices, especially with regard to the emancipatory potential of religion.[15] Nevertheless, in this situation, which Enwerem described, it is very easy to see religion as the reason for violence, as Enwerem's next point demonstrates. He maintains, "No longer do many Nigerians look at issues in the country from the purview of ethnicity as they used to do in the not so distant past. Now, government policies and actions and the motives behind them are largely seen through the lens of religion."[16] Of course, such a charge might not lack historical validity. Yet I will argue:

(1) It is true that religion in Northern Nigeria triggers violence. However, we must not let that myth eclipse other dimensions, which are equally important: political, economic, and ethnic violence.

(2) While I am not disputing the role of religion in conflicts in Northern Nigeria and the nation at large, I want to stress that religion is a double-edged sword: it contributes to the violent situation. Yet it is equally the

---

14. Enwerem, *A Dangerous Awakening*, ix, xi, 2.
15. Enwerem, *A Dangerous Awakening*, 2.
16. Enwerem, *The Politicization of Religion in Modern Nigeria* (York University, North York, Ontario, July 1992), iv.

The Impact of Ethnic, Political, and Religious Violence on
Northern Nigeria, and a Theological Reflection on Its Healing

46

contributing *solution* to violence, as Kimball and Kukah in their works
have indicated. There is therefore the need to hold religion in a dialectical
tension and in a connecting link to the other variables of the phenomenon
of violence in Northern Nigeria.

(3) I do not think it is a wise move to conclude impetuously that violence in Nigeria is primarily caused by religion. Such a move is extremely
dangerous to the moral health of the nation. In fact, it can be disastrous
to other communities in the global village if we think that only one or
two religions are our problem today. Simply put, limiting the phenomenon
of violence that has overwhelmed the Nigerian state in recent decades to
religion alone will conceal the larger context of the impacts of violence. It
will obscure the other dimensions involved in the issue: the socioeconomic,
sociocultural, sociopolitical, and socioreligious-cum theological dimensions of the problem. In the next section I will try to capture the ethnic,
political, and religious sentiments, which provide a much-desired picture
of the issue at stake: violence is a three-legged phenomenon in Northern
Nigeria. I will attempt to draw from a catalogue of overwhelming evidence
of religious violence, ethnic violence, and political violence in Nigeria and
other relevant contexts.

1.2 The Commercialization of Religion

Economic corruption stands at the center of ethnic, religious, and political
struggles in Nigeria. Thus it is not only the politicization of religion or the
mixing of religion with absolute truth claims that is the reason for violence
in Nigeria, but also the commercialization of religion. Certain strands
of Pentecostalism and Charismaticism have been accused of turning the
Church into a commercial venture. If this is true they must answer Jesus'
inquiry in Luke 19:46: *How dare you turn my Father's house into a market!*
James Cone has reminded us that we live in a world in which society is

> [D]efined according to the socio-economic interests of
> the rich. Preaching the gospel, doing Christian theology,
> and speaking the truth are interrelated, and neither can be
> correctly understood apart from the liberation struggles of the

poor and marginalized. . . . The church of Jesus Christ is that community that can read the signs of the time, seeing God's struggle in the struggle of the poor.[17]

My driving concern is to speak the truth with love and courage, and to care for the poor and voiceless. Thus I argue that one of the issues at stake in regard to violence in Nigeria is the commercialization of ethnicity, politics, and religion.[18] Landed property has become a precious commodity in Nigeria. A plot of land in the city of Jos cost N250,000 or about $2,000 U.S. dollars. Politics has become a lucrative business. A counselor receives N150,000—about $1,200 U.S. dollars a month. The church has become a lucrative business: some pastors drive very expensive cars such as limousines or SUVs. They live in mansions like kings. This is why some government men and women, professionals and academic professors are leaving their jobs to start churches. Some entrepreneurs are turning their business places into churches for this same economic reason.[19]

The economic problem is not limited to Christianity. Rather, it is for this very reason that Islam in Nigeria is divided along principles, not sects per se, because of two people: the former Sultan of Sokoto Ibrahim Dasuki, who is from *darika* (traditional, fundamentalist, and conservative form of Islam); and the late Shehu Yar'aduwa of the *Izala* group (moderate, more liberal branch of Islam in Nigeria). The legend has it that the two men would go to Saudi Arabia to raise money for the building of the national mosque in Abuja only to come back and put the money in their personal accounts (Dasuki) or pay fanatical Islamic Imams (Yar'aduwa) to pit the poor Muslims against their non-Muslim brothers and sisters. In summary,

---

17. James H. Cone, *Speaking the Truth: Ecumenism, Liberation, and Black Theology* (Grand Rapids Michigan: Wm. B. Eerdmans Publishing Company, 1896), vii.

18. I am aware as Cone says that "speaking the truth" can be politically dangerous in a society defined according to the socio-economic interests of the rich.

19. Rev. Andrew Tella, *Interview*, on February 8, 2007. Tella, a Cameroonian, has three churches, a theological college, and a seminary in Lagos. He narrated how people go to the extent of buying fake theological certificates because they want to be able to travel to the West and North America. He lamented how there is a shallow Christian ethic in most of the churches in Africa. The first reason is that most of the pastors use deception and the members get carried way by their deception. Second, people have wrong motives for getting into the pastoral ministry.

violence is a means of concealing cases of economic corruption and injustice. By and large, Nigerian violence keeps some people in business. It helps attract sympathy from the Middle East in the case of Muslims and from the West and North America in the case of Christians.

1.3 The Impact of Mammon vs. Jihad

Mammon helps and also shapes our world. Studies have shown that the world today is under siege by mammon (money). This is because a very strange thing has happened: many people have forgotten that money was made for humans and not humans for money.[20] Consequently, money has become the master and humans are the slaves. This is why, as a study conducted by Tom Riddlell, et al., observes, "Our world continues to face the crisis of a unique giant who has consistently been the determinative focus of all societies. No country is immune to economic-cum political power crises. Thus even the richest country in the world today, America, is facing this crisis."[21] Riddlell and his associates' study describe the tension:

> [Over] two hundred years after the beginnings of the United States as an independent nation, we Americans live in one of the most technologically and economically advanced countries in the world. Our complex economic system produces and distributes goods and services to us daily and provides us with a high standard of living. And yet we are not satisfied, because we, personally and collectively, have many economic problems.[22]

In the context of the continuing turmoil, violence and confusion of the twenty-first century, the situation in our world deserves some attention. Why do people want political power, religious power, and ethnic power? Why is the question of ethnic relevance and identity in Nigeria becoming

---

20. As Jesus points out in Mark 2:27, "The Sabbath was made for man [human beings] not man for the Sabbath."
21. Tom Riddlell, Jean Shackelford, and Steve Stamos, *Economics: A Tool for Understanding Society*, 2nd ed. (California: Addison-Wesley Publishing Company, 1982), xi.
22. Riddlell et al., *Economics: A Tool for Understanding Society*, xi.

the reason behind violence and ethnic cleansing? The answer to these and many other issues lies in the need to appreciate their economic undercurrent. Economic greed is promoting social and economic injustice, resulting in the amassing of huge wealth and salient destruction of innocent lives and properties. Thus Jesus' words in the Sermon on the Mount are crucial in times of mixed motives for doing things in a world that has become more and more lethal against itself:

> Watch out! Be on your guard against all kinds of greed; a man's life does not consist in the abundance of his possessions. (Luke 12:9)

> No one can serve two masters. Either he will hate the one and love the other, or he will be devoted to the one and despise the other. You cannot serve God and Money. (Matt. 6:24)

Loyalties to economic power and the seeking of political dominance are responsible for the crises of political power in Nigeria, particularly but not exclusively in Northern Nigeria. Leaders refuse to relinquish power even when the country's constitution says otherwise. One of Nigeria's founding fathers, and Nigeria's first democratic president, the late Dr. N. Azikiwe, is reported as telling his people that the reason he was retiring from politics after sixteen years of active political involvement was because "an individual leader, by his unwillingness to step down at the right moment, could bring misfortune to himself and to the nation."[23] While this is true, many of our leaders in Africa—and in Nigeria in particular—do not pay heed to this warning.

In summary, I argue that the impact of violence is very broad, very holistic, and even elusive. This is because violence is sin. Therefore, the bottom line is that violence opens the door to widespread deception, distortion, corruption, exploitation, oppression, and "domination in all forms

---

23. Richard L. Sklar, *Nigerian Political Parties: Power in an Emergent African Nation* (New Jersey: Princeton University Press, 1963), 86.

of human relationships—with God, with one's self (and family), within the community and between others and the environment." Käe Mana observes:

> We see fratricidal violence as an element inherent in culture and in its basic mechanisms. Violence reveals itself not only in political institutions and in the higher realms of power, but also in everyday relationships where social groups, communities or ethnic groups, base their relationships with others on the principles of exclusion and the extermination of all who are different.[24]

Hence, in order to show the extent of the impact of violence it should be noted that politicians use economic and political power not only to engender the situation of violence but also to whip up the situation of exclusion. They adopt the principle of divide and rule; exclusion has the connotation of discrimination between groups.

Discrimination in the choice of who gets economic and social developments exemplifies exclusion. In areas hardest hit by waves of violence in Northern Nigeria this sad phenomenon of the politics of exclusion largely generates hostility, animosity, antagonism, and ethnic loyalties. These circumstances perpetuate because those socioeconomic and sociopolitical situations of ethnic, political, and religious violence and the intolerance of difference enable corrupt elite and the rich in the Northern region and the country at large to get away with injustice, exploitation, and suppression of human aspirations and the general abuse of human rights.

The tribes have risen to political mobilization but it has just provided the opportunity for their wise, understanding, and so-called respected people to feed their obsession with possessions. The moral energy to hold politicians and government officials accountable is enervated because of the situation of violence, which is killing not just people but even their moral and economic bases. It makes it difficult to know who are the wise,

---

24. Käe Mana, *Christian and Churches of Africa Envisioning the Future: Salvation in Jesus Christ and the Building of a New African Society* (Yaoundae; Great Britain: Editions Clâe, 2002), 33.

understanding, and respected men and women who could overcome the inclination to pit Nigerians against each other for their political, religious, economic, and ethnic power interests. We must search for those who will be inclusive, not exclusive—people who will fairly judge disputes between their brothers (either host or settlers) and aliens rather than those who only use their wisdom to siphon public funds to foreign banks.

Political, religious, and ethnic elite who encourage the exclusion of other people on the basis of religion, politics, and ethnicity are supposed to lose the respect of their people, particularly the valued electorate. This is because they do not mean well. But unfortunately, because of ethnic, religious, and political affiliations, they are celebrated as heroes or heroines.

The socioeconomic condition described above has its global context. Generally, mammon helps shape much of the world today, resulting in all forms of violence. Benjamin R. Barber illuminates the global situation and its interconnectivity to local players. We are facing two human situations, which Barber personified as *Jihad vs. McWorld,*

> In the tumult of the confrontation between global commerce and parochial ethnicity, the virtues of the democratic nation are lost and the instrument by which it permitted peoples to transform themselves into nations and seize sovereign power in the name of liberty and the commonweal are put at risk.[25]

The risk lies in the fact that "neither jihad nor McWorld aspires to rescue the civic virtues undermined by its denationalization practices; neither global markets nor blood communities service public goods or pursue equality and justice."[26] Instead, "Jihad pursues a bloody politics of identity, McWorld a bloodless economic profit [which send societies to dire poverty and premature deaths]. Belonging by default to McWorld, everyone is a consumer; seeking a reposition for identity, everyone belongs to some tribe.

---

25. Benjamin R. Barber, *Jihad vs. McWorld* (New York and Canada: Times Books, 1995), 7.
26. Barber, *Jihad vs. McWorld*, 7–8.

52

The Impact of Ethnic, Political, and Religious Violence on
Northern Nigeria, and a Theological Reflection on Its Healing

But no one is a citizen. Without citizens, how can there be democracy? How can there be justice and peace in Northern Nigeria?

In summary, the impact of violence is not limited to what happens at the spur of the moment: it goes before and beyond the present situation. It is intrinsically linked to the chain of ethnic, political, and religious violence of the past, which have always been caused by economic forces. Therefore, the whole phenomenon should be seen as a network that has been largely influenced by economic corruption in our country and the world at large. Having established that the bottom line of violence in Northern Nigeria is economic corruption, I will proceed to examine this triadic connection.

2. The Triadic Connection of Violence

Violence is not disjointed, as we tend to think. Rather present violence interacts with past violence. Violence—whether ethnic, political or religious—is better grasped by going beyond a single dimension to the other related dimensions. In this section I attempt to examine three variables, which are hardest hit wherever injustice exists: religion, politics, and culture. The point is that the past still lives on through some elements of religious ideologies and theological convictions. For instance, in Northern Nigeria, during times of violence these past ideas are retrieved.

It seems as if today the reason why religion is seen as a cause of violence is because people of faith are "pouring new wine into old wineskins," resulting in the skins bursting. People of faith are sewing "a patch of unshrunk cloth on an old garment," resulting in "the new piece" pulling "away from the old" (Mark. 2:21–22).

A Nigeria adage says, "*Da tsohon zuman ake maganin sabo.*" That is, it is with old honey that the medicine for catching new bees for new honey is made. Jesus' teaching about old cloth and new, of course, discredits this saying. Old wineskins cannot stand the test of our times, as studies have demonstrated. The question that every religion must ask is, "Is it lawful for a religion to determine when to do good or evil, to save life or to destroy it?" For Christians, what does it means to "be merciful as God is merciful?"

The political analysis of religious violence owes much to Max Weber's insight that the legitimacy of the state is rooted in violence.[27] Since religion is the only entity besides secular nationalism that can give moral sanction to the use of violence, it holds the potential of being fundamentally competitive with it.

It should be no surprise then, "that religious violence has erupted in those parts of the world where the legitimacy of the nation-state has been questioned: Ireland, India, Sri Lanka, Israel, Lebanon, Northern Nigeria, and elsewhere in South Asia and the Middle East."[28] We need to realize, as Elias points out, "The standard of what society demands and prohibits changes; in conjunction with this, the threshold of socially instilled displeasure and fear moves; and the question of sociogenic fears thus emerges as one of the central problems of the civilizing process."[29]

Violence is not only perpetrated by people of faith in the church, mosque, or temple. It is also perpetrated by the elite, the rich, and by government officials. These categories of people in our society pit the common and poor people against one another. The Usman dan Fodio's *jihad* of the early nineteenth century in Nigeria, which started with the intention of transforming Islam,[30] was later catapulted to political violence, resulting in Islam being reformed and transformed into a mass state religion.[31] Therefore, as Matthew H. Kukah and Toyin Falola demonstrate, "What made up the former Northern region had a well established political structure erected under the banner of the Islamic religion."[32] The non-Muslim ethnic groups in the North are now seeking political breathing space, which is causing Muslims to unleash burning anger upon them.[33] The Muslim elite who have enjoyed using the non-Muslims for their political agenda

27. Harold G. Coward, and Gordon S. Smith, *Religion and Peacebuilding* (New York, Bristol: State University of New York; University Presses Marketing, 2004), 123.
28. See Norbert Elias, *The Civilizing Process: The Development of Manners: Changes in the Code of Conduct and Feeling in Early Modern Times* (New York: Urizen Books, 1978), xiii.
29.
30. Jerome H. Berkow "Hausa" in *Muslim Peoples: A World Ethnographic Survey*, eds., by Richard V. Weeks (Westport, Connecticut, London: Greenwood Press, 1978), 152.
31. Berkow, "Hausa," 152.
32. See Falola and Kukah, *Religious Militancy and Self-Assertion*, 15–16, 29.
33. Johnstone, et al., *Operation World*, 493.

54

The Impact of Ethnic, Political, and Religious Violence on
Northern Nigeria, and a Theological Reflection on Its Healing

are now threatened by the political mobilization that the non-Muslims are engaging in. In short, these elite do not want the political independence of the ethnic tribes in the North because that has been their secured political hegemony or monopoly.[34] In essence, the elite in the North are threatened by the challenge of pluralism in contemporary Northern Nigeria. Northern Nigeria is indeed caught up in the spiral cobweb of religious politicization because of economic corruption.

Thus some scholars have simplistically concluded that violence is caused by the phenomenon of politicizing religion.[35] Others, like Niels Kastfelt, believe that religion has been part of politics in Nigeria. To him "what is newly introduced is radical violence."[36] Perhaps what Kastfelt forgets is to connect the dots between the ethnic, political, and religious dimensions of violent confrontation that have also been part and parcel of the Nigerian history.[37] Kastfelt seems to situate the blame on the amalgamation of the South and the North by the British. His analysis here has a built-in weakness because it fails to understand the peculiarity of the northern hegemony, which was founded on a slave-based social structure. However he is helpful in pointing to the fact that

> [I]n Northern Nigeria, and especially in the Nigerian Middle
> Belt, in the 1950s the politicization of religion was first seen in
> the relations between Christians and Muslims. In the Middle
> Belt, during the period of decolonization, political conflicts
> were primarily formulated in religious and ethnic terms, with
> the so-called ethnic minorities—most of them with a strong

---

34. Alias, *The Civilizing Process*, 7.
35. See Enwerem, *The Politicalization of Religion in Modern Nigeria: The Emergence and Politics of the Christian Association of Nigeria (CAN)*, and *A Dangerous Awakening: The Politicalization of Religion in Nigeria*.
36. Enwerem, *The Politicalization of Religion in Modern Nigeria*, ix.
37. Enwerem, *The Politicalization of Religion in Modern Nigeria*; Kastfelt writes, "The politicization of religion is nothing new. . . . The historical roots of this tragic development, which has threatened to tear Nigeria apart along religious lines, are partly to be found in the 1950s with the emergence of constitutional regionalism and regionally based political parties. Since then ethnic, religious, and regional loyalties have been decisive and formative elements in Nigerian politics."

Christian political leadership—fighting to maintain their independence of Muslim Hausa-Fulani hegemony.[38]

As a matter of fact, Kastfelt believes that "the same structure of political conflict, with its conjunction of religious and ethnic interests, is repeated in many of the violent confrontations of the 1980s and 1990s, those of Bauchi in 1991 and Zangon Kataf in 1992 being typical examples."[39] In short, violence has left its indelible imprint on us to the extent that, as Kastfelt points out, in Northern Nigeria "local conflicts are translated into religious loyalties and interpreted within the historical antagonism between Christian ethnic 'minorities' and Muslim Hausa-Fulani."[40] In Northern Nigeria violence has formed a community—ethnic, political, and religious—of resistance. This sense of community points to the fact that the world is not loosely connected as we usually imagine. Rather, ethnicity, religion, and politics are intrinsically connected. The belief in a dichotomized world is flawed and unsubstantiated. The reality is, as Larry L. Rasmussen points out, "The world around us is also within. We are an expression of it; it is an expression of us. We are made of it; we eat, drink and breathe it."[41]

Since we are not always conscious of the fact that our past haunts us, a chain of events that have some linkage with the past always hardest hits us. Consequently, Rasmussen notes:

> The problems we thought the golden age had solved thus reappear all over again. Yet now they surface with global reach: mass unemployment, severe cyclical slumps, the spreading distance between rich and poor in a confrontation of limousine plenty with homelessness, and limited state revenues for limitless expenditures. Thus people's fears of breakdown heighten.[42]

---

38. Enwerem, The *Politicalization of Religion in Modern Nigeria*, ix.
39. Enwerem, *The Politicalization of Religion in Modern Nigeria*, x.
40. Enwerem, *The Politicalization of Religion in Modern Nigeria*, x.
41. Larry L. Rasmussen, *Earth Community Earth Ethics* (New York: Orbis Books, 2003), xiv, xi.
42. Rasmussen, *Earth Community Earth Ethics*, 3.

Citing Dietrich Bonhoeffer and Maria von Wedemeyer,[43] Rasmussen notes, "The insistence of the biblical religions is correct . . . The universe in its essence has justice and love as its foundation, and it is our alienation from a just and loving totality that feeds our deep frustration with the order of things."[44] What does this all mean to a study of the impact of violence on faith communities in Northern Nigeria? In essence it means that we cannot grasp the impact of violence when we still see the world in bits and pieces. The intent of this chapter is not only to show the role of economic corruption in the scheme of things but also to clearly demonstrate that violence has a triadic source: ethnic, political, and religious. Therefore my task in this chapter has been to point to the economic corruption as the clearest-connecting link.

3. Conclusion

This chapter has primarily endeavored to encapsulate the argument that violence is more complex than religious idiom and bloated categorization can offer. I have therefore attempted to outline the dimensions of violence that are usually eclipsed when we hastily see religion as the cause of violence in Northern Nigeria. I have argued that violence is complex. It is like roosters who crow, cows that low, and sheep that bleat. In other words, violence has many faces or ties. But the truth is that violence is a symptom of what is really going on in society. This chapter has identified economic corruption and political power, as well as politicization and commercialization of religion in Northern Nigeria as the real sources of violence. The bottom line is economic pursuits have been given primacy over and above the pursuit of God.

Although there are several factors causing violence in Northern Nigeria, economic corruption is one of the overwhelming causes of violence. In the past our people built fortified cities for protection from both human and

---

43. *Braubriefe: Zelle* 92 (Munich: Beck, 1992), 176.
44. Rasmussen, *Earth Community Earth Ethics*, 13.

animal predators. Today, people are obsessed with the desire to pile up or hoard money to gain power and control over their fellow men and women.

Violence is whipped up by a brood of corrupt elite who stand in the place of their colonial masters and take advantage of poor and frustrated youths for their individual interests. In retrospect, our elite used to struggle for the interest of one Northern region. But now violence has created ethnic, political, and religious divides. Consequently, a spirit of obsessed desire to make easy money and to gain political and economic power that allows the elite to grasp political dominance and economic monopoly has crippled Northern Nigeria. They then use these acquired resources as tools for the perpetuation of their hold on power and control to the detriment of their rivals and the poor masses. They neglect the causes of the orphans, the widows, and the poor and the rights of the marginalized. Thus, the region is bent over and cannot straighten up at all. Is there any hope? Yes! In such situations the components that are urgently needed are economic justice and honesty, and legal and institutional restraint on greed. These measures will undoubtedly produce fruits that bring praises to God, resulting in blessings to our fellow human beings. Violence has kept us bound for too long. The task for a just or egalitarian Northern Nigeria is the task of every Nigerian living in Northern Nigeria.

> O Northern Nigeria, Northern Nigeria, how long will you continue to kill and murder innocent victims, destroy businesses, properties and your places of worship! When will you stop destroying yourself and your land so that you can begin to gather your children together, as a hen gathers her chicks under her wings! If you have the will you can do it!

Finally, in this chapter I have tried to engage in the debate of whether or not religion is our problem. My conclusion is yes and no. Yes because history shows that religion has been a cause of violence in the past and still does. No because religion is also a solution to the problem of violence. in fact, the problems include ethnic hostility and grievances that are economically and politically motivated. Therefore, ethnic power sharing is crucial.

The good thing is that no one ethnic group has the majority. Rather, several ethnic groups make up the region.[45] This can, if carefully used, help avoid domination by one group—by organizing a balance of power and a shared voice in the legal, economic, and political arrangements.

In the next chapter I shall concentrate more on deepening our understanding of the possible root causes of violence in Northern Nigeria. That is, I shall attempt to take the issues I have noted in passing in the present chapter to a deeper level.

---

45. Turaki, *The British Colonial Legacy in Northern Nigeria*, 72.

CHAPTER 4

Understanding the Root Causes of Ethnic, Political, and Religious Violence in Nigeria

Introduction

The primary aim of this chapter is an assessment of the root causes of ethnic, political, and religious violence in Nigeria. One of the consequences of violence is that it prevents self-questioning and self-criticism. Ironically, the political elite and some intellectuals want to maintain the status quo by convincing the citizenry that religion and ethnicity are the two monsters that prevent nation building. Assuming that is the case, a follow-up question is, "Are religion and ethnicity the only problems that trigger violence in Northern Nigeria?" This question is crucial because violence in Northern Nigeria has become endemic. All has overwhelmingly felt its impact.

Therefore, I am taken aback by the fact that our political elite and some students of social and political engineering in Nigeria are gambling with human life by seeking a shortcut to solving the problem of violence. It is dangerous to single out religion and ethnicity as the only key problems bedeviling our Nigerian nation. I see the move as a singular act with a built-in attempt by government to cover up the economic decay, which is sending millions of people into dire poverty and causing future violence, which will continue to send people to the grave prematurely.

Religious and ethnic rhetoric has largely been used as a hasty solution to an elusive threat. I shall attempt to outline the causes of violence by examining the following: (A) the broad climate of the threat: (1) the humanist agenda in Nigeria, (2) the religious cause, (3) the political cause, (4) the economic cause, and (5) the ethnic cause; (B) and a vignette of some practical situations of violence in Northern Nigeria. This approach is intended not only to illuminate the threat but also to work toward a solution to violence.

1. The Broad-Based Analysis of the Perceived vs. Real Threat

By paying attention to the broader context of violence, I shall attempt to outline in detail some of the salient perceived or real threats, which are triggering violence in the Northern region.

1.1 The Humanist Agenda in Nigeria

As we may be aware, humanists in the West and North America have been at the forefront of technological invention and application. Their successful influence in technology and its application has given them impetus to face other areas of crucial importance, including religion. Their thesis is that religion is the *opium* of the people. From this standpoint their goal is to liberate the human mind from superstition and dogma. They oppose any obstacles to freedom of inquiry. As they have seen technology's continuous expansion, the transformation of our power over nature and the provision of new, exciting, and awesome options for the human species, they hope to transform our view of religion.

They have persistently tried to pluck human beings from the hand of God. As Paul Kurt, himself a humanist, points out, "In general, humanists have heralded the wise application of technology to nature and society. And technology on the whole has benefited humankind. It places the power to solve human problems and to redress human ills in our hands, *rather than leaving it to some absent deity or providence*" (italics mine).[1] He further points out,

> What is especially surprising today, given the rapidity of scientific, technological, economic, political, and moral change on a global scale, is the persistence of ancient religious systems: Hinduism, Judaism, Christianity, Islam, etc. These systems provide belief in a supernatural deity or deities and also in the idea of human salvation and obedience to divine commandments. Humanism is nontheistic, and it rejects these supernatural doctrines and provides a naturalistic humanist alternative. The central issue concerns the meaning of life and the role of the human persons on this planet.[2]

In "Agenda for the Humanist Movement in the Twenty-first Century" (Editorial), Paul Kurt argues, "In the contemporary world the pace of social change is enormous. This, I submit, provides unparalleled opportunities for humanism."[3] In order to take advantage of the opportunity that violence in Nigeria provides, the humanists are making a frantic effort to convince Nigerians that religion is a bad idea; they use Marx's slogan, "the opium of the masses." Generally, the present human situation—which includes, but is not limited to, the history of religious violence—is providing philosophical opportunity for the humanist agenda to come to fruition.

What many Nigerians do not realize is that our causes of violence are not disconnected from the humanist's project. The naturalist humanist's goal has been to discredit religion in the world. We must not forget that "Humanism draws upon the physical, biological, social, and behavioral sciences in order to explain how nature operates and why human beings behave the way they do."[4] The humanist project is gaining ground in Nigeria. Hence, I insist, the usual argument that seeks to make us buy into

1. Kurt, *Free Inquiry*, 3.
2. Kurt, *Free Inquiry*, 6.
3. Paul Kurt, *Free Inquiry*: "Agenda for the Humanist Movement in the Twenty-first Century" in *High Beam Research* www.highbeam.com (Editorial), June 22 1995, 1.
4. Kurt, *Free Inquiry*, 6.

The Impact of Ethnic, Political, and Religious Violence on
Northern Nigeria, and a Theological Reflection on Its Healing

62

the idea that religion is the only problem bedeviling our society must be discredited if we want a way out of the impasse we have found ourselves in Nigeria. The humanist category is a reminder of the fact that the causes of violence in Northern Nigeria are multifaceted.

1.2 An Analysis of the Sources of the Threat

Following Reinhold Niebuhr's argument, Glen Stassen has postulated that we need scientific data to substantiate ethical analysis.[5] Niebuhr's point is that

> Sociologists, as a class, understand the modern social problem even less than the educators. They usually interpret social conflicts as the result of a clash between different kinds of "behavior patterns," which can be eliminated if the contending parties will only allow the social scientist to furnish them with a new and more perfect pattern, which will do justice to the needs of both parties.[6]

For Niebuhr, "only a very few sociologists seem to have learned that an adjustment of a social conflict, caused by the disproportion of power in society, will hardly result in justice as long as the disproportion of power remains . . ." This disproportionate power creates the situation of the "inherited group."[7] Niebuhr believes "Lack of an understanding of the brutal character of the behavior of all human collectives, and the power of self-interest and collective egoism in all interest group relations" is responsible for the failure to provide checks and balances of disproportionate power.[8]

Niebuhr further maintains, "They do not see that the limitations of the human imagination, the easy subservience of reason to prejudice and passion, and the consequent persistence of irrational egoism, particularly in group behavior, make social conflict inevitable in human history, probably

---

5. Seminar class comment, Winter, 2004.
6. Reinhold Niebuhr, *Moral Man and Immoral Society* (Louisville: Westminster John Knox Press, 1960), xvi.
7. R. Niebuhr, *Moral Man and Immoral Society*, xvii.
8. R. Niebuhr, *Moral Man and Immoral Society*, xvii.

to its end."[9] Niebuhr sees power as the biggest source of the threat to human flourishing. But what does this mean to Northern Nigeria? It means, among other things, revisiting the religious dimension of the threat in Northern Nigeria.

1.2.1 The Religious Dimension of the Threat

Religion must be redefined. What is religion? Simply put, religion is a belief in a superpower, a higher power or infinite controlling power, especially in a personal God or gods entitled to obedience and worship. Islam and Christianity are one of the "Religious movements that are classified as world religions."[10] Let us take each in turn.

1.2.1.1 Islam

Historically the Hausa-Fulani land encountered Islam between the fourteenth and fifteenth centuries. But Islam did not meet a religious vacuum. Rather it spread to the detriment of hitherto indigenous African religions. Islam was catapulted to Northern Nigeria through the activities of itinerant-Muslim traders from the east (*wangawara*) who, as W.F.S. Miles points out, "enthusiastically praised their faith along with their wares."[11] It spread like wildfire, first and foremost in the urban cities where they concentrated their trading. By the middle of the eighteenth century it had spread to rural areas as a result of Muslim missionaries' efforts to convert commoners and the rural people to Islam.[12]

(1) The Islamic Jihad in the Context of Northern Nigeria

Islam spread in Nigeria, thanks to Usman Dan Fodio's *jihad*, which was launched in 1804. *Jihad* is defined as a *holy war* waged by Muslims in defense of the Islamic faith against individuals, organizations, or countries regarded as hostile to Islam. It is usually connected with a pursuit of *Shari'ah's*

---

9. Niebuhr, *Moral Man in an Immoral Society*, xx.
10. Ruth A. Tucker, *Another Gospel: Alternative Religions and the New Age Movement* (Grand Rapids: Academia Books, 1989), 20.
11. William F. S. Miles, "Shari'ah as de-Africanization: Evidence from Hausaland" in *Africa Today*, March 22, 2003, 2.
12. Miles, "Shari'ah as de-Africanization" *Africa Today*, 2.

The Impact of Ethnic, Political, and Religious Violence on
Northern Nigeria, and a Theological Reflection on Its Healing

64

full-fledged application. *Shari'ah* or *shar'* is defined as path. *Shari'ah* can be compared to the Christian Canon law. That is, it is a technical term for the canon law of Islam.

Shari'ah is considered to be divinely established and not developed by human experience or reasoning. Its bases are the Qu'ran, tradition, and *jam'* (consensus) and *oiyas* (analogical reasoning on basic of the above).[13] According to Brandon,

> It is designed to govern the whole of life of Islam adherents. Therefore it ought to be strictly followed by orthodox Muslims. But in modern times the *Shari'ah* has suffered considerably. Some Islamic countries have terminated the *Shari'ah* regimes of their countries. [For example], in 1927 Turkey abandoned it. Instead, Turkey adopted Swiss family law. Egypt and Tunisia also followed suit, resulting in the abolition of *Shari'ah* courts in those countries.[14]

The *Shari'ah* is intended to govern all aspects of life, which include, among others, doctrine, practice, morality, and politics. "It has not claimed to be able to deal with inward belief, judging wholly on basis of outward action. Actions are divided into five classes: (1) obligation (*fard, wajib*); (2) recommended (*mandūb*); (3) prohibited (*harām, mahzūr*); (4) disapproved (*markrūh*); (5) legally indifferent (*mubāh*)."[15]

Kimball's study provides more insight into the concept of *jihad*. Kimball defines *jihad* as literally meaning, "struggling in the way of God." All Muslims are enjoined to engage in *jihad*.

Given the prevalence of violence in the Muslim community many believe that violence is justified—even required—as punishment. In Islamic contacts with "the world of conflict" (*dar al harb*) outside the Islamic world, violence is permitted for defensive purposes and as a tool in subduing an

---

13. S.G.F. Brandon, "Shari'ah," in *A Dictionary of Comparative Religion* (New York: Scribner, 1970), 552.
14. Brandon, *A Dictionary of Comparative Religion*, 552.
15. Brandon, *A Dictionary of Comparative Religion*, 552.

enemy of the faith. Conflict of the latter sort is known as *jihad*, a word that literally means "striving" and is often translated as "holy war."[16] This concept (*holy war*) has been used to justify the expansion of Muslim states into non-Islamic areas.

> But Muslim law does not allow *jihad* to be used to justify forcible conversion to Islam: the only conversions regarded as valid are those that come about nonviolently, through personal persuasion and change of heart. Yet in recent years Muslim political activists have employed the notion of *jihad* in justifying militant political acts. According to an influential Egyptian author, Abd Al-Salam Faraj, *jihad* is every Muslim's "neglected duty" to defend the faith—violently, if necessary— in the social and political spheres.[17]

This sort of emphasis has eclipsed the fact that *jihad* is a personal striving to socioeconomically, sociopolitically, and socioreligiously please Allah. That is to say, the term *holy war*, which is widely used in Western media and among some Muslims, includes one of the ways this obligatory duty has been and is being promulgated.[18] However, Kimball points out that this is not the whole story. There are two kinds of *jihad*: the "greater *jihad*" and "lesser *jihad*." Kimball contends, "The outward struggle in defense of Islam is not the biggest challenge. The greater *jihad* is the inner struggle to overcome selfish and sinful desires, the strong tendencies that inhibit human beings from doing what they know to be right."[19] Muslims, like all human beings, tend to forget the inner struggle. Their outward struggle overshadows the inner struggle. Hence, they also confuse the struggles for economic and political power with religious struggle. In Northern Nigeria violence, in most cases, is not in defense of the religion but rather in pursuit of political and economic power. As Kimball further insists, "Frequently,

---

16. Jonathan Z. Smith, and Scott William Green, eds., *The HarperCollins Dictionary of Religion* (San Francisco: HarperCollins Publishers, 1995), 1123.
17. Smith and Green, *The HarperCollins Dictionary of Religion*, 1123.
18. Kimball, *When Religion Became Evil*, 173.
19. Kimball, *When Religion Became Evil*, 174.

the savage attacks and murderous intrigue took place among Muslims vying for power."[20] This is not just any power; it is political power and economic dominance.

(2) The Intriguing Connection of Jihad and Economic Power

Scholars have often wondered why the Usman Dan Fodio *jihad* had such enormous success within the shortest time.[21] The *jihad* started as a war against the Hausa-Fulani aristocracies that had allegedly corrupted Islam. However, because commoners fought it later turned to looting and confiscating other ethnic groups' property and land. That is to say, a divine mission got turned to the service of the evil one because of economic interests.[22]

Generally, raiding has been embedded in the history of nomadic and seminomadic peoples from the east with which the Hausa-Fulani in Northern Nigeria share a culture. They have been involved in what is known as "Razzias." As Wevers explained, this is the military form of the nomad and seminomad.[23] Muslim raiding activities were characterized by plundering and carrying away of victims as captives. It is no wonder that during the slave trade period in West Africa much of Northern Nigeria became a slave-trading and/or selling center. That the *jihadists* employed this method demonstrated that it had political and economic ulterior motives rather than only religious reform. This background provides a helpful insight into the contemporary *Shari'ah* discourse. If one put the *Shari'ah* debate in Nigeria into this larger perspective one cannot help but realize that its sole purpose is not just the purification of religion, as its agitators claimed. Rather, it is an opportunity for the corrupt aristocrats and politi-

---

20. Kimball, *When Religion Became Evil*, 175.
21. See Jerome H. Berkow, "Hausa" in *Muslim People: A World Ethnographic Survey*, ed. V. Weeks (Westport, Connecticut, London and England: Greenwood Press, 1978), 152.
22. See, Walter Rauschenbusch, *Christianity and the Social Crisis* (New York: The Macmillan Company, 1908), 253–254. See also Kukah, *Religion, Politics and Power*, 2.
23. Wevers, "War, the Ideas of" in *The Interpreter's Dictionary of the Bible*, 802. Wevers explains, "The Razzias or raid has been from time immemorial the military form of the nomad and seminomad. The Ayyam el-'Arab in the Jahihiyah period find their modern center parts in clan raids among the tribes of the Arabian Peninsula (where Islam first took its roots). Settled states found the sudden raids of such tribes (this explains why the jihad swept and spilled over all major parts of Nigeria and West Africa) highly discomforting."

cians to reclaim their credibility before the poor populace in Hausa-Fulani lands.[24] In order to make sense of this scenario one has to understand the internal crisis of Islam in Nigeria.

(3) The Internal Crisis of Islam in Nigeria: A Case Study of the Izala Scenario

In Nigeria, Islam has allegedly "sewn a patch of unshrunk cloth on an old garment." That is, "many pre-Islamic practices and beliefs coexisted with the ostensibly Koranic-based counterparts."[25] It was against this background that a brand of Islam, Sunni, started confronting those contradictions.

The "Islamic purists," as Miles called them, or Islamic reformists, took the responsibility of ridding Islam in Hausaland of its moral decadences. They declared jihad against the "decadent custodians of the faith."[26] Out of that group sprang up Izala—a sect in Islam that seeks a return to the glorious days of Islam. According to Bernard Lewis,

> It was historically started by Muhammad ibn 'Abd al-Wahhab (1703–1792). Al-Wahhab was a theologian from the Najd area of Arabia, which was ruled by local Sheikhs of the House of Saud. Al-Wahhab was the founder of this renewed spirit of Islam, which has had incredible impact on the younger generation of Islamists all over the world.[27]

---

24. William Miles writes, "In what was to become northern Nigeria, the jihadists downgraded women's status, power, and wealth by suppressing *bori* (a spirit-possession cult) and promoting seclusion. Women of the aristocracy had enjoyed important roles in *bori* (including titled positions) until the largely female cult was forced underground. Seclusion, by forcing married women off their farmlands (and thereby out of public view) deprived them of an important source of income" (*Africa Today*, "Shari'ah as de-Africanization," 2003), 6.

25. Miles, "Shari'ah as de-Africanization" *Africa Today*, 2.

26. Miles, "Shari'ah . . ." *Africa Today*, 2.

27. Bernard Lewis, *The Crisis of Islam: Holy War and Unholy Terror* (Great Britain: Clays Ltd, St Ives Plc, 2003), 103.

The teaching of Wahhabism includes, among other things, a "rejection of modernity in favor of a return to the sacred past. It has a varied and ramified history in the region and has given rise to a number of movements."[28]

In Northern Nigeria, it has given rise to a radical movement known as *Izala*. The activities of the Izala sect become deathly pronounced in the 1970s and 1980s. Izala exposed the internal conflicts Islam has been experiencing in Northern Nigeria. It was a situation wherein the younger generation of Islamic scholars in Northern Nigeria was looking back to the past and drawing lessons from such reformists as al-Wahhab in Saudi Arabia and Sheik Shehu Usman Dan Fodio, the founder of the Sokoto Caliphate. It was a conflict largely between the young generation of Islamic scholars and the old school of Islam in Nigeria. In other words, these younger theologians were pitting their ideas against those of traditional Islam, which was allegedly a concoction of the pre-Islamic beliefs, practices and traditions of the past. This was why, in the late 1980s, such disparate group as the Maitatsine in Kano began to emerge.

The internal conflict created a rift in Northern Nigeria. This is the background against which the introduction of Shari'ah in the Northern region in 1999 was made palatable. A look at this past helps us to understand the present: Shari'ah was introduced to gain political momentum. Shari'ah implementation was a calculated ploy to unify a divisive Islam: Shari'ah is what unifies a divided Islam in the North.[29] As Miles aptly points out, "Underlying the strictly juridical changes in Nigerian Hausaland has been the emergence of a theopolitical movement for Islamic reform."[30] As Miles further explains, "Izala is known as Association for Elimination of Innovations in Religion and for Reinforcement of the Sunnah."[31] Although Ismalia Idris founded this movement in 1978, it was the late Sheikh Abubakar Gumi who actually brought it to its national recognition.[32]

Gumi dreamed of the restoration of the Sokoto Caliphate. Thus Gumi's primary concern was the full implementation of Shari'ah across the whole

---

28. Lewis, *The Crisis of Islam*, 103.
29. See Kukah, *Religion, Politics and Power*, 1.
30. Miles, "Shari'ah . . ." *Africa Today*, 6.
31. Miles, "Shari'ah . . ." *Africa Today*, 6.
32. Miles, "Shari'ah . . ." *Africa Today*, 6.

nation, thanks to his predecessor Sheikh Shehu Usman dan Fodio. He and his followers saw the Nigerian Constitution as anti-Islamic. According to them it was inherently Christian and hence anti-Islamic because it exemplified the West's calculated plan to undermine Islam. As such, merely adapting Western-derived jurisprudence to Shari'ah principles was, for Gumi, "logically untenable and culturally demeaning."[33]

The background to Gumi's argument is the colonialists' conquering of the Sokoto Caliphate. The *Jihadist* agenda was the establishment of Islam's hegemony in Nigeria; i.e., Usman dan Fodio chiefly wanted to fashion an Islamic nation state solely run by Shari'ah. This desire was, in part, achieved through the establishment of the Sokoto Caliphate. But the British, who felt the only way they could impose their supremacy in Northern Nigeria was by suppressing the supremacy of the Sokoto Caliphate, prematurely truncated it.[34] This singular act was a great setback to dan Fodio's dream for Islam.

Gumi was committed to a realization of this dream in Nigeria. But to some extent, Gumi's vision ran counter to that of the core group, Izala, whose main commitment was launching an onslaught on the Muslim elite who had allegedly corrupted Islam. Thus, as Miles notes,

> Promoting Shari'ah itself was not Izala's original or primary mission. With its more than two million Nigerian followers, the movement nevertheless created an overall cultural and political atmosphere conductive to radical institutional change in an Islamist direction. Although the movement was socially expansionist, it still enjoys a particularly urban sensibility.[35]

That is to say, Izala's essential aim was the purging from Islam its alleged evil, local practices. These practices were hitherto assumed and seen as pure Islam, while in reality they were nothing but *haram* (forbidden).

---

33. See Toyin Falola, *Violence in Northern Nigeria* (Rochester, New York: University of Rochester Press, 1998), 124–126.
34. Matthew Hassan Kukah, *Religion, Politics and Power in Northern Nigeria* (Ibadan, Owerri, Kaduna, and Lagos: Spectrum Books Limited, 1993), 115.
35. Miles, "Shari'ah . . ." *Africa Today*, 6.

These include, among other things, impure excrescences such as "Sufi Brotherhood (*tariqa*), believers' networks that promote devotion to elders and the veneration of saints."[36] Within the context of the Islamic crisis, Miles notes that "the principal (and often rival) brotherhoods are the Qadariyya associated with Usman dan Fodio himself and the Tijaniya (a mercantilistic network stretching well into Senegal), introduced by Alhaji Umar Tall in the 1830s and popularized by Ibrahim Niasse a century later."[37] In short, in pursuit of their goal to purify Islam, Izala launched an internal *jihad* against Sufism in Nigeria, resulting in a struggle over denominational power in local mosques. These struggles led to the establishment of separate Izala mosques in the region.

Izala weighed in against all popular practices of Islam that favor superstitious ritual (such as amulet wearing) over against literalist study and understanding of the Koran. By extension, Izala favors an "individualism in which people hope . . . to extricate themselves from the tutelage of the religious and moral authorities."[38] Izala sets out to purge faithful Muslims in Nigeria of the evil amongst them.

The younger generation showed contempt for the practices and organizations of the older generation. This is the background against which we can understand the Shari'ah phenomenon in Nigeria. Shari'ah's implementation helped Muslims overcome their internal tension. It was partially meant to redirect attention from this internal crisis to a perceived external enemy—the West (and, by extension, Christians in Nigeria). This will become clearer if we put the Izala scenario in Northern Nigeria in its global perspective.

---

36. Miles, "Shari'ah . . ." *Africa Today*, 6.
37. Miles, "Shari'ah . . ." *Africa Today*, 6.
38. Ousmane Kane, "Izala: The Rise of Muslim Reformism in Northern Nigeria" In *Accounting for Fundamentalisms: The Dynamic Character of Movements*, eds. Martin E. Marty and R. Scott Appleby, (Chicago and London: University of Chicago Press, 1994), 494 as quoted by Miles. See also Muhammad Sani Umar, "Changing Islamic Identity in Nigeria from the 1960s to the 1980s: From Sufism to Anti-Sufism" in *Muslim Identity and Social Change in Sub-Saharan Africa*, ed. Louis Brenner. Bloomington and Indianapolis: Indiana University Press, 1993), 178.

(5) The Global Context of Izala

Violence is not limited to local players. It persists in most societies because of conflicting human interests. This human problem is aggravated by international or global politics.[39] Ricardo Rene Laremont noted that during the Cold War the United States and the Soviet Union were the major causes of war in Africa: "as evidenced by proxy wars in Namibia, Angola, and Mozambique, the warrior factions were encouraged by the then Superpowers: the United States and the Soviet Union."[40]

However, with the demise of the Soviets from the scheme of things "the Western powers of the United States, France, and Great Britain have concomitantly retreated from Africa and lowered the importance of Africa's geo-strategic role."[41] Now that the West is no longer behind the scenes, it means that the questions must be freshly asked: what is the cause of violence in the continent, and in Nigeria in particular? Who is behind the violence? Has the withdrawal of the West given room to a new encourager of violence behind the scenes? Scholars from the African ethnic perspectives have concluded, "Violence and war occur in Africa because of irreconcilable ethnic differences and conflict."[42] But with the new development in Nigeria this is not the only reason for violence—it is just the tip of the iceberg.

A new generation of Muslim youth wants to modernize, but not in Western terms. They want to see Muslims take advantage of the many opportunities that the world provides today to further the values of the Islamic religion in opposition and utter rejection of Western values that they perceive as the primary cause of Islam's decline. In 1994 a top Saudi official explained, "[I]slam for us is not just a religion but a way of life. We Saudis want to modernize, but not necessarily westernize."[43]

---

39. Ricardo Rene Laremont, ed., *The Causes of Warfare and the Implications of Peacekeeping in Africa* (Portsmouth, NH: Heinemann, 2002), 3.
40. Laremont, *The Causes of Warfare*, 4.
41. Laremont, *The Causes of Warfare*, 4.
42. Laremont, *The Causes of Warfare*, 4.
43. Bandar bin Sultan, *New York Times*, July 10, 1994, 20 as quoted by Samuel P. Huntington, *The Clash of Civilization and the Remaking of World Order* (New York: Simon and Schuster, 1996), 110.

A distinguished Islamic scholar, Ali Hillal Desouki, sees the Resurgence as characterized by efforts to reinstitute Islamic law in place of Western law. Such efforts include, among other things,

> [T]he increased use of religious language and symbolism, expansion of Islamic education (manifested in the multiplication of Islamic schools and Islamization codes of social behavior e.g., female covering, abstinence from alcohol, and increased participation in religious observances, domination of the opposition to secular governments in Muslim societies by Islamic groups, and expanding efforts to develop international solidarity among Islamic states and societies.[44]

Seen from the perspective of the global context, Izala is a broad-based renewal. As Huntington notes, "In its political manifestations, the Islamic Resurgence bears some resemblance to Marxism, with scriptural texts, a vision of the perfect society, commitment to fundamental change, rejection of the powers that be and the nation state, and doctrinal diversity ranging from moderate reformist to violent revolutionary."[45] Their overarching goal is fundamental reform.

(6) Summary

The foregoing analysis of Islam in Northern Nigeria has yielded some conclusions.

(1) Religious violence in Northern Nigeria results from a transferred anger. This is a region that prior to the coming of the British enjoyed Islamic hegemony over the inhabitants of the region. The historical data indicate that Islam thrived in Northern Nigeria and beyond. Abdullahi attested to the phenomenal growth: "Islamic religion has been part and parcel of the culture and tradition of the inhabitants of contemporary Northern Nigeria." Although Islam's arrival in the region dates back many centuries,

---

44. Huntington, *The Clash of Civilization and the Remaking of World Order*, 111.
45. Huntington, *The Clash of Civilization*, 111.

it was the Sheik Usman Danfodio's *jihad* that transformed Islam into an institution to be reckoned with in Nigeria.

Danfodio successfully founded an Islamic state known as the Sokoto Caliphate; its structures and institutions were guided by the teaching and practice of Islam. It was so well organized that when the British came to the North, they decided to use indirect rule. As Abdullahi argues, "The main reason why the colonial masters used indirect rule in the north was because of the administrative system they found in place which was established by the Sheik and his lieutenants under this government." Although the British in principle used indirect rule because they found a civilized and more structured administration, in practice they did two things:

First, they truncated the Islamic system of administration in the region. This act went against the religious and political wishes and aspirations of the Hausa-Fulani peoples. Thus the British were perceived by the Hausa-Fulani as an occupation army, resulting in "widespread resentment across the people against the white men and all they brought." The phrase "all they brought," in part, alludes to Christianity. This is why that same anger today is transferred to Christians living in Northern Nigeria. They are seen as traitors and collaborators with the West.

Second, on the flip side of the coin, indirect rule meant a bombshell for non-Muslim minorities in the region. Professor Yusufu Turaki argued that one of the major reasons for continuous violence in Nigeria is because of the British policy of indirect rule in the North.[46] Eghosa E. Osaghae also noted that the British policy of indirect rule handed over the non-Muslim ethnic minorities to the powers that be in the north: the emirates. The British colonialists left the minorities at the mercies of the Hausa-Fulani Emirs.[47] This impacted not only the non-Muslims in the northern region but even in the whole country.

The British colonialists helped reinforce the goal of permanent enslavement of the non-Muslims not only in Northern Nigeria but in the country

---

46. Yusufu Turaki, *The British Colonial Legacy in Northern Nigeria: A Social Ethical Analysis of the Colonial and Post-colonial Society and Politics in Nigeria* (Jos, Nigeria: Challenge Press, 1993), 41–42.
47. Eghosa E. Osaghae, *The Cripple Giant: Nigeria Since Independence* (Bloomington: Indiana University Press, 1998), 2.

at large. Legend has it that even when the predominantly Christian Middle Belt sought to be guaranteed a separate region from the north, the British refused to grant the demand. These are today the problems bedeviling our society.[48]

Thus while other ethnic minorities in Nigeria experienced only British colonialism, their counterparts in Northern Nigeria experienced double colonialism, i.e., Hausa-Fulani and British. The North became a superpower in Nigeria and did exactly what other superpowers usually do: meddled into other peoples' affairs. The U.S. and Soviet meddling in Africa's affairs led to wars, as Huntington has pointed out. The Hausa-Fulani did the same in Nigeria. As Eghosa demonstrated,

> The wars and crises in the West (western region of Nigeria) were instigated and fuelled by the meddling of Fulani *jihadists,* whose sphere of influence spread to Oyo and other northernmost parts of the West, and European traders and colonialists who, particularly since the era of the slave trade, pursued manipulative and divisionist strategies to gain trade advantages and retain political-cum-military control in the region; [even though] in terms of political organization, the groups in the West ranked next to the centralized theocracies of the Islamised parts of the North.[49]

In spite of this historical evidence of Muslims' strong hold in Nigeria, most of them today do not agree that colonialism was to their advantage. The primary reason is because they do not want to accept responsibility for violence. They face two challenges: arrogance and the crisis of Islam's perceived decline in the world.

(2) Violence persists because of Muslim unwillingness to accept responsibility for the violence. Nobody is willing to accept the blame. John Boer argues that

---

48. See Turaki, *The British Colonial Legacy in Northern Nigeria,* 72.
49. Osaghae, *The Crippled Giant,* 3.

From the Muslim perspectives, the major context of the riots is the colonial imposition of a Christian-secular establishment that has deranged Nigerian Muslim spirituality and institutions. It has created the anger and frustration that marks the Muslim community in Nigeria and that is ever ready to explode at the slightest provocation.[50]

Boer suggests that one of the reasons is what he calls "the claim of innocent suffering." According to Boer, "Muslims resent the accusation that they are the cause of Nigeria's problems." In his words,

> There is strong resistance among Muslims against seeing themselves as cause, against accepting any blame or responsibility for riots. They are not the ones to have started the colonial process. Muslims generally think of themselves as either innocent or provoked to such an extent that the provocateur must be held responsible, even if Muslims took the initiative.[51]

In the aftermath of Shari'ah implementation in 2000 and its attendant violence in Northern Nigeria, Obed Minchakpu told of Sheikh Ahmed Sanusi Gunbi's remark: "Muslims in Nigeria are tired of unnecessary criticisms and outright attacks on us and our religion by those who should know better." Similarly, another Islamic leader, Alhaji Balarabe, says, "We are therefore prepared to shed blood to defend our religion." The assumption is that this is their right to religious freedom. But is it really religious freedom? In "Nigeria on the Brink of Religious War," a reflection on Northern states' adoption of Islamic law, which resulted in increasing Christian-Muslim tensions, Minchakpu argued that "Many Muslim religious leaders are unbending." He cited Sheikh Abubakar Jibrin, the imam of Fasfam Mosque in the northeastern city of Sokoto as saying, "It is on the basis of freedom

---

50. John Boer, *Muslims: Why the Violence?* In Studies in Christian-Muslim Relations, Vol. 2, 77–78.
51. Boer, *Muslims: Why the Violence?*, 78.

The Impact of Ethnic, Political, and Religious Violence on
Northern Nigeria, and a Theological Reflection on Its Healing

76

of worship that people in these states, who are predominantly Muslims, want to be governed by the laws of their religion." Thus, violence persists in Nigeria because nobody seems to be willing to take responsibility for the problem of the country. This refusal to accept responsibility is itself concealed in spiritual arrogance. Social criticism is crucial to any community's moral vision.[52]

(3) Violence persists because of Nigerians'—including Muslim Nigerians'—unwillingness to accept failure. When nobody wants to accept responsibility for a problem, the next line of action is to shift the blame. The West and North America, in particular are blamed for Islam's decline today. As Lewis writes, "American paramountcy, as Middle Easterners see it, indicates where to direct the blame and the resulting hostility."[53]

Arrogance is a universal affliction. The Christians in Nigeria are not immune to it, either. In the meantime I must ask the question, why did the Islamization project—in part—fail in Nigeria and elsewhere? Alasdair MacIntyre's explanation of why the Enlightenment project in the West partially failed provides some insights. Referring to the Enlightenment project, MacIntyre argues that lack of self-questioning is responsible for much of human moral blindness.[54] MacIntyre points out that when we look at the eighteenth century we will discover that Scottish moral philosophers (Hume and Smith) "were the least self-questioning, presumably because

---

52. See arguments on the necessity of social criticism. Michael Walzer reminds us of a crucial reason why criticism is usually best done within the community of shared understanding: "No doubt, societies do not criticize themselves; social critics are individuals, but they are also, most of the time, members, speaking in public to other members who join in the speaking and whose speech constitute a collective reflection upon the conditions of collective life" (*Interpretation and Social Criticism*, [Cambridge, Massachusetts, and London: Harvard University Press, 1987]), 35. Walzer disagrees with those who think criticism requires radical distance. His reason is simply this: "Radical detachment has the additional and not insignificant merit of turning the critic into a hero" (36). Walzer's conclusion therefore is criticism must be done in the community. Nevertheless those outside can criticize but their criticism will only be minimal. For Walzer, criticism is the product of cultural "elaboration and affirmation," 40.
53. Lewis, *The Crisis of Islam*, 97.
54. Alasdair MacIntyre, *After Virtue* (Notre Dame, Indiana: University of Notre Dame Press, 1981), 54–55.

they were already comfortable and complacent within the epistemological framework of British empiricism."[55]

In Northern Nigeria the Islamic elite are comfortable with the way things are and therefore complacent. They are, in many ways, similar to the British moral philosophers as described by MacIntyre. However, they specialized in the art of using religious language to pit the poor or the oppressed against each other. In short, Northern Nigerian, Muslim elite have tried to shield their people against Western infiltration. Thus it is not true that Islam failed to achieve its goal in Nigeria because of British truncation of the Caliphate system. The main reason is because their moral philosophers "were the least self-questioning." They felt that indirect rule gave them the security they needed. Thus they were presumably already comfortable and complacent within the epistemological scheme of Islamic theocracies. But the issue of lack of self-criticism is in itself one of the critical causes of violence in Nigeria.

When it comes to the problem of self-criticism, the Christian community is not immune.[56] In the next section I attempt to dissect the Christian dimension of the issue at stake.

1.2.1.2 Christianity

Mainstream Christianity came to the Northern region of the country mostly through the coast: the Southwest and the Southeast coastal areas. Roman Catholic—particularly Portuguese—missionaries arrived the coastal areas of Nigeria in the late seventeenth century. But the founding of many churches in Northern Nigeria is traceable to the eighteenth century revival in the Church of England, which gave birth to the Church Missionary Society (CMS [now Church Mission Society]) in 1799. There were also missionaries from North America, Sudan Interior Mission, (SIM [now Society of International Ministries]) which came to the Northern region through the Southwest in 1893 and gave birth to the Evangelical

---

55. MacIntyre, *After Virtue*, 55.
56. Luke 24:46–47.

Church of West Africa (ECWA) in 1956. Turaki tells us that SIM was one of the first missions that came to Southern Zaria in 1910.[57]

Generally, mainstream missionaries in Nigeria made hard decisions and many mistakes. Believers were required to break completely with the past. Polygamists were forced to renounce their wives. Those who failed were regarded as outcasts or backsliders. The missionaries emphasized the importance of spiritual encounter and true repentance as the necessary indicators of Christian life. The African cultures and histories were assumed and seen as unredeemable and/or taboos. Consequently, the African believers were uprooted from their cultures and histories: they were left culturally, socially, and spiritually dangling in mid-air. Thus, in most cases, they remain babes and immature Christians for years.

This situation became clearer when the wave of Charismatic and Pentecostal movements swept through the continent of Africa from Europe and North America in the 1970s. Pentecostalism presented unprecedented challenge to the mainline churches in Nigeria. Most importantly, the Charismatic and Pentecostal movements revealed the weakness of the church: the church was tested and found wanting.

The Charismatic and Pentecostal movements in Nigeria, which took their origin from the worldwide spread of the Pentecostal, and charismatic movements from Northern America and Britain in the 1960s sought to contextualise African Christianity. The younger generation of Christians became dissatisfied with the way things were in the mainline churches, which worship like Euro-American worshipers. They were therefore looking for something authentically African. As a result, Matthew Ojor tells us, "In Nigeria the charismatic movements initially arose among college students and university graduates in the early 1970s, emphasizing. The Pentecostals doctrines of baptism of the Holy Spirit and spread in tongues as means of revitalizing the lives of Christians."[58] The Pentecostal and Charismatic movements presence in Nigeria expose the shoddy foundation

---

57. Turaki, *The British Colonial Legacy in Northern Nigeria*, 111.
58. Matthew Ojo, "The Contextual Significance of the Charismatic Movements in Independent Nigeria" in *Africa: Journal of the International Institute*, Vol. 58, No. 2, 1988, 192.

of Christianity in Nigeria, particularly in the Northern region. The major challenge that the scenario of Pentecostalism and Charismaticism indicated was Christian's lack of clarity about the meaning of Christianity; that is, what the Church is all about.

Therefore I want to be very clear about what I mean by Christianity. By Christianity I am referring to the Christian Church. And by Christian Church I am recognizing, as H. Richard Niebuhr demonstrates, that "the Church is not the only human community directed toward the divine reality; its uniqueness lies in its particular relation to that reality, a relation inseparable from Jesus Christ. It is related to God through Jesus Christ, first in the sense that Jesus Christ is the center of this community directed toward God."[59] Hence the Church must be willing to align with Jesus Christ to fulfill God's will and purpose for this earth.

Like Johann Baptist Metz, my starting point is that missiologically speaking, we are standing at the end of the European-centered era of Christianity. One of the outstanding features of Christianity since the turn of the twenty-first century has been the incredible desire of Christian churches to fulfill Jesus' priestly prayer for unity: "that they may be one." This concern has given impetus to the unprecedented global trend in ecclesiology that raises the question, "What makes a church church?"[60] Intriguingly, this question is being asked by all and sundry in that those in the perceived margin (church laity) are seeking to know their true lot in the church as well as in society; and that attitude is making it difficult for the so-called established churches today to continue doing "business as usual."[61] The Christian community's mission is to model humanity's need of repentance and forgiveness. Hence it is not just the Muslims who need to take responsibility for the problems of the north. But neither the Muslims nor the Christians seem willing to do so. This has evidently revealed, in part, the magnitude of the impact of violence on our values and perspectives.

---

59. H. Richard Niebuhr, *The Purpose of The Church and its Ministry* (New York, Hagerstown, San Francisco, London: Harper & Row, Publishers, 1956), 20.
60. Veli-Matti Kärkkäinen, *Ecumenical, Historical & Global Perspectives: An Introduction to Ecclesiology* (Illinois: InterVarsity, 2002), 9.
61. Sunday B. Agang, "Ecumenical Suspicion in Africa", an unpublished seminar research paper presented to Dr. Veli-Matti Kärkkäinen, Winter Quarter 2003, 2.

Arguably, this general situation of refusing to accept responsibility is embedded in humanity's nature. That is why, as Jared Diamond points out, lack of self-questioning is "today the reason even though segments of Western society publicly repudiate racism; yet many (perhaps most!) Westerners continue to accept racist explanation privately or subconsciously. In Japan and many other countries, such explanations are still advanced publicly and without apology."[62] For the Christian community "the crucified Christ is the test of faith. He is the stumbling block set by God to cause the downfall of those who look for righteousness on the merits of their own pious works. But he is also the sign of salvation for all who put their faith and trust in him."[63] Christians' arrogance is unfounded for they still have fewer prerogatives. Their only claim to belong to the people of God is their faith in Jesus Christ. Thus as Hans Küng aptly points out, "Self-glorification, scorn, mockery, pride, any sort of revenge against . . ." non-Christians "indicate a total misunderstanding of the situation."[64] But the church is often under siege by external and internal crises, as the analysis below demonstrates.

(1) The Internal Crisis of Christianity in Nigeria

Like Islam in Nigeria, Christianity has its own side of the story. In the 1970s and 1980s there was internal rancor between the mainline churches (hereafter Euro-American Missionary Established Churches [EAMECs]) and the fast growing Charismatic-Pentecostal or Indigenous churches (hereafter African Independence Churches [AICs]). The AICs saw the EAMECs as traitors. EAMECs had adopted the Western cultures that the Euro-American missionaries brought, resulting in cultural uprooting. Consequently, the AICs are allegedly embarking on a quest for the renewal of African Christianity. In the late 1970s and 1980s they became a threat to the mainline churches. Thus the AICs look at the EAMECs as spiritually dead churches.[65]

---

62. Jared Diamond, *Guns, Germs and Steel: The Fates of Human Societies* (New York; London: W. W. Norton & Company, 1999), 19.
63. Hans Küng, *The Church* (New York: Sheed and Ward, 1967), 144.
64. Küng, *The Church*, 145.
65. Agang, "Ecumenical Suspicion in Africa," 10.

AICs teachings included, among other things, embracing the African worldview, exorcising demons, healing miracles, prosperity, and speaking in tongues as the public sign of being genuinely "born again." The EAMECs in Nigeria nicknamed the AICs "born again." The EAMECs see the AICs as their Muslim counterparts see the Izala. There is a certain animosity caused by mistrust and prejudice. The mistrust is partially due to the way some of the AICs were started. Many AICs in Nigeria are started as ecumenical fellowships,[66] with prayers or Bible studies. At first, potential attendees are told that the meeting is nonchurch or nondenominational. Such a gathering, in the beginning, may meet on Friday afternoons or Saturday evenings. But down the road, as the leader gains the confidence of the attendees, the meeting will be shifted to Sunday morning instead of the usual Friday afternoon or Saturday evening.[67] Gradually, a church is started, and the EAMEC members by now have been enticed with an attractive position in such a gathering, which obligates them to stay even when a new name of the church is announced. Consequently, AICs' attitude encourages EAMEC pastors and elders to have a long-term bitter hatred and deep anger toward their members and also toward the AIC leaders.

It is this bitterness that generates labeling and stereotyping with a view of ridiculing or reducing the other to nothingness. S.I. Moboea observes that some of the EAMEC regard the AIC not as "churches but [as] subverts of the gospel, or sects." He argues that the AICs encourage dual membership, which is causing serious confusion today in Africa. Some EAMEC members are EAMEC members during the day and AIC members, even co-leaders, at night. "These people yearn for the caring and personal identity that exists within the AICs but are lacking it in the historical church, with its cold, stereotyped and one-sided leadership."[68] In addition, I believe most early AICs were a result of dissatisfaction with what was going on with the mission that usually wanted to assert control and, when defection happened, those who defected were persecuted and regarded as outcasts.

---

66. See also Veli-Matti Kärkkäinen, *Toward Pneumatological Theology*, 39.
67. Agang, "Ecumenical Suspicion in Africa," 35.
68. Kärkkäinen, *Toward Pneumatological*, 126.

This attitude makes it difficult for any cordial relationship between those who broke away and those who stayed with the mission.

Like Izala, their Islamic counterpart, AICs have some strength: enormous desire for independence, autonomy and the freedom to express religious faith and carry out religious practices in ways and manners that are deeply meaningful in Africa.[69] This is a positive development as long as it is done with a genuine motive. For as Victor E.W. Hayward observes, "Human motives are almost invariably mixed."[70] Our human fallen nature often impinges on our vision and thus causes us to seek interior motives that exclude others who do not share our aspiration and perspective. The AICs' loyalty and interest in appropriating the manifold power of the Holy Spirit tends to distort their understanding of why Christian unity is important. They often forget that Christian unity is embedded in Christ's vision for his Church. AIC members, in fact, tend to think that being filled with the Holy Spirit guarantees infallibility. Hence they look down on those who do not speak in tongues and label them as "dead churches."

In summary, the AIC versus EAMEC case study has brought to light the underpinning factors of violence in Nigeria. We continue to engage in self-defense or self-covering. The Church ought to do better than it has done. But it has also had its problems. The Pentecostal and Charismatic churches have abhorred the mainline churches and vice-versa. I believe that the labeling is a sign of pride. Historically, when the Church forgets that it is "the already and not yet," it has tended to claim absolute truth, resulting in the lack of tolerance of those who differ. As Küng writes, "In all ages the Church has been partly responsible for the rise of great heresies, and nearly always by neglecting or even by obscuring and distorting the Gospel."[71]

Similarly, Jürgen Moltmann has argued that when the Church fails to engage in self-criticism it faces the danger of decay. The question that the church should not fail to ask is, "How can we live in community not only with one another but also with people who differ?" Paul alluded to this

---

69. E.W. Hayward Victor, ed., *African/Madagascar Independent Church Movements* (London: Edinburgh House Press, 1963), 27.
70. Victor, *African Madagascar Independent Church Movement*, 27.
71. Küng, *The Church*, 247.

problem when he wrote, "Accept one another, then, just as Christ accepted you, in order to bring praise to God" (Rom. 15:7). Acceptance is a key ingredient in human interpersonal interaction—with acceptance we feel the joy of being human. That is, as Moltmann correctly observes,

> When others look at us in a friendly way, we feel alive and vital. When others recognize us just the way we are, we feel fulfilled. . . . Acceptance is the atmosphere of humanity. Where acceptance is lacking, the air becomes thin, our breathing falters, and we languish. Therefore we are repulsed by the indifferent glance, hurt by disregard, and humanly destroyed when others deny us.[72]

The Church in history has tended, especially when it has become aligned with external powers, to become impatient with its enthusiasts and those who differ. This is what Küng points out when he says, "The establishing of the State Church from the time of Constantine brought with it a time of *violent opposition* to heretics. It had become increasingly the custom to measure heresy not primarily against the message of the Gospel, but against particular theological doctrines and systems, against 'orthodoxy.'"[73]

The Gospel that Küng is referring to here is nothing short of dealing with one another on the basis of what Christ has done instead of on the basis of our preconception of who is "in" and who is "out." Paul was addressing a situation wherein the Jewish Christians were looking down on the Gentile Christians. Perhaps the Jewish Christians felt they were privileged Christians while the Gentile Christians had to come by grace.[74] But Romans is Paul's careful rebuke to such preconceived notions. Both Jewish and Gentile Christians have the same way of coming to Christ: by God's grace!

---

72. Jürgen Moltmann, *The Open Church: Invitation to a Messianic Lifestyle* (London: SCM Press, Philadelphia: Fortress Press, 1978), 27.
73. Küng, *The Church*, 249.
74. Moltmann, *The Open Church*, 28.

The situation in Northern Nigeria is a bit different because it is not about Jewish and Gentile Christians. Nevertheless, it is similar in the sense that it is about the Church trying to exclude others on the basis of their doctrine and mode of worship. It is a situation in which names are called and stereotypes are formed. The Church tends to find it difficult to be the community of hope, love, faith, justice, and peacemaking. History is repeating itself in Northern Nigeria. As Küng argues,

> It is true that the opponents of heresy in the Church had from early times abandoned the prime commandment of love in their setting of questions of faith, and had abused and reviled those who held different notions and beliefs. The sowing of hatred was bound to lead to a bloody harvest. The church in power soon abandoned the tolerance for which the persecuted Church had pleaded and with the help of the "Christian" state it began to persecute those who pleaded for tolerance. . . . The Gospel of Jesus Christ on which the Church bases itself makes it completely impossible to turn aside from love even for a moment and even for the sake of the unity of the Church. It is love, after all, which holds the body of Church together.[75]

In the final analysis, whoever alienates others alienates himself. Thus Moltmann asks a pertinent question, "What is the reason for this alienation from each other in which we allow others to suffer and in which we ourselves also finally suffer?"[76] He suggests two reasons. First, "The reason is that we accept others, even our neighbors, only on our own turf and view them only with our own preconceptions. And thus we do not at all seek the other but only ourselves in the other. We leave the other alone and remain alone ourselves."[77] Second, "We accept and treat each other only in terms of reciprocity: 'you scratch my back and I'll scratch yours.'"[78] In that case,

---

75. Küng, *The Church*, 253.
76. Moltmann, *The Open Church*, 29.
77. Moltmann, *The Open Church*, 29.
78. Moltmann, *The Open Church*, 29.

people whose life, "thoughts, feelings, and desires are different from ours, make us feel insecure."[79]

Paul recognizes this tension. This is why he makes Christ the basis of our attitude toward each other. Accept one another, "as Christ accepted you" (Rom. 15:7). We can break with our human limitations only when we grasp the depth of what Christ has done for us. Recognizing how Christ has embraced us just as we are will move us away from our notions of who is "inside" and who is "outside."

Finally, the Christian ecumenical suspicion analyzed above can contribute to the impasse of reconciliation and just peacemaking in Northern Nigeria. That is, if the Church has not been able to set its house in order, how can it set about creating just peace in society? The strategic nature of the Church in Nigeria and the global community requires that it thinks of creating a community of hope, love, justice, peace, and righteousness in a society infested by violence like northern Nigeria.

1.2.2 The Economic Dimension of the Threat

Nigeria is a money-centered society. The well being of the society is defined by this market philosophy. Yet decision makers have largely neglected the impact of economic policies on society's social capital.[80] They tend to forget that since the discovery of oil in 1956s, 80 percent of Nigerian economic mainstay has shifted from agriculture to white-collar jobs. Thus, to have no employment spells doom for anyone who finds himself in that situation; in a society that has moved from family-centered society to a money-centered society, unemployment means hopelessness and frustration.

Unemployment creates a great deal of distress that is easily ignited at the slightest provocation. Paul E. Lovejoy and Pat Ama Tokunbo William maintain that Nigerians have had to grapple with enormous social, political, religious, and economic forces. These forces have given the military every reason to perpetuate their hegemony in Nigeria. Consequently, Lovejoy, et al., point out,

---

79. Moltmann, *The Open Church*, 30.
80. David C. Korten, *Globalizing Civil Society: Reclaiming our Right to Power* (New York: Seven Stories Press, 1998), 56.

The maintenance of full-fledged military rule required increasing repressive measures against its opposition. The political situation reached a stalemate. The contending forces among the economic and religious elite within Nigeria have since been contesting control over the economy. Often this struggle has been perceived in religious terms. These conflicts have many-times degenerated into violence; conditions of insecurity have increased as the different factions within the country have attempted to corner for themselves the vestiges of state power. Solutions to the problems underlying this instability have remained elusive because political, religious, class, and ethnic factors have to be considered. This complexity has enabled the military government to manipulate the situation for its purposes. Nigerians who can no longer endure the situation have been forced to leave the country in multitudes.[81]

The paradigm shift from a family-cum-agrarian society to a market-cum-money-centered society explains why corruption is largely a barrier to Nigeria's social, political, and economic developments. The military and some civilian/political leaders in Nigeria can be likened to raiders whose intention is to plunder the nation's economic resources. Their attitude has proved that they are economic raiders who see the Nigerian economy as something to be plundered and taken as spoil.

The pace of corruption in a world that is flattened by a technological and globalized economy is increasing. It is networked into transnational corporations who are also involved in this game. This double raiding and plundering that is going on today is making life unbearable for the poor in Northern Nigeria and elsewhere. People are in great distress; the result is a chain of reaction and resistance that wells up not only in violence against oppressive regimes but also against other poor people in the society. In short, the overall economic decline is affecting every sphere of life, especially

---

81. Paul E. Lovejoy and Pat A. T. Williams, eds., *Displacement and the Politics of Violence in Nigeria* (New York: Leiden, 1997), 34.

"the religious establishment."[82] This results in increased competition and tension, as individuals struggle to maintain their positions or to acquire new ones. Youth unemployment is creating unimaginable frustration, hopelessness and violence in Northern Nigeria.

1.2.3 The Political Dimension of the Threat

As the liver is to the human body, the Northern region is to Nigeria; whatever affects it affects the country at large. As Leo Dare demonstrates, "political instability has been a chronic problem both before and after political independence from Britain. Population displacement has been a major factor of recent Nigerian history."[83]

1.2.3.1 The Broad Sociopolitical Situation

The broad political situation of Nigeria portrays a political climate saturated with policies that have inhibited the realization of the goal of independence. Both military and civilian leaders treat their subjects as spoils. Given that the British in part, created the situation, these military and civilian leaders are perpetuating the inhumane treatment of Nigerians and Africans at large.[84]

(a) The Colonial Context

Some authors tend to overemphasize the impact of Colonial Policies in Northern Nigeria, blaming it for all problems and therefore not accepting their own responsibility. Abdullahi argues that the British policies in Northern Nigeria were detrimental to the Islamic educational system. But this is not wholly true. The point is, as Eghosa tells us, "Most parts of the North were shielded from Western influences, especially education and Christian missionary activities, in accordance with a pact Lugard was said to have signed with the emirs." This policy was the enabling environment

---

82. See Frederick De Jong, et al., eds., *Islamic Mysticism Contested: Thirteen Centuries of Controversies and Polemics* (Leiden, Boston and Köln: Brill, 1999), 243.
83. Leo Dare as cited by Lovejoy E. Paul, et al., *Displacement and the Politics of Violence in Nigeria* (Leiden; New York: Brill, 1997), 35.
84. Wole Soyinka, *The Open Sore of a Continent: A Personal Narrative of the Nigeria Crisis* (New York, Oxford: Oxford University Press, 1996), 96.

for an educational gap between the Christian southwest and even to some extent the Middle Belt that is part of the North but not the so-called "core" North. For example, "by 1912 there were only 34 primary schools in the North compared with the South's 150 primary schools, and ten secondary schools (the first in the North was established in 1922)."[85] These are past situations whose impacts interact with present violence in Northern Nigeria. It is the reason the Southern region abhors the Northern leadership. It is also the reason the Core North is violent toward the Middle Belt, which they have tried to subjugate to their tutelage.

(b) The Beginnings of Nigeria Wars

Between the late 1950s and early 1960s oil was discovered off Port Harcourt and a movement for Igbo independence began. In January 1966 a group of Igbo army majors murdered the federal Prime Minister, Sir Alhaji Abubakar Tafawa Balewa; the Premiers of the Northern and Western regions; and many leading politicians. In July, a group of Northern officers retaliated and installed General Gowon as Head of State. A massacre of several thousand Igbo living in the North followed.

Attempts to work out constitutional provisions failed, and in May 1967 the military governor of the Eastern region, Colonel Ojukwu, announced his region's secession and the establishment of the republic of Biafra. Civil war between the Hausa and Igbo peoples erupted, and Biafra collapsed in 1970. General Gowon was deposed in 1975.

(c) Military and Civilian Leaders' Roles

Africa has been home to many military coups. As Harvey J. Sindima rightly notes, the military usually comes in as the messiahs of the nation. In his words, "The reasons that are often given for staging a coup are

---

85. However, according to Eghosa, by 1957 when many of the restrictions on Christian missionary activities in the North had been relaxed, especially in the Middle Belt areas, the number of schools increased to 2,080 primary with 185,484 pupils and eighteen secondary with 643 students. Comparative figures for the South were: 13,473 primary with 2,343, and 317 pupils and 176 secondary with 28,208 students (Ngou, 1989:84) as quoted by Eghosa, *Crippled Giant*, 5.

the deterioration of the economic and political situation of a country."[86] Ironically, civilian leaders sometimes create an inviting political situation by not serving the interests of the citizenry. Sindima explains,

> Military intervention is not entirely the fault of soldiers . . .
> For instance, when a civilian government is weak and feels
> threatened by the opposition or dissidents and then calls in
> soldiers instead of seeking a political solution; it makes soldiers
> feel that they have the power to unify the state.[87]

Yet the question that ought to be answered is whether the military is any better than their civilian counterparts in Nigeria. The answer is, simply, no. It is no because military rulers are sometimes worse than their civilian counterparts. Sindima points out, "Nigeria has had several coups: 1966, 1975, 1983, and 1985."[88] If the military rule was better than democratic rule Nigeria would have not been in the situation it finds itself today. Due to economic greed and other selfish interests, both civilian and military rulers have often succeeded in institutionalizing corruption in Nigeria. Military governments (despite their claim to moral authority) in all their years in power in Nigeria, have failed to produce a cleaner, honest, and efficient government. Instead, they spread corruption to all spheres of society.

The point is that military in Nigeria has had every opportunity to demonstrate that it is the messiah it claimed to be, but it has failed. As Sindima notes,

> There have been so many coups, so many soldier-rulers who
> have ruled. If military governments had moral integrity, as
> they claim, Nigeria would have the cleanest government in
> Africa. On the contrary, corruption and political instability

---

86. Harvey J. Sindima, *Religious and Political Ethics in Africa: A Moral Inquiry* (Westport, Connecticut, London: Greenwood Press, 1998), 46.
87. Sindima, *Religious and Political Ethics*, 47.
88. Sindima tells of how in Nigeria military governments have fought each other for long periods, from 1966–1979 and from 1985 to 1998, *Religious and Political Ethics*, 46.

continue to plague the country in astronomical proportions. There is corruption within the military itself.[89]

For instance, "Before President Ibrahim Bangidan left office, he had money worth 5 million U.S. dollars. His predecessor Sani Abacha before his mysterious death had money worth 8 million U.S. dollars."[90] The military's usual excuses for a coup include, among other things, corruption and mismanagement. Yet when they are given the opportunity to demonstrate their capability to salvage the nation, the army also falls victim to corruption. Innocent citizens bear the consequences of such irresponsible leadership and interruption of democracy. For instance, in 1979 the military government organized multiparty elections. Corruption and unrest precipitated more military takeovers, in 1983 and 1985, when General Ibrahim Babangida became Head of State. Table 1 (below) shows the catalogue of events.

The social and political crisis continued and Sanni Abacha took over as head of state in November 1993. He dismantled many existing political institutions and re-instituted the 1979 military constitution, but continued to insist that a civilian government would eventually be installed. Abiola returned to Nigeria to campaign for democracy and was arrested in 1994. In 1995 the government announced that civilian rule could not be introduced before 1997, but lifted the ban on political activity. However, in October 1995, nine pro-democracy activists were charged with murder and were executed, provoking international outrage. As a result, Nigeria was suspended from the Commonwealth. Social unrest has persisted. Following Abacha's death in 1998, General Abdulsalami Abubakar became President. He released the remaining political prisoners and restored democratic rule. In subsequent elections General Obasanjo was elected President and Nigeria was readmitted to the Commonwealth in 1999.

89. Sindima, *Religious and Political Ethics*, 51.
90. Sindima, *Religious and Political Ethics*, 51.

1.2.3.2 The Shape and Pattern of Nigeria's violence from the Eleventh to Twenty-first Century

Political violence has continued to destroy the Nigerian state. In the April 14, 2007 elections Nigerians went to the poll to elect governors for the 36 states and houses of assembly members. The election was marred by violence, irregularities, and rigging. Consequently, fifty-two people were killed nation wide.[91]

Table 2 (below) shows the shape and pattern of violence in Nigeria, particularly in the North, from the Eleventh to the Twenty-First Century. This table demonstrates that Nigeria's violence is often tied into the social-historical situation in which every Nigerian lives. That means that it is critical and, in fact, necessary for us to deal more adequately with the social complexity and conflict in Northern Nigeria's society.

TABLE 2
A CENTURY LEGACY OF CONFLICT
(Source: distilled from B.B.C. *News Africa: Country profile: Nigeria*)
(www.bbc.africannews/nigeria.com)

DATE	KEY EVENTS
Circa 800 BC	Jos Plateau settled by Nok—a Neolithic and iron age civilization
Circa Eleventh Century onwards	Formation of city states, kingdom and empires, including Hausa Kingdoms and Borno dynasty in north, Oyo and Benin kingdom in south
1472	Portuguese navigators reach Nigerian coast

---

91. In one of the national newspapers, *Vanguard*, Sunday, April 15, 2007, it was reported that "Violence mars polls 52 people killed." That is to say, "Amid violence in many states of the country, Nigerians went to the polls yesterday to elect governors for the 36 states and members of the Houses of Assembly. About 52 persons lost their lives to the violence that characterized the polls with the highest toll coming from Rivers States where seven policemen and four soldiers were killed by suspected militants who attacked two police stations at Mino Okoro and Elelenwo."

92

The Impact of Ethnic, Political, and Religious Violence on
Northern Nigeria, and a Theological Reflection on Its Healing

DATE	KEY EVENTS
Sixteenth to Eighteenth Centuries	Slave trade: Millions of Nigerians are forcibly sent to the Americas.
1809	Single Islamic state—Sokoto caliphate—is founded in north
1830s–1886	Civil wars plague Yorubaland, in the south
1850s	British establish presence around Lagos
1861–1914	Britain consolidates its hold over what it calls the Colony and Protectorate of Nigeria, governs by "indirect rule" through local leaders
1922	Part of former German colony Cameroon is added to Nigeria under League of Nations mandate
1960	Independence, with Prime Minister Sir Abubakar Tafawa Balewa leading a coalition government
1962–63	Controversial census fuels regional and ethnic tensions
1966 January	Balewa killed in coup. Major-General Johnson Aguyi-Ironsi heads up military administration
1966 July	Ironsi killed in counter-coup, replaced by Lieutenant-Colonel Yakubu Gowon
1967	Three eastern states secede as the Republic of Biafra, sparking bloody civil war
1970	Biafran leaders surrender, former Biafran regions reintegrated into country
1975	Gowon overthrown, flees to Britain, replaced by Brigadier Murtala Ramat Mohammed, who begins process of moving federal capital to Abuja
1976	Mohammed assassinated in coup attempt. Replaced by Lieutenant-General Olusegun Obasanjo, who helps introduce American-style presidential constitution
1979	Elections bring Shehu Shagari to power

DATE	KEY EVENTS
1983 January	The government expels more than one million foreigners, mostly Ghanaians, saying they had overstayed their visas and were taking jobs from Nigerians. The move is condemned abroad but proves popular in Nigeria
1983 August	Shagari re-elected amid accusation of irregularities
1983 December	Major-General Muhammad Buhari seizes power in bloodless coup
1985	Ibrahim Babangida seizes power in bloodless coup, curtails political activity
12 June 1993	Nigeria's freest and fairest elections ever
1993 June	Military annuls elections when preliminary results show victory by chief Moshood Abiola
1993 August	Power transferred to Interim National Government
1993 November	General Sani Abacha seizes power, suppresses opposition
30 May 1994	National Democratic Coalition (NADECO) formed to oppose military rule
12 June 1994	Abiola arrested after proclaiming himself president
16 June 1994	Abiola jailed for treason. Country becomes ungovernable and economy goes into freefall
29 September 1994	Provisional Ruling Council dissolved—Abacha passes new draconian laws to insulate himself from popular anger
1995	Ken Saro-Wiwa, writer and campaigner against oil industry damage to his Ogoni homeland, is executed following hasty trial. In protest, European Union imposes sanctions until 1998, Commonwealth suspends Nigeria's membership until 1998
1998	Abacha dies, succeeded by Major-General Abdulsalami Abubakar, Chief Abiola dies in custody a month later
1999 May 29	Parliamentary and presidential elections. Olusegun Obasanjo sworn in as president

DATE	KEY EVENTS
2000 February 21–25	Adoption of Islamic or Sharia law by several northern states in the face of opposition from Christians. Tension over the issue results in hundreds of deaths in clashes between Christians and Muslims
2001 February	Tribal war in Benue state, in eastern-central Nigeria, displaces thousands of people. In October, army soldiers quash the fighting, kill more than 200 unarmed civilians, apparently in retaliation for the abduction and murder of 19 soldiers
2001 October	Nigerian President Olusegun Obasanjo, South African President Mbeki and Algerian President Bouteflika launch New Partnership for African Development, or Nepad, which aims to foster development and open government and end wars in return for aid, foreign investment and the lifting of trade barriers to African exports.
2002 January	Blast at munitions dump in Lagos kills more than 1,000
2002 February	Some 100 people are killed in Lagos in clashes between Hausas from mainly Islamic north and ethnic Yorubas from predominantly Christian southwest. Thousands flee. City's governor suggests retired army officials stoked violence in attempt to restore military rule
2002 March	Appeals court reverses death sentence against woman found guilty of adultery. Islamic court in north had ordered she be stoned to death
2002 October	International Court of Justice awards the disputed Bakassi peninsula to Cameroon, but Nigeria is adamant that it will defend its right to the valuable land mass
2002 November	More than 200 people die in four days of rioting stoked by Muslim fury over the planned Miss World beauty pageant in Kaduna in December. The event is relocated to Britain

DATE	KEY EVENTS
2003 April 12	First legislative elections since end of military rule in 1999. Polling marked by delays, allegations of ballot rigging. President Obasanjo People's Democratic party wins parliamentary majority
2003 July	Nationwide general strike called off after nine days after government agrees to lower recently increased fuel prices
2003 August	Violence between Ijaw and Itsekiri people in Delta town of Warri kills about 100 people, injures 1,000
2004 May	State of emergency is declared in the central Plateau State after more than 200 Muslims are killed in Yelwa in attacks by Christian militia; revenge attacks are launched by Muslim youths in Kano
2005 May	Muslims attacked and killed Christians in Kaduna
2006 February	More than 157 people are killed when religious violence flares in mainly-Muslim towns in the north and in the southern city of Onitsha

The above table shows that far from bringing peace and prosperity, the end of British rule in Nigeria left the country open to chaotic violence. Yet the impacts of these crises seem to be quickly forgotten by those who think religion and ethnicity are our only major threats. Granted, religion and ethnicity are the problem. But if religion and ethnicity are a part of the problem, then they must be a part of the solution.

1.2.3.3 The Ethnic Dimension of the Threat

The colonialist fusion of diverse histories, which took place for the sake of political convenience and so-called unity, has backfired in Nigeria. We are reaping the consequences of a colonial legacy of diverse histories intermingled in Nigeria. Moltmann points out how industrialization and European imperialism has led to this sad human experience.[92]

---

92. Jürgen Moltmann, *The Experiences of Theology: Ways and Forms of Christian Theology* (Minneapolis: Fortress Press, 2000), 123.

This fusion has left an indelible legacy of slavery in Northern Nigeria. It was one of the approaches that handed over the pagan tribes in the Middle Belt into the cruel hands of the Northern Hausa-Fulani hegemony. But the question is, why would other human beings want to enslave others? Is anyone free from slavery? First, I wish to underscore the fact that everyone in the North is a slave to something. But we continue to deny this sad reality. We are like the Jews of Jesus' day who denied the reality of Roman occupation: "We are Abraham's descendants and have never been slaves of anyone" (John 8:33). They pretended to forget the history of prolonged occupations of world imperial regimes over the centuries. Jesus retorted, "Everyone who sins is a slave to sin" (John 8:34). Occupation is a violation of human rights. As such, it is a sin against humanity. So the occupiers are often slaves to their own acts.[93]

1.2.3.4 The Legacy of Institutionalized and Globalized Slavery

In Northern Nigeria, without slavery of the minorities, the North would not have survived. Violence in Nigeria today is also the legacy of slavery. Years of enslavement of the pagan population in Northern Nigeria have profoundly infected the souls of the Hausa-Fulani with this disease of violence. It is manifested in Nigeria's form of racism institutionalized by the British.[94] Even today, the Hausa-Fulani involvement in slave raiding and trading has had a tremendous impact on their view of non-Muslims.

Given that, as Berkow tells us, Islam is the sole mark of identity to Hausa-Fulani[95] in Northern Nigeria: to be human is to be a Muslim; people of different religious persuasions are seen as nonpersons, sub-human, or people of inferior values and capacities. One's own self-esteem is based on one's religion, ethnicity, and political status. In this legitimating function, religion, ethnicity, and politics "become dangerous means of psychological warfare waged by the ruler over the ruled. As 'second-class citizens' the people belonging to this dominated group are denied civil rights; as itiner-

---

93. Moltmann, *The Experiences of Theology*, 190.
94. See Turaki, *The British Colonial Legacy in Northern Nigeria*, 64–65.
95. Berkow, "Hausa" in *Muslim People*, 151.

ant workers they are kept permanently dependent and homeless, they are open to every violent action. The feelings of superiority cherished by the dominating race then produce feelings of inferiority among the races that are dominated. Religious, ethnic, and political racism always have two sides: they are both a psychological mechanism of self-righteousness on the one hand and on the other an ideological mechanism for the domination of others. Thus Moltmann is right, "Racism [of any kind] destroys humanity on both sides."[96]

The Muslim racist displays superhuman pride in his Islam and is yet obsessed by an inhuman fear. Those who assume that to be human is to be Muslim destroy their own humanity.

1.2.3.5 The Scenario of Displaced People

Nigeria is home to many forms of displacement. But displacement does not feature as a cause of violence in most analysis. Nigeria is a country in which there are displaced people both within and without. From within, many people live as displaced people in their homeland, and from without, there are refugees from neighboring countries who end up living in Nigeria, either legally or illegally. Lovejoy tells us that "Nigeria has received refugees from Chad, Ghana, Togo, and Nigeria—victims of poverty, drought, and general economic decay. But also, Nigeria's capacity to generate outward population flow is enormous."[97]

Since the 1950s Nigeria has witnessed mass migration of rural youths to the cities. This phenomenon makes these cities a breeding ground for violence. Both internally and externally displaced people have been factors of continuous violence in Northern Nigeria. People have dreams that remain unfulfilled, resulting in grave frustrations that generate all kinds of social reactions.

---

96. Moltmann, *The Experiences of Theology*, 197.
97. Lovejoy, et al., "Displacement and the Politics of Violence in Nigeria" *Journal of Asian and African Studies*, Vol. 32, no. 1–2 (Leiden: Brill, 1997), 6.

1.2.3.7 Poverty

Violence feeds on poverty. That is to say, violence is often a direct result of poverty. In a *Punch* editorial from February 1, 2006, Zayyad I. Muhammad points out, "Rampant violence is fed by poverty, injustice, and unemployment. Except economic succor is allowed to trickle down to the grassroots, and a level political playing field is ensured, tackling the problem of insecurity in the country will remain a mirage."[98] These observations acknowledge that poverty is truly a deep-rooted cause of violence in Northern Nigeria. Our politicians have determined to keep the poor in perpetual poverty so that they will continue to hold unto political and economic power unchallenged. Therefore, for the sake of their selfish ambition they ignore economic, social, and political contradictions, which are at the heart of the festering insecurity in the country.

The poor have lost their economic base. That is, since Nigeria's discovery of oil in the late 1950s, their economic mainstay has been displaced. Worse, white-collar jobs are hard to come by. Thus, tens of thousands of unemployed youths are roaming the streets of our urban cities. To them, violence is not only an opportunity for releasing their frustration and hopelessness but also for looting and plundering. Besides, in most cases, politicians and other wily individuals take advantage of the situation by manipulating these youths for their destructive mission in the country. The youths are denied the right to work and by extension the right to meaningful participation in building the nation.[99] This partially explains why violence persists unhindered in Northern Nigeria.

1.2.3.7 The Crisis of Freedom: Political Mobilization

In Northern Nigeria we are faced with a situation, which can rightly be called the crisis of freedom. In the past people enjoyed the freedom of moving from one region of the country to another. There was open land and virgin land where they could move to settle and farm. This is no longer the case. The available land is impoverished. Violence has made some parts

---

98. Zayyad I. Muhammad, "Poverty and Violence," *Punch*, February 1, 2006, 1.
99. See Jürgen Moltmann, *On Human Dignity: Political Theology and Ethics* (London: SCM Press Ltd, 1984), 37.

of Northern Nigeria very dangerous to live in. The shift away from freedom of land and space has left Nigerians in Northern Nigeria with only one option: political freedom.

Therefore, among the causes of violence in Nigeria's Northern region, political mobilization plays a significant role. Some studies conducted on the tribal groups of Nigeria's Middle Belt illustrate the upsurge for political determination among the various tribes. Considering most of these tribes were conquered by the Islamic *jihadists* and made to serve the Islamic traditional rulers and Emirs, one can see why this engenders violent reactions against and by those Hausa-Fulani rulers who have enjoyed unhindered hegemonic monopoly over those tribes.

Political mobilization is known as "the emancipation of the Middle Belt Peoples." The founding fathers of this vision ardently pursued the dream of political and economic emancipation for the Middle Belt People.[100]

The quest for political and economic deliverance from the Hausa-Fulani began even before Nigeria gained independence from the British: while Nigeria was struggling for independence from the British, non-Muslim tribes in the Northern region were also seeking independence from the brutal and lethal rule of the Hausa-Fulani rulers. After Nigeria gained independence from Britain, the country's leadership sensed the weight of this tension all over the country. This was the background against which states were created. For the Middle Belt tribes who had been surrounded by Muslims in the Northern region, their first priority was not creation of states but creation of a separate region from the Muslim-occupied North. The British and, thereafter, the national leaders who succeeded them rejected this desire. Instead, states were created during General Yakubu Gowon's military regime. As Ibrahim James suggests,

> The creation of states appears to have caught the Middle Belt Movement off guard as it completely altered the historical and probably the political context of the Middle Belt Movement. As the historical and probably the political context of the

---

100. James, ed., *Settler Phenomenon in the Middle Belt and the Problem of National Integration in Nigeria*, 67.

The Impact of Ethnic, Political, and Religious Violence on
Northern Nigeria, and a Theological Reflection on Its Healing

100

Movement changed, the Movement had to readjust its position and redefined its objectives within the context of the Middle Belt strategic position in Nigeria. The Middle Belt Movement appeared to have lost its momentum and became denuded of ideals and energy to sustain its struggle for the complete emancipation of all its territories and its peoples.[101]

Thus, in retrospect, the creation of states was essentially the pouring of new wine into old wineskins. Instead of just a region, everybody desired their state and their own local governments. The dicey sociopolitical and socioeconomic situations have been compounded by military and civilian regimes that have restricted the political participation of the larger population of the country. "Public office was treated as a route to personal and ethnic gratification, and contending political factions employed fraud, patronage, and violence to gain advantage."[102] Finally, the politicians who served only themselves and their ethnic groups have contributed enormously to this demand for states and the resultant ethnic, political, and religious tension and violence.

1.3 An Anatomy of Nigeria's Federalism

The wicked man craves evil; his neighbor gets no mercy from him.

—Proverbs 21:10

When justice is done, it brings joy to the righteous but terror to evildoers.

—Proverbs 21:15

A wise man [or woman] attacks the city of the mighty and pulls down the stronghold in which they trust.

—Proverbs 21:22

---

101. James, *Settler Phenomenon in the Middle Belt*, 67.
102. Peter M. Lewis, Pearl T. Robinson, and Barnett B. Rubin, *Stabilizing Nigeria: Sanctions, Incentives, and Support for Civil Society* (New York: Century Foundation Press, 1998), 44.

Nigeria's federalism was fashioned on three faulty premises: that when government is brought nearer to the people their complaints will be reduced; that state creation is a way of reducing ethnic competition and encouraging participation; and, that unity is a way of encouraging simple equality in Nigeria.[103] This is to say, one of the reasons Nigeria opted for a federal system was to foster regional and ethnic unity. But this was based on the above premises. Thus, the magic such political, economic, and social arrangements were expected to perform has not happened. Rotimi T. Suberu reminds us why the system is failing:

(1) Core political institutions, especially the presidency and the National Assembly, work as rivals. They "tend to block each other, employing mechanisms of parliamentary democracy (such as the timing of elections, or the instrument of impeachment) in a highly manipulative way."[104]

(2) "Politics" in Nigeria continues to be largely a competition among personalities, rather than programs and visions; it continues to be a playground for numerous big men (and few big women), many of whom regard political engagement primarily as an investment that will pay off after electoral success. In effect, political competition in Nigeria's fourth Republic has exacerbated the numerous lines of regional, ethnic, and religious conflict, and more political violence threatens to arise during the 2007 elections.

(3) Nigeria installed a federal political system to contain and manage this variety of conflicts, but by 2006, the federal order had once again barely come to fruition.[105]

One of the profoundest weaknesses of Nigeria's "federalism" is the neglect of the socioeconomic and sociopolitical predicaments of the minorities. Thus I argue that the causes of violence in Northern Nigeria also include the clash between different ethnicities. Nigerian history is characterized by

---

103. A.B. Akinyemi, P.D. Cole and Walter Ofonagoro, eds., *Readings in Federalism* (Lagos: Nigerian Institute of International Affairs, 1979), 191.
104. Suberu T. Rotimi, *Federalism and Ethnic Conflict in Nigeria* (Washington D.C.: United States Institute of Peace Press, 2001), xxvi, 247.
105. For more information see Axel Harneilt-Sievers' article on "Suberu, Rotimi T. Federalism and Ethnic Conflict in Nigeria" in *Africa Today Magazines*, Sept. 22, 2002 www.highbeam.com, 1–3.

a focus on the major ethnic groups or their elite. That approach has left what is happening at the grass roots level unanalyzed. In connecting dots between ethnic, political, and religious violence, those at the periphery, who make up the greater percentage of the Nigerian state, must be brought to the center of the discussion.

I shall proceed to define ethnicity albeit, as Elizabeth Isichei points out, "we are prisoners of the label we use." The word ethnicity is encompassing. It generally means ethnic affiliation or distinctiveness. But it can also mean civilization, society, mores, traditions, customs, or way of life. Generally, in a postmodern world, religion is becoming inherently linked to ethnicity. In postmodern society our local and global dreams are modifying and multiplying our conception of ethnicity. In *Global Dreams,* Richard J. Barnet and John Cavanaugh noted, "[G]overnments, families, and tribal structures are thrown into crisis by the sweeping changes of late-twentieth-century society."[106] Arbuckle aptly notes, "Ethnocentrism is a dynamic at work in every culture and subculture."[107] He further points out,

> Cultural identity requires that people feel pride in their group's achievements, and believe that other cultures have something to learn from their group. Unchecked, this group pride can go over the brink into prejudice and discrimination against people who are different, and then it ceases to be a positive value.[108]

Ironically it leads to false conclusions such as "our way of life is *the* way to live to be protected at all costs." The next step is to require other members of minority cultures or subcultures in the vicinity to be assimilated. People that do this forget, as Isichei argues, that "ethnic identity is not necessarily the same thing as the language one speaks. Fulani families which speak Hausa, but not Fulfulde, still retain a strong sense of Fulani identity

---

106. Richard J. Barnet and John Cavanaugh, *Global Dreams: Imperial Corporations and the New World Order* (New York, London, Toronto, Sydney, Tokyo, and Singapore, 1994), 137.
107. Arbuckle, *Religious Violence*, 16.
108. Arbuckle, *Religious Violence*, 17.

and some Kanuri, such as the "Lafia Beriberi', speak only Hausa. . . . Many peoples of the Jos Plateau and Benue valley are known by the names given them by the Hausa."[109] Above all, the name of ethnic groups changes over time. For example the Kaje has changed to Bajju.

Ethnicity is sometimes, but not always, identifiable with language. It is facile to identify it with culture, but as Isichei observes, "The more one studies the structures and attitudes of traditional Nigerian societies the more one is struck by their profound similarities."[110] Isichei cites the work of S. F. Nadel who made his point with reference to the Nupe:

> You ask a Nupe man what all Nupe have in common. As a rule he will enumerate the same few traits. All Nupe, he will say, have the age-grade associations, all Nupe have the *guru* cult. . . . The age-grade associations are common both to Nupe and Hausa. The rank system is common all over Northern Nigeria. . . . The *guru* cult exists also among Gbari, Gara, Basa, and Kom.[111]

In the case of Northern Nigeria, the definition of Hausa culture presents a special problem. This problem is connected with the assimilation processes that have taken place over the years in the region. The hyphenated name, *Hausa-Fulani,* is a perfect example. Two distinct ethnic groups—Fulbe and Hausa—have now been assimilated. Jerome Berkow argues that the Hausa is not an ethnic group. He writes, "It would be misleading to speak of the Hausa as a tribe or ethnic group."[112] This is because, according to him, "These terms suggest a cultural homogeneity which Hausa-speaking groups lack."[113] Thus their sole identity is the religion—Islam. Berkow notes, "A large part of the Hausa identity involves being a Muslim."[114] That

---

109. Elizabeth Allo Isichei, *A History of Nigeria* (London and New York: Longman, 1983), 12.
110. Isichei, *A History of Nigeria*, 12.
111. Isichei, *A History of Nigeria*, 12.
112. Berkow, "Hausa," in *Muslim People*, 151.
113. Berkow, "Hausa," in *Muslim People*, 151.
114. Berkow, "Hausa," in *Muslim People*, 152.

104

The Impact of Ethnic, Political, and Religious Violence on
Northern Nigeria, and a Theological Reflection on Its Healing

explains why the Muslim ethnic groups in the North seem to expect that
non-Muslim ethnic groups become assimilated to Islam.

The term *Fulani* is the name given to them by the Hausa people, another
ethnic group in northwest Nigeria. Appiah et al., explain, "Approximately
half of the Fulani live among the Hausa as a ruling class though they have
adopted many Hausa customs, as well as the Hausa language."[115] This is
why the hyphenated *Hausa-Fulani* term is used to describe the ruling class
in Northern Nigeria whose culture has been emerged in Islam since the
fourteenth century.[116]

The Hausa ethnic group on the other hand is a population composed
of 7 million ethnic Hausa and augmented by 4 million of the Fulani. The
Fulbe and the Hausa not only intermarry and mutually assimilate each
other's culture but the intermarriage actually has blurred the distinction
between the two groups.[117] Mahdi Adamu writes:

> The person should be fluent in the Hausa language, and in all
> his dealing with Hausa people should use it as his first language.
> . . . The prospective assimilant should be either a Muslim or
> bear a Muslim name; at the very least, he should use a name,
> which is distinctly associated with the Hausa people. . . . The
> person should have historical claim to Hausa ethnicity.[118]

In order to be considered a Hausa ethnic group you have to be merged
into the Hausa and Fulani culture and religion. But as Isichei points out,

> Hausa identity is a complex cultural package. It is not essential
> for a Hausa to be Muslim, as witnessed by the Abakwariga
> of the Benue valley or the Maguza[wa] south of Kano. It is
> possible to become a Hausa by assimilation, a process much in

---

115. Appiah and Gates, *The Dictionary of Global Culture*, 230.
116. Berkow, "Hausa," in *Muslim People*, 152.
117. Appiah and Gates, *The Dictionary of Global Culture*, 230.
118. Cited by Isichei, *A History of Nigeria*, 12.

evidence in central Nigeria in this century. A Hausa is defined
by his language, lifestyle, and to some extent by his religion.[119]

Generally, three major groups, Hausa-Fulani, Yoruba, and Igbo, have
overshowed the rest of the ethnic minorities. But the study conducted by
Britannica World Data in 1983 demonstrates that Nigeria's ethnic composition includes, among other things, the following: "Hausa 21.3%; Yoruba
21.3%; Igbo 18.0%; Fulani 11.2%; Ibibio 5.6%; Kanuri 4.2%; Edo 3.4%;
Tiv 2.2 %; Ijaw 1.8%; Bura 1.7%; Nupe 1.2%; other 8.1%."[120] Besides,
since the Nigerian civil of the late 1960s the Igbo ethnic group has not
regained its political significance. That is why since 1967 to date the presidency rotates between Hausa-Fulani and Yoruba ethnic groups.

In summary, the Hausa-Fulani ethnic groups dominate Northern
Nigeria. Yet while increasingly assuming greater homogeneity, Hausa-
Fulani still reflect a certain degree of ethno-linguistic and religious diversity.
It is also true that the minor ethnic groups are out of the picture of the
scholarship of Nigeria. That is, most history has been written about the
Igbos, Hausa-Fulani, and Yoruba to the detriment of the other tribes that
live within them.

This attitude has led to the infamous underrating of the political significance of these smaller ethnic groups and their exclusion from the political
power of the country. But with time some of these tribal groups have grown
in population and size to the point that they are crying out for liberation.
They want to lift the feet of their oppressors off their necks so that they can
breathe normally as dignified human beings. Although many small ethnic
groups have long been assimilated and absorbed by successive waves of
migration and settlement, there are still groups in the region that can be
reckoned with.

Berkow's study shows that Arabs and their descendants, along with the
Arabized population, are to be found throughout Northern Nigeria, and
since the Hausa are the majority, it is safe to say that they constitute an

---

119. Isichei, *A History of Nigeria*, 13.
120. *Britannica World Data* (Chicago: Encyclopaedia Britannica, Inc., 1990), 687.

The Impact of Ethnic, Political, and Religious Violence on
Northern Nigeria, and a Theological Reflection on Its Healing

106

overwhelming majority in the Northern region.[121] However, increasing migration is taking place. James's study demonstrates that violence forces ethnic groups to migrate to a safer haven. According to James, these core areas—Kaduna, Abuja, Jos-Abuja, Abuja-Ajaokuta, Abuja-Minna, Abuja-Makurdi—are already experiencing some rural-urban and rural-rural migrations from the core Northern states of Borno, Yobe, Jigawa, Kano, Katsina, Zamfara, Bauchi, Gombe, and from the Southern states, Cross River, Akwa Ibom, Abia, Imo, Anambra, Enugu, Ebonyi, Delta, Rivers, Edo, Oyo, Ogun, Osun, Ondo, Ekiti and Lagos.[122]

Given that the population density, the population and settlement patterns of the Middle Belt and the Northern region as a whole have long been influenced by migrations, ethnic violence has become an embedded phenomenon in Nigeria before and after independence. At first, this phenomenon was more conspicuous amongst the major ethnic groups—Yoruba, Hausa-Fulani, and Igbo—who were vying for political monopoly of land and taxpayers. The situation reflects a general manipulation of historical facts to the detriment of the minorities. The class divide in Nigeria is so deep that it influences even the way Nigeria's history is written. Nigeria's history focuses largely on the wealthy. Isichei best described this scenario. She argues that the history of Nigeria is biased and one-sided. She writes,

> Conventional history, in Nigeria, tends to focus around political and military narrative, on the one hand, and fairly specialized economic analysis on the other. Much Nigerian history is unconsciously and unintentionally elitist in conception, focusing on the rich man in his castle, to the exclusion of the poor man at his gate.[123]

Yet as James' work demonstrates, this development has threatened the survival of the original settlers resulting in the phenomenal increase in incidence, scale, and intensity of land disputes, boundary disputes, and

---

121. Berkow, "Hausa," in *Muslim People*, 151.
122. James, *Settler Phenomenon in the Middle Belt*, 114.
123. Isichei, *A History of Nigeria*, 13.

chieftaincy disputes. James's study shows that these disputes have impacted all of the eight typologies of settlement he covered in his research. These include, among other places, those who are in the area most hit by violence in the Northern region:

(1) Settlements that have developed around Hausa Trading Colonies, for example, Zangon Kataf in Kaduna State;

(2) Settlements that have developed around Hausa Farming Colonies, e.g. Tingo and Waduku in Lamurde Local Government Area of Adamawa State;

(3) Settlements that have developed as centers or towns of Hausa-Fulani foundation consequent to the Islamic Jihad of Sheikh Usman Dan Fodio, e.g. Jema'a-Kafanchan in Kaduna State;

(4) Settlements that have developed as a result of commercial mining activities, e.g. Gero near Bukuru in Jos South Local Government Area of Plateau State.[124]

The ethnic groups that make up Nigeria tend to look down on each other, resulting in distrust and suspicion.[125] As Nelson aptly points out,

> Northerners were long regarded by southern Nigerians, particularly the Igbos, as tradition-bound and ultraconservative. Lines of class distinction in the north were rigidly drawn, and ultimate authority rested in the hands of the Fulani emirs, who assumed control over the Muslim Hausa after an early nineteenth century jihad (holy war). By contrast the traditional sociopolitical values of southerners prove more adaptable to the process of modernization initiated by the British.[126]

Once people begin to treat their fellows as different the consequences can be disastrous. As Harold D. Nelson further maintains,

---

124. James, *Settler Phenomenon in the Middle Belt*, 114–115.
125. Harold D. Nelson, *Area Handbook for Nigeria* (Washington: American University Foreign Area Studies, 1972), xxiv.
126. Nelson, *Area Handbook for Nigeria*, xxiv.

The Impact of Ethnic, Political, and Religious Violence on
Northern Nigeria, and a Theological Reflection on Its Healing

108

> Because of the differences among the various areas of
> the country based on language, religion, economics, and
> sociopolitical values, two kinds of nationalism emerged.
> Modern nationalism, having a unified republic as its goal, was
> championed by a small number of people who were members
> of the new educated elite. Most of them came from the ranks of
> the civil service, the military officer corps, and the professions.
> The vocal adherents include a number of politicians and most
> students. The other form of nationalism espoused loyalties
> owed to traditional ethnic entities or regional amalgams of
> related ethnolinguistic groups.[127]

This is why, as Nelson also points out, from the outset of independence
the country was faced with ethnic and regional tensions as basic distrust
grew between the slowly developing north and the more advanced south.
The commoners and traditional elite of the north regarded southerners,
particularly the Igbos and other peoples associated with them, as aggressive heathen (non-Muslim), proud, disdainful of northern customs, and
disrespectful of established authority.

In addition, southerners aroused opposition among members of the
northern elite because, having taken advantage of educational opportunities, they were able to capture most of the available positions in government
and the more modern forms of private enterprise, thus depriving younger
northerners of the few salaried positions open to them.[128] "Northerners
came to fear that Igbo were attempting to dominate the country through
control of the civil service and, consequently, of the federal government."[129]
According to Nelson it was "in this climate of ethnic and regional animosity, four coups d'état and a costly civil war occurred in the decade from
1966 to February 1976."[130]

---

127. Nelson, *Area Handbook for Nigeria*, xxv.
128. Johnstone, et al., *Operation World*, 493.
129. Nelson, *Area Handbook for Nigeria*, xxv.
130. Nelson, *Area Handbook for Nigeria*, xxv.

It is against this background that I undertake an analysis of the embedded history of ethnic violence in Northern Nigeria. James' previously mentioned study catalogued some of the most notorious disputes as shown in Table 3. Today settler versus host communities' communal conflicts characterizes Northern Nigeria. Grievances from past conflicts also played into the current conflicts. Sometimes these conflicts are personified as religious-cum political violence as the table below demonstrates. The majority of non-Muslim minority ethnic groups are found in what is known as the Middle-Belt of Nigeria (the Middle-Belt is also part of what is known as Northern Nigeria). That is, it is part of the geographical northern region of Nigeria. The table below illustrates how violence in Nigeria takes complex and elusive dimensions. Ethnic, political, and religious variables characterize it.

TABLE 3

**MIDDLE BELT: SETTLER VERSUS HOST COMMUNITIES'
COMMUNAL CONFLICTS**

(Source: Distilled from James Ibrahim's analysis of the Middle Belt Tribes)

TYPE OF CONFLICT	DESCRIPTION OF CONFLICT
● Territorial/ Ethnic	Land dispute between Kadara Host communities and Hausa settler community
● Territorial/ Ethnic	Land and boundary dispute between the Gbagyi and Koro host communities and the Hausa-Fulani settler community
● Territorial/ Ethnic	Land and boundary dispute between the Kahugu autochthonous community of Kauru high land complex and Gure immigrant community
● Territorial/ Ethnic	Land disputes between the Kataf host community and the Hausa-Fulani settler community
● Territorial/ Ethnic	Land and boundary disputes between the Pushil people Pankshin LGA and the Fier Mwaghavul people of Mangu LGA

TYPE OF CONFLICT	DESCRIPTION OF CONFLICT
■ **Political**	Chieftaincy disputes between the Igbira on the one hand, and the Bassa, Gbagyi, Gade and Agatu on the other on the Ohinoye Chiefdom in Toto and Umaisah and the perceived domination and hegemonic control of the chiefdom by the Igbira
♦ **Religious**	Clashes between Muslims and Christians as a personification of the conflicts between Fantsuam, Bajju and Kaninkon host communities and the Hausa-Fulani settlers of Jema'a Dororo now in authority in Kafanchan
♦ **Religious**	Violence between Muslims and Christians, wherein the former set numerous church buildings on fire and damaged property belonging to Christians. [This is an example of] the inverted personification of the conflict between settler and host community conflict
● **Territorial/ Ethnic**	Communal conflict between Kurama local inhabitants of Lere and the Hausa settler community
♦ **Religious**	Religious riots between Muslim and Christian students resulting in the destruction of the Christian Chapel's Foundation walls.
● **Territorial/ Ethnic**	Land and Boundary disputes between the Tivs-settler community and the non-Tiv host community of Awe LGA: Alago, Mighili, Gwandaras, Hausa and Fulani
♦ **Religious**	Land disputes between the Bwatye-Bachama host community and the Hausa settlers of Tingno and Waduku, Kabawa, Gyawana
♦ **Religious**	Communal Violence between the Zar-Saiyawa host community and the Fulani settler community of Tafawa-Balewa later Bauchi town

TYPE OF CONFLICT	DESCRIPTION OF CONFLICT
■ Political	Land and chieftaincy (chiefdom demand between Kataf host community and the Hausa settler community of Zangon Kataf town
♦ Religious	Inter-religious war between Muslims and Christians in Kaduna town spilling over to Zaria, Ikara
● Territorial/ Ethnic	Communal conflict between the Tiv-settler communities and the Alago, Mighili, Gwandara, non-Tiv host communities of Awe LGA
● Territorial/ Ethnic	Inter-ethnic violence between the Tiv-settler community and the non-Tiv hosts communities of Awe LGA
● Territorial/ Ethnic	Communal conflict between the Tiv-settler community and the Jukun host community in the Wukari, Ibi, Bali, Bantaji, LGA of Taraba State
● Territorial/ Ethnic	Inter-ethnic conflict between the Hausa-Fulani settler community and the Berom, Afizere and Anaguta host communities over the appointment of Sanusi Mato as the Chairman Jos North LGA
■ Political ● Territorial/ Ethnic	Communal conflict between the Igbira, on the one hand, and the Bassa, Gade, Gbayi and the Agatu over the rotation of the Chieftaincy Title of the Ohinoyi of Toto
■ Political ● Territorial/ Ethnic	Communal conflicts between the Berom, Afisere and Anaguta host communities and the Hausa Fulani settler community of Jos town over Local Government Chairmanship elections
● Territorial/ Ethnic	Inter-ethnic conflict between the Chamba/Jukun versus the Kuteb in Takun and Ussa LGA of Taraba State
● Territorial/ Ethnic	Inter-ethnic conflict between the Igbira and the Bassa, the Gade and the Gbayi over control of Toto and Umaisah Districts of Toto LGA of Nassarawa Sate

TYPE OF CONFLICT	DESCRIPTION OF CONFLICT
● Territorial/ Ethnic	Communal conflict between the Hausa-Fulani settler community and the Berom host community over the control of Fadamaland personified by a dispute over "garden eggs" yallo.
● Territorial/ Ethnic	Inter-ethnic conflict between the Igbira and the Bassa, and the Gbagyi over control of Toto and Umaisha.

131

This table gives a clear picture of the intrinsic connection between ethnic, political, and religious violence in Northern Nigeria. Although some past or recent violence is not recorded here, what we have here is enough to show that religious, ethnic, and political violence are inseparable. Most of the violence is labeled as ethno-political and religion is mentioned in only a few of the cases, but almost all also brought religious loyalties into the struggles. The economic aspect is often concealed. Therefore the task of teasing out the impact of violence in Northern Nigeria is complex. However, it is a task that must be carried out if peacemakers and policy makers are going to be able to bring effective transformation to Northern Nigeria. As James Cone once said,

> [T]he gravity of the problem of violence in this society and the world and the urgency of the need to find ways to control and eliminate its most destructive manifestations require all responsible persons to face this issue squarely, speaking forcefully and frankly. No one person, group, or nation can

131. The above table is taken from the analysis of James Ibrahim, *Settler Phenomenon in the Middle Belt and the Problem of National Integration in Nigeria* (Jos, Nigeria: Midland Press, 1998), 115–117. However, I have added some vital information that makes it clearer and better as well as demonstrates that violence is not always religious as some school of thoughts would want us to believe. Thus the information I have added, explaining what kind of violence (for example, territorial/ethnic, political, or religious), underlines the fact that violence is not only multifaceted nor limited to one dimension. Its extent and impact cannot be overstressed.

eliminate violence alone. All persons [Muslims, Christians, and traditionalists] concerned about the survival and health of human beings must join together to renounce violence or it will devour us all.[132]

From the above analysis I attempt to draw the following conclusions:

(1) This ethnic, political, and religious situation makes it difficult for politicians to work for the interest of all groups that they are elected to represent because an environment of rivalry and unhealthy competition and hatred has been created. In the midst of confusing and overwhelming problems the politicians have concentrated on building their own empires and not on building bridges and developing communities.

(2) In retrospect, our elite used to fight for the interest of the whole Northern region. But now violence has created ethnic, political, and religious divides. Consequently, those with an obsessed desire to make easy money and to gain political dominance, economic power, and personal control over their fellow humans have crippled Northern Nigeria. Thus the region is bent over and cannot straighten up at all. To provide a conducive environment for checks and balances against wanton use of economic and political power, there must be peace and justice.

Therefore it is significantly important to emphasize that we need to avoid violent approaches to our desperate, life-affecting needs. The safest way is nonviolent direct action. It is nonviolence that will set us free from our infirmity. Nonviolence will straighten us up and we will be able to produce fruits that bring praises to the One whom we claim as our God as well as blessings to our fellow humans and the whole ecosystem. Violence has kept us bound for too long. But nonviolence will set us free.

(3) Nigerian history has focused on the Northern elite, to the detriment of the commoners and those on the periphery of Northern Nigeria both within Muslim and non-Muslim communities. Consequently, the tribes are fighting to gain social, economic, and political relevance and identity. This is personified in land and chieftaincy disputes. But the reality is the

---

132. James H. Cone, *Speaking the Truth*, 62.

ethnic groups are fighting to reach a point where they can have a significant role in the scheme of things in the region as well as in the country.

In summary, Nigeria's threat is not limited to religion and ethnicity. As Moltmann notes, "Human persons are not one-dimensional beings. They always live and suffer simultaneously in many different dimensions."[133] He explains the five dimensions as follows:

> (1) The struggle for economic justice against the exploitation of some people by other people; (2) the struggle for human rights and freedom against the political oppression of some people by other people; (3) the struggle for human solidarity against the cultural, the racist, and the sexist alienation of people from people; (4) the struggle for ecological peace with nature against the industrial destruction of nature by human beings; [and] (5) the struggle for assurance against apathy in personal life.[134]

Moltmann concludes: "These five dimensions hang so closely together that there can be no economic justice without political freedom, no improvement of socioeconomic conditions without overcoming cultural alienation, and without personal conversion from apathy to hope."[135] I suppose John N. Paden is right, "The Key to a workable three tier of federalism [federal, state and local areas] is an appropriate balance of functions and responsibilities between the larger political unit, the component states, and the local areas."[136] These political arrangements should be encouraged as a matter of urgency to ensure and assure the balance use of power: checkmate the infamous and blatant use of political power to amass wealth to the total disadvantage of the masses.

---

133. Moltmann, *On Human Dignity*, 110.
134. Moltmann, *On Human Dignity*, 110.
135. Moltmann, *On Human Dignity*, 110.
136. John N. Paden, "Sokoto Caliphate and Its Legacies" Nigerian *Sunday Tribune*, February 25, 2007, 1.

2. A Case Study of Some Selected Practical Situations of Violence in Northern Nigeria

Many relevant studies have been conducted to assess the causes of violence in Northern Nigeria. This chapter builds on those studies but goes beyond them to other windows that point to where the problem really lies.

In his study of three basic religious conflicts in Northern Nigeria in the 1980s and 1990s and how they impacted nation building, Rotgak I. Gofwen identified the following occurrences in Northern Nigeria: the Kafanchan crisis in 1987 (my hometown); the Kano crisis of 1991; and the Kaduna Shari'ah crisis in February of 2000 (in which my cousin was killed). I shall attempt to re-examine Gofwen's analysis and conclusions.

2.1 Kafanchan Crisis, March 1987

The immediate cause of the Kafanchan Crisis was the alleged misinterpretation of Koranic verses at a weekend Easter conference organized by the Christian students of College of Education Kafanchan. The invited guest speaker was a recent convert from Islam to Christianity and a student at Ahmadu Bello University Zaria. He wanted to demonstrate his ability to use both sacred texts effectively. Thus, he was trying to quote both the Bible and the Koran simultaneously. The Muslim students at the school took offense by the way he was indiscriminately using the Koranic verses. The conflict that ensued led to a violent attack on the Christian students. It immediately became lethal and spilled over to other parts of the state. As Gofwen's study suggested, "This crisis, even though brought under control in Kafanchan town, it later engulfed almost the entire Kaduna State."[137] Gofwen contended, however, that there were remote root causes. These included, among other things, political, social, economic, and religious factors.

Of the political factors that played into the conflict, Gofwen writes,

---

137. Rotgut Gofwen, *Religious Conflicts in Northern Nigeria and Nation Building: The Throes of Two Decades 1980–2000* (Kaduna: Human Rights Monitor, 2000), 91.

For a very long period, there had been grievances about the imposition of persons as political heads in areas of Southern Kaduna where the indigenous community perceives them as alien. Specifically, there were complaints by the Southern Kaduna people, that the feudal system resulting from the appointment and imposition of Hausa/Fulani people as village or district heads offended their culture and feelings, and subjected them to the domination of people who were different from them politically, socially and religiously. The grievances laid the foundation for the 1989 suspicion, bitterness, and frustration.[138]

The government set up an investigation committee. The committee asked both the Christian and Muslim communities to submit memoranda. Part of the memoranda submitted to the probe panel by the Student Affairs Officer of the College of Education concludes, "[T]he Sunday Kafanchan uprising was a way of showing dissatisfaction with the Government by those brains behind it."[139] Some of the respondents argue that the remote cause lies in "the increasing polarization of Nigerians along religious lines,"[140] particularly, "Since the OIC [Organization of Islamic Countries] issue was raised to the level of national debate last year, there have been much less veiled attempts by certain Moslem leaders to generate and sustain a climate of religious animosity between Moslems and Christians."[141]

Gofwen's analysis showed that violence has both immediate and remote causes that need to be understood. It demonstrates that past grievances often play a role in fueling present violence. The current outrage results from the inherent bitterness and resentment of the Hausa-Fulani's alleged grievous treatment of their non-Muslim cousins who are minorities living in the region. Of course, some of the causes of violence may or may not be well founded because they get personified as political, religious, and ethnic

---

138. Gofwen, *Religious Conflicts in Northern Nigeria*, 92.
139. Kaduna Riots, '87 A Catalogue of Evens, 1987: 31 in Gofwen, *Religious Conflict in Northern Nigeria*, 2000, 92.
140. Gofwen, *Religious Conflicts in Northern Nigeria*, 92.
141. Gofwen, *Religious Conflicts in Northern Nigeria*, 93.

masks. Thus, without unmasking the inherent link between contemporary and past grievances, the desired result—peace and just peacemaking—will be difficult to reach.

Gofwen also argues that there is social disorientation in Southern Zaria. According to Gofwen,

> Based on the long-standing relationship of hostility associated with conquest, the indigenous communities felt that the Hausa/Fulani groups have excluded them from traditional rulership. On the other hand, the indigenous communities are of the feeling that despite being part and parcel of the society, they have been completely sidelined from the administrative management of the local government council. Furthermore there was a feeling of inequitable distribution of education and social amenities by the Southern Zaria communities when compared to other parts of the state.[142]

This is an overwhelming list of complaints. It indicates that the causes of violence in Northern Nigeria cannot be reduced to a single index of the situation's gravity. Rather, the complaints are multitiered and complex. Therefore, while the causes of violence must be treated case by case, the other layers must be also considered.

The underlying economic factors are very illuminating. Gofwen observes that the people of Southern Zaria have argued that the area is denied certain economic activities that give hope to a society. This includes, for example, the siting of industries. The northern part of Kaduna has concentrated industries while the southern part of the state has none. This situation has contributed enormously to the problem of youth unemployment.[143]

Regarding the effect of the Structural Adjustment Programme (SAP), Gofwen argues,

---

142. Gofwen, *Religious Conflicts in Northern Nigeria*, 98.
143. Gofwen, *Religious Conflicts in Northern Nigeria*, 98.

The Impact of Ethnic, Political, and Religious Violence on
Northern Nigeria, and a Theological Reflection on Its Healing

118

During Ibrahim Babangida's regime, the International Monitory Fund (IMF) and World Bank succeeded in convincing the nations to implement the policies of the Structural Adjustment Programme [SAP] with the assumption that it would bring hope to the teeming population of unemployed youth in Nigeria by creating jobs.[144]

But as Gofwen observed, the government white paper discovered that "the introduction of the SAP had led to untold hardship for the people and the folding up of Several Businesses, resulting in unemployment and idleness."[145]

The government's conspicuous identification with a certain religious persuasion was seen as responsible for the crisis. Nigerian leaders, particularly from the Core North, who were Muslims, tended to pit the nation and its religious communities along a religious divide. This was in pursuit of the strategy the British colonialists had used: "divide and rule." As Gofwen noted, during the investigation of the cause of the Kafanchan crisis Christians expressly pointed out:

It is our fervent belief that the present administration of President Ibrahim Babangida is largely responsible for the current pervasive atmosphere of religious intolerance in the country, which has recently manifested clearly and alarmingly in the religious riots in Kaduna State. This is so because since the inception of the administration, some specific wealthy Moslems, Islamic scholars and Emirs have been making explosive religious utterances and even calling for an Islamic State. In the face of all what has government done?[146]

---

144. Gofwen, *Religious Conflicts in Northern Nigeria*, 98.
145. Gofwen, *Religious Conflicts in Northern Nigeria*, 98.
146. Gofwen, *Religious Conflicts in Northern Nigeria*, 99.

Other causes that have been expressed include ignorance, poverty, multi-ethnic hatred, religious intolerance, and idleness.[147] In my field research a question was asked whether there is an alternative to violence in Northern Nigeria. Most Christians answered *no*, because they believe that Christianity equates to tolerance while Islam personifies intolerance. Some of these factors are hard to understand without elucidating them. I suppose this is what happens when you have two large religious communities—each claiming to number 60 million—with missionary visions that force them to compete for more numbers. Intolerance is the name of the social dynamic that develops.

2.2 Kano Crisis, October 1991

The 1991 Kano crisis was not the first time Kano had experienced crisis. The plain truth is that the history of Kano is embedded with violence: Kano dates back to the sixth century, following Maguzawa settlement around the Dala, Gwauron Dutse, and Fanisau hills. "In the early 19th century, the Fulani *Jihad* was waged against Kano by Usman dan Fodio and that ended the *Ha-e* dynasty and brought the establishment of the Fulani dynasty." Thereafter, the British, under the command of Colonel Morland, attacked Kano.

The ethnic composition of Kano shows some diversity, which is what one would expect to find in most of the states in Northern Nigeria. The following table shows some examples of the ethnic composition of Kano.[148]

---

147. Gofwen, *Religious Conflicts in Northern Nigeria*, 100.
148. This information was provided by my interview, on March 19, 2006, with Adulrazaque Bello, a journalist with Nigeria's newspapers and media.

TABLE 4
THE COMPOSITION OF KANO
(Source: distilled from Kano online www.kanoonline.com)

Ethnic composition:	Mostly Hausa and Fulani; others include the Igbo, Yoruba, Kanuri, Arabs, Nupe, and Tiv
Languages:	Hausa predominates. English is the official language. Arabic is also spoken.
Religion:	Islam is the principal religion
Population:	5.6 Million (1991)

The 1991 Kano crisis resulted from a report that Reinhardt Bonnke, a German evangelist, was in Kano for evangelistic outreach whose intent was to discredit Islam. The unemployed-poor youth in Kano were therefore mobilized to do everything at their disposal to stop the program. Gofwen tells us:

> A day after this incident and the date for the beginning of the crusade—Monday 14th October—it was noticed that by 9:00AM, Muslim youths largely composed of almairis (Islamic Mallams disciples) had started gathering at the Kofa Mata Eid-ground. The choice of the venue was indicative of the seriousness of the gathering.[149]

For those familiar with Kano, this venue is primarily used for important occasions, including Islamic festivals and when the Emir of Kano addresses his subjects. It was from there the violent mob proceeded to the Emir of Kano's palace to protest the presence of Reinhardt Bonnke in Kano.

Ironically, the protesters headed for the Kofar Mata Central Mosque, assembled there for their afternoon prayers and thereafter engaged in violent attacks on the residents of Sabon Gari, a non-Muslim community of Kano. According to Babarinsa, "The targets of the rioters, as it was in the past,

---

149. Gofwen, *Religious Conflicts in Northern Nigeria*, 103.

were mostly Southerners and Christian Northerners. The rioters moved from street to street, killing people, setting vehicles and houses on fire."[150] Of course this crisis, like most crises in the north, had its antecedents.

The remote causes of this crisis are situated in the historical fact that prior to this, Kano had suffered from the onslaught of a fundamentalist Islamic group, which in 1980 threw the state into upheaval. This was known as the Maitatsine Sect, a militant Islamic group that attacked moderate Muslim groups in Kano. Consequently, the crisis that engulfed the state led to the murder of 4,177 people, including policemen. Following these events Islamic fundamentalism remained a security threat in Kano and the nation.

In addition, Gofwen states, "Protesters alleged that government is 'hostile' towards Islam. According to them, earlier in the year, the government had refused permission for the renowned South-African-born Islamic preacher, Ahmed Deedat, whom they invited to visit Nigeria and preach. For the protesters, this denial was tantamount to Kano State government hostility towards Islam."[151] In other words, the government's move generated future violence.

2.3 Kaduna Shari'ah Crisis, February 2000

In Northern Nigeria, Kaduna State has been a center of political, religious, and ethnic violence. The state is also the most ethnically diversified:

> Kaduna State forms a portion of the country's cultural melting pot. Apart from six major ethnic groups found in the state, there are over twenty other ethnic minority groups, each with its language and arts or religion different from the other. Works of art and pottery (e.g. the "Nok Terracotta") found in the southern parts suggest that it is a major cultural center. Among the major ethnic groups are Kamuku, Gwari, and Kadara in the west, Hausa and Kurama to the north and Northeast. "Nerzit" is now used to describe the Jaba, Kaje,

---

150. *Tell* Magazine Oct. 28, 1991: 13 in Gofwen, *Religious Conflicts in Northern Nigeria*, 104.
151. Gofwen, *Religious Conflicts in Northern Nigeria*, 107.

Koro, Kamanton, Kataf, Morwa, and Chawai instead of the derogatory term "southern Zaria people." Also, the term "Hausawa" is used to describe the people of Igabi, Ikara, Giwa, and Makarfi LGAs, which include a large proportion of rural dwellers that are strictly "Maguzawas."[152]

Historically, Kaduna is a state full of fragmented societies. In fact, Kaduna epitomizes the whole North. Simply put, like other states in Northern Nigeria, an awful lot of cultural uprooting has occurred in Kaduna State. As Gofwen notes, "Prior to Colonial conquest, the present day Kaduna town was traditionally inhabited by the Gbagyi people."[153] Kaduna derived its name from the Hausa word "Kadudna," which means, "crossing the River of Snails."[154] However, these original inhabitants were uprooted from their land and sent to the outskirts of the city. The situation is comparable to what Americans did to the Native American population of North America. The growth and development of the city has been vividly captured by John N. Paden:

Official British perspectives on the growth of Kaduna may be summarized as follows: in 1913 Kaduna was selected by Lugard to be the Capital not just of the north, but of the whole of Nigeria. For practical reasons, including cost, Lagos continued to be the capital. At the time, Kaduna was Savanna bush and a resting place for Crocodiles (kada, in Hausa). Hence the name "Kaduna." Zungeru had been the seat of government in the early days, but in 1917 government activities were shifted to Kaduna. It was near to Zaria, where the military headquarters was located at the time. The railway line to Zaria passed through Kaduna, which was more congenial to expatriates because of its climate and water supply. By 1956, Kaduna is

---

152. This information comes from the Kaduna website called *Kaduna Online web*.
153. Gofwen, *Religious Conflicts in Northern Nigeria*, 107.
154. John N. Paden, *Ahmadu Bello, Sarduna of Sokoto: Values and Leadership in Nigeria* (London; Portsmouth, N.H: Hodder and Stoughton, 1986), 319.

a town of about 30,000, and serves as an administrative and military base . . . Kaduna is also the major center of rail traffic in the north, with the largest junction, handling about 250 trains a week. This facilitates the large influx of southerners. . . . In short, by 1956, Kaduna is a town of soldiers, railway men, administrators, educational institutions, and southern migrants.[155]

Kaduna is one of the hottest political, economic, and religious hot-button states in Nigeria. The Shari'ah agitation, which besieged the North at the reintroduction of democracy on May 29, 1999, led to the violent killing of innocent victims. Against the backdrop of the onslaught of Shari'ah implementation strategy, the Kaduna situation reveals insights into the multifaceted nature of violence. It shows that in Northern Nigeria the rich, who sponsor unemployed youths to destroy the lives of innocent victims, often cause violence.

During my field research I saw the pathetic situation of the rural areas of the Northern states. By merely seeing the rate of underdevelopment, one cannot help but conclude that the rich have always thrived on the labors of the poor. Despite the fact that the Governor of Zamfara State was the first to declare the controversial Islamic law, Shari'ah, the State is one of the most underdeveloped in the Northwest. What did he do with the money that he got from Saudi Arabia and other Muslim countries in the Middle East for propagating Islam in the country? His people are in debt more than ever before.

The Economic and Financial Crime Commission (EFCC) chaired by Nuhu Ribadu, probed thirty-two governors for financial crime allegations. On September 27, 2006, Ribadu (himself a Muslim) told the Nigerian people on national network news (NTA) that among the thirty-two governors being probed for financial corruption, the governor of Zamfara State was the most corrupt. Ironically, he was still seen and celebrated as a hero because he had blinded the eyes of his people with Shari'ah law

---

155. Paden, *Ahmadu Bello, Sarduna of Sokoto*, 319.

124

The Impact of Ethnic, Political, and Religious Violence on
Northern Nigeria, and a Theological Reflection on Its Healing

implementation. Politicians generally know how to appeal to the deepest concerns and familiar experiences of the poor and misdirect their attention away from their injustice and corruption. The subjects get trapped in their arrogance.

Micah, the Prophet, is right that when people refuse to "do justice and love kindness and to walk humbly before the Lord" it results in violence. "For the rich men of the city are full of violence, her residents speak lies."[156] Obsession with materialism and economic as well as political power leads to lies and all sorts of cover-ups. The case of Shari'ah crisis of February 2000 and the post-Shari'ah crisis have shown how deception played into the psyche of Nigeria's sociopolitical radar. "To the pure," writes the Apostle Paul, "all things are pure, but to those who are corrupted and do not believe, nothing is pure. In fact, their minds and conscience are corrupted."[157] Some Nigerian politicians are always liars and evil brutes.

3. Conclusion

Northern Nigeria's condition is very elusive. The problems are many and feed into each other in an endless and vicious circle. Political problems produce economic crises, which cause civil unrest, ethnic prejudice, and linguistic tensions "as people scramble for what is an ever-diminishing national economic pie."[158]

Violence is multifaceted: every situation has both immediate and remote causes. This is why the question of the impact of religious, political, and ethnic violence becomes very significant. We must be able to understand how causes of violence are, in most cases, connected to past injustice, either perceived or real. Hence, I have attempted to trace the possible causes of violence in Northern Nigeria.

---

156. Micah 6:8, 12.
157. Titus 1:15.
158. Sindima, *Religious and Political Ethics in Africa*, 13.

First, people no longer feel a sense of belonging in the political and economic scheme of things. Every ethnic group wants to be recognized because such acknowledgment has political and economic values attached.

Additionally, in the absence of jobs and employment, the teeming population of graduates and undergraduates sees politics as an avenue to employment. No wonder politics is becoming a do-or-die affair. Generally, the attitude of politicians does not help. Personal economic goals take priority over religious commitment to society.

Materialism and individualism are no longer the exclusive monopoly of Western and North American societies. In the *Guardian Newspapers*, February 1, 2006, Femi Olawole points out that "Almost all the young people, including elementary school pupils, appeared to be daily equipped with the latest news about America. There is therefore the desperate urge to tailor personal styles and business goals along every trend that emanates from God's own country." This obsession encourages corruption and the lack of satisfying the yearnings of their people when they achieve political positions. For in most cases, politicians who are elected into office do not go there as the people's representatives. As Lewis states, "Divisions arise from ethnic and regional distinctions, personal ambition, and a degree of ideological contention. These fissures are intensified by a system whereby politicians compete as much, if not more, for support from military rulers as from the voters."[159] This also creates and encourages political, ethnic, social, and religious rifts and socioeconomic divides.

When Nigeria was subdivided into regions, the struggle was limited from region to region. No longer is the fight is limited to just a state; it trickles down to local government areas and districts. This greatly impacts the social dynamic; it metamorphoses to religious group rancor. This rancorous situation is undoubtedly heightening a sense of difference.[160] Hollenback suggests,

---

159. Peter Lewis, et al., eds., *Stabilizing Nigeria: Sanctions, Incentives, and Support for Civil Society* (New York: Century Foundation Press, 1998), 65.
160. David Hollenbach, *The Common Good and Christian Ethics* (Cambridge; New York: Cambridge University Press, 2002), 14.

[A]wareness of diversity is a prominent fact in daily experience.
When difference generates conflict, fear grows. And such fear
makes further conflict more likely. This raises the specter that
we have fallen into a downward spiral in which awareness of
differences leads to conflict, which in turn leads to fear, more
conflict, more defensive boundaries, and onward to deepened
perceptions of difference.[161]

Yet another cause of violence is the polarization between rich and poor.
Hollenbach tells us that "Aristotle and many after him have long argued
that societies with a large middle class are less subject to internal conflict
than those polarized between rich and poor."[162]

The Christian denominations are also lured into the oppressive political
structures of the country. Some denominations have adapted the system
of zoning, which the government has used as another assumed solution to
the problem. Self-assertion is on the increase because people are no longer
interested in staying together. It is a chaotic social environment that breeds
violence in all spheres of life. This trend gets confused with the general phenomenon of social decay as well as economic and political breakdown. A
great deal of the problem originates from a lack of a sense of human rights.

Finally, the country's military rulers have governed without accountability. Lewis tells how "political participation has been stringently curtailed,
human rights abuses have been endemic, and the traditionally independent
media have been partly curbed. Most of the population does not enjoy
access to the political arena."[163]

The long-term risks continue to threaten the stability of Nigeria's nation-
hood. For example, "Nigeria continuously experiences intense situations of
politically motivated murders. The political atmosphere has been such that
assassination of people like Harry Marshal, A.K. Dikigbo, Bola Ige, and

---

161. Hollenbach, *The Common Good*, 21.
162. Hollenbach, *The Common Good*, 23.
163. Lewis, et al., eds., *Stabilizing Nigeria*, 55.

Chuba Okhadigbo are believed to be the deliberate handiwork of selfish politicians."[164] Zayyad I Muhammad is right:

> Political elite sometimes may not be directly involved in the assassination of their political opponents, but illiterate political thugs who every so often are employed to do the job of intimidating political opponents may sometimes cross the line to the extent of taking a life; thinking it would score a political point to their pay-masters.

Given that economic and political goals override religious commitments, leaders do not hesitate to employ assassinations or provoke ethnic or religious tensions among the populace in pursuit of a political goal.

---

164. Lewis, et al., eds., *Stabilizing Nigeria*, 55.

CHAPTER 5

Understanding the Impact of Violence on Christians's Christology: Moltmann's Experiential Contribution

The primary goal of this chapter is to demonstrate that violence shapes our theological perspectives and values. In the pages that follow, I shall explore Jürgen Moltmann's Christology, looking at how violence affected his theological perspectives and values, but also to ask what lessons Northern Nigeria can learn from Moltmann's experiences. I believe this approach will provide a window of opportunity to do a deeper reflection on the kind of theology that is being developed, unnoticed, in Northern Nigeria and the country at large. I shall then conclude the study with an exposition of Moltmann's concept of the way of Jesus, which is variously called "creative love" (Moltmann), "compassionate love" (Glen Stassen), and "love of the other" (Jesus). I shall be attempting to answer the question, "How does the way of Jesus speak to the present day violence occurring in Northern Nigeria?"

I am aware that many scholars have undertaken the task of interpreting the work of Jürgen Moltmann through essays, articles, and books on his theology. Richard Bauckham, M. Douglas Meeks, and Miroslav Volf, just to name a few, interpret his theological project. They have helped us grasp the thrust of Moltmann's theology. Yet there is still much to be explored, particularly regarding the ways in which violence explicitly and implicitly shaped Moltmann's theology. One of the few scholars who has specifically attempted to give attention to how violence impacted Moltmann's theology, and by extension Christology, is his former student Miroslav Volf.[1] Volf, who had given a lecture on the need "to embrace our enemies as God has embraced us in Christ," was confronted by Moltmann's penetrating question, "[But] can you embrace a *četnik*—the ultimate other, so to speak, the evil other?"[2] Moltmann's question triggered awareness in Volf's mind of the existence of "tension between the message of the cross" on the one hand and "the world of violence" on the other. He realized that because we are surrounded by the reality of "a world of injustice, deception, and violence," Christians tend to fall prey to the temptation of either assigning "the demands of the Crucified to the murky regions of unreason [or] abandon[ing] the struggle for justice, truth, and peace."[3]

Volf has set the stage for a continuous careful application of Moltmann's experiences to our contemporary social issues. While Volf has given us the tools to grapple with violence in our own social milieu, his work has, however, left much to be desired, particularly in speaking to Northern Nigeria, which has been engulfed by ethnic, political, and religious violence.

In this book, my hypothesis is that war and its attendant violence cause people to lose sight of the wider and fuller picture of their social conditions or circumstances. Put simply, violence distorts people's perspectives and values. The question, therefore, is, "How has violence shaped Moltmann's theological perspectives and values, particularly his Christology?" If, as Matthew reports, Jesus Christ is our only teacher—"You have one teacher, the Christ" (Matt. 23:10)—I claim that it is appropriate to investigate what Christ taught Moltmann in his experience of violence during World War II and thereafter. But there is no point in just analyzing Moltmann's experiences without seeking to see how we might learn some vital lessons from his experiences. How can grappling with Moltmann's experience contribute to our grasp of Christology in a world full of social ills? What does he have to say, for example, to questions such as, "Can Christians in Northern Nigeria

1. Miroslav Volf, *Exclusion & Embrace: A Theological Exploration of Identity, Otherness, and Reconciliation* (Nashville: Abingdon Press), 1996.
2. Volf, *Exclusion & Embrace*, 9.
3. Volf, *Exclusion & Embrace*, 10.

(where there have been decades of religious, ethnic, and political violence between the Muslims and Christians) embrace a non-Christian person, particularly a Muslim?" and "Can a Muslim embrace a non-Muslim person, particularly a Christian?" It all comes down to the fundamental question, "Is there light at the end of the tunnel?" Or to borrow Moltmann's central theme, "Is there hope?"

I shall attempt to examine these questions as I try not only to grasp the development of Moltmann's theological journey, but also to tease out Moltmann's concrete contribution to an understanding of ethics and theology in a violent environment. I will explore insights from Moltmann's theme of entering into suffering, discuss Moltmann's Christology in conversation with African Christologies, and conclude with precise lessons from Moltmann's Christology, a critique and a careful application of Moltmann's contribution to the general situation in Northern Nigeria.

1. The Beginnings of Moltmann's Theological Journey

Jürgen Moltmann is Professor Emeritus of Systematic Theology at the University of Tübingen in Germany, where he started teaching in 1967. He was the Robert W. Woodruff Distinguished Visiting Professor of Systematic Theology at United Methodist-related Candler School of Theology at Emory University in Atlanta for ten years, beginning in 1983. Moltmann's work has won many national and international awards, including the 2000 Louisville Grawemeyer Award in Religion for his book *The Coming of God: Christian Eschatology*. Moltmann belongs to the Reformed Church of Germany. Hence he speaks from within a reputable religious community and tradition. His works have had an indelible impact on the Christian community both inside and outside Germany.

1.1 Encountering Jesus Christ

Every theology has its impetus. Moltmann's Christology was birthed through what he describes as "struggle": "For me, Christian faith began with a despairing search for God and a personal struggle with the dark sides of 'the hidden face' of God."[4] In 1945 during the horror of the war in which 40,000 people in Moltmann's hometown faced the wrath of "Operation Gomorrah," Moltmann came face-to-face with the terrifying reality of death. Although Moltmann came from a secular home, he could not help but cry out, "My God, where are you?" and the question, "Why am I alive and not dead like the rest?" has haunted him ever since.

The consequence of this experience was that Moltmann had a personal encounter with Jesus: "I found that comfort in the Christ who in his passion became my brother in need, and through his resurrection from the dead awakened me too to a living hope."[5] In *Experiences in Theology*, Moltmann recounts the experiences that led him to an understanding of what Christ meant and still means to him, as well as to the rest of the world:

> My experiences of death at the end of the war, the depression into which *the guilt of my people plunged me*, and the inner perils of utter resignation behind barbed wire: these were the places where my theology was born. They were my first *locus theologicus*, and at the deepest depths of my soul they have remained so (italics mine).[6]

Since then Moltmann's primary objective for studying theology has been Christ and his crucifixion. He wanted to find out whether or not truth can be found in Christ and what sort of truth that is.[7] Moltmann has a passion for theology because he has "a passion for the kingdom of God."[8] This birthed a willingness to dialogue with people of different theological, social, political, and scientific persuasions.[9]

In order to grasp Moltmann's overarching theological project, we must situate it in its context. This context is the whole period before, during

---

4. Moltmann, *Experiences in Theology*, 3.
5. Moltmann, *Experiences in Theology*, 4.
6. Moltmann, *Experiences in Theology*, 4.
7. Moltmann, *Experiences in Theology*, 4.
8. Moltmann, *Experiences in Theology*, 8.
9. Moltmann, *Experiences in Theology*, 8, 18.

and after the Second World War. Although Moltmann has tended to be subjective in his approach to theological issues, he has not let circumstances eclipse the wider and fuller context of God's activities in creation. I suspect that Moltmann's subjectivity is largely connected to the impact of violence on his life.

Generally, a careful reading of Moltmann's work reveals how violence has continued to be the reality with which Moltmann lives year in and year out. In Moltmann's words, "The experiences of the life of a prisoner have left a lasting mark on me." These and other experiences shook him and drove him to the cross. "Moltmann was able to see the cross and resurrection as an event of universal eschatological promise in which Jesus was identified with the godforsakenness of all reality in hope of the eschatological resurrection of all reality."[10] Hence it is clear that Moltmann not only sees Jesus as his divine brother but also the brother of all those who face a world of persistent contradictions and sufferings. The suffering of Christ includes everyone's sufferings.[11]

In summary, when other people were still "looking for Jesus, who was crucified," Moltmann found this Jesus, who tells those whose hopes have been shattered by human violence, "Do not be afraid. Go and tell my brothers" that there is yet hope (Matt. 28:5–10). Likewise, our present situation can best be described as "afraid yet filled with joy," because in Christ's resurrection, hope is reborn. This hope in Jesus Christ is what has kept Moltmann going. It is a better hope that introduces humanity to the power of an indestructible life. In fact, Moltmann rightly says, "To be human is to hope."[12] But it is not just any hope—hope in God and his promises. Geiko Müller-Fahrenholz points out, "So the leading concepts are 'God's faithfulness and promise.'"[13] Moltmann remained firm in his hope even when he realized that instability, both inward and outward, was

---

10. Richard J. Bauckham, *Moltmann: Messianic Theology in the Making* (Basingstoke, U.K: Marshall Pickering, 1987), 6.

11. Jürgen Moltmann, *The Crucified God: The Cross of Christ as the Foundation and Criticism of Christian Theology* (Minneapolis: Fortress Press, 1993), x.

12. Bauckham, *Moltmann: Messianic Theology in the Making*, 10.

13. Geiko Müller-Fahrenholz, *The Kingdom and the Power: The Theology of Jürgen Moltmann*, ed., Muller-Fahrenholz Geiko (London: SCM Press, 2000), 47.

growing, German political, economic, ethical, and religious systems were more vulnerable than many people thought and the longing for security in all spheres of life was growing as well. This longing welled up in questions for which answers were sometimes hard to come by.

1.2 Questions Raised by World War II

In 1995, during a service in London, Moltmann spoke about his World War II experiences and their effect:

> In July 1943 I was an air force auxiliary in a battery in the center of Hamburg, and barely survived the fire storm which the Royal Air Force's "Operation Gomorrah" let loose on the eastern part of the city. The friend standing next to me at the firing predicator was torn to pieces by the bomb that left me unscathed. That night I cried out to God for the first time: "My God, where are you?" and the question "Why am I not dead too?" has haunted me ever since, but to be a survivor is hard. One has to bear the weight of grief; *it was probably in that night that my theology began,* for I came from a secular family and knew nothing of faith.[14]

Clearly, the Second World War raised some significant questions for Moltmann. Moltmann's faith was confronted with demanding questions: "How can one believe in God 'after Auschwitz?'" Why had so many German churches and German Christians refused to join the confessing church in its opposition to Hitler's regime and the Nazi ideology? Why was the German church so reluctant to confess its guilt and to reform itself after the war?

Attempting to find theological meaning in this existential dilemma, Moltmann was attracted to the theologies of Karl Barth and Dietrich Bonhoeffer. Both Barth and Bonhoeffer had, in one way or the other, reflected deeply on the circumstances surrounding the Christian faith during

---

14. Müller-Fahrenholz, *The Kingdom and the Power,* 16

the war and after it. Barth sought to protect the identity of Christian faith against a fascist state and against churches that either actively or passively supported that state, and Bonhoeffer risked his life to oppose Hitler and, from a prison cell in a concentration camp, began to formulate theological thoughts that dealt with the question of how one can believe in God in a secular and unjust world. Moltmann continued that tradition by arguing that Christian faith by its very nature needs to assume responsibility for the world in which it lives. On the one hand, Moltmann criticizes churches that used the word "God" to justify political and economic structures. On the other hand, he encouraged them to be true to their confession of Jesus Christ as Lord by being therapeutically and critically involved in the conflicts of their world.[15]

The hard questions that Moltmann asked enabled him to develop his theology into several basic components. These components include, among other things: Trinitarian view of God, theology of the cross, doctrine of salvation, eschatology (hope), ecclesiology, pneumatology, and ecology.

In short, Moltmann's experiences and questions actually have helped him to develop a theology from an ecumenical standpoint. He realized that God is not "a particularist God."[16] I think this approach is what makes him the best-known German-speaking academic theologian at the end of the twentieth century.[17] Finally, experience is Moltmann's starting point. That is to say, Moltmann's theology is "experimental theology." The question is whether Moltmann's perception of Christology, and the image of man in which it is usually crystallized, can serve as a reliable starting point for an attempt to gain an understanding of human beings' responses to violence. What then is Moltmann's central thesis?

1.3 Moltmann's Central Thesis

Moltmann's central thesis is *hope*. This is obviously the foundation of his theology. Many scholars rightly call him the father of the theology of hope. For Moltmann hope is not just a future reality but also a present one: Hope

---

15. See also Musser, 1996, 304–5.
16. Moltmann, *Experiences in Theology*, 14.
17. Bauckham, *Moltmann: Messianic Theology in the Making*, 1.

"does not take things as they happen to stand or to lie, but as progressing, moving things with possibilities of change."[18] The words of the old hymn, "On Christ the solid rock I stand," best describe Moltmann's theological motif. Moltmann stands on a rock—"the Crucified Christ." From this standpoint, Moltmann sets hope in juxtaposition with promise. This is what gives him an edge over many of his contemporaries.

Moltmann was brought up in an era when chaos, conflict, and despair deeply engulfed human history. Thus it is not surprising that *hope* became his overarching theological theme. Moltmann sought to provide an alternative to the thick cloud of darkness and despair that engulfed his contemporary society. He simply contends that there are yet possibilities for transformation. Hence Moltmann rejects the idea of the *completion* of history in favor of the *redemption* of history. Accordingly Moltmann states, "Hope makes us ready to bear the 'cross of the present.' It can hold to what is dead, and hope for the unexpected."[19] But how do the promise and hope work together?

Promise inspires hope. In Moltmann's view, as Richard Bauckham points out, "the cross and resurrection of Jesus both represent total opposites: death and life, the absence of God and the presence of God, godforsakenness and God's glory." However, Moltmann is clearly aware that "Jesus, the crucified and risen one, remains the same person in this total contradiction."[20] Moltmann uses the words promise and hope interchangeably or even interdependently. He sees promise as the source of hope. Yet Moltmann does not see Jesus as a fulfiller of God's promises, as it is usually assumed. The promise is for the eschatological transformation of the whole of reality. Hence "Christian hope, which puts its trust in this promise, necessarily thrusts believers into the worldly reality for whose future they hope."[21]

But how does promise inspire hope and affect us directly as individuals? According to Moltmann, God "promises life for the dead, righteousness for the unrighteous, freedom for those in bondage." God's promise "offers

---

18. Jürgen Moltmann, *Theology of Hope: On the Ground and the Implications of a Christian Eschatology* (London: SCM Press, 1967), 25.
19. Moltmann, *Theology of Hope*, 31.
20. Bauckham, *The Theology of Jürgen Moltmann*, 100–101.
21. Bauckham, *The Theology of Jürgen Moltmann*, 101.

hope where the immanent prospects of the world offer no hope."[22] This promise inspires hope, which likewise inspires love—the embrace of the other. Consequently, Moltmann writes, "Where in faith and hope we begin to live in the light of the possibilities and promises of this God, the whole fullness of life discloses itself as a life of history and therefore a life to be loved. . . . In love, hope brings all things into the light of the promises of God."[23]

This fits nicely with Moltmann's central thesis found in his seminal work, *Theology of Hope*: "There can be no Christology without eschatology and no eschatology without Christology."[24] It is against this background that Moltmann argues, "Christian eschatology speaks of Jesus Christ and *his* future" and "Eschatology sets out from a definite reality in history and announces the future of that reality, its future possibilities and its power over the future."[25] Moltmann tells us that "the resurrection of Jesus from the dead by God does not speak the 'language of facts,' but only the language of faith and hope, that is, the 'language of promise.'"[26] How does violence shape these central theological perspectives and values? The plain truth is that Moltmann has remained remarkably aware of the impact of violence on society. Thus Moltmann consistently brings the work of Jesus Christ to bear on the present situation of society.

Moltmann is determined to make Christ's life, ministry, death, and resurrection count in the present scheme of things, to the surprise of his contemporaries' disparate thoughts about Christology. Two lines of antithesis dominate Moltmann's thought. First of all Moltmann contrasts the cross and the resurrection, setting them in apparent tension. The second antithesis is the dialectical relationship between the present and the future. Moltmann demonstrates that the idea of eschatology for the present social reality was not widely grasped by much of the Christian community in Germany, and perhaps elsewhere.[27]

---

22. Bauckham, *The Theology of Jürgen Moltmann*, 101.
23. Moltmann, *Theology of Hope*, 31, 32.
24. Bauckham, *The Theology of Jürgen Moltmann*, 100.
25. Moltmann, *Theology of Hope*, 102.
26. Moltmann, *Theology of Hope*, 1967, 173.
27. In *The Christian Century*, Jeffrey Gros rightly points out in his article, "Spirit of the

When some Christians were challenged by the aftershocks of the Second World War, they were quick to think that Jesus has no social and political relevance in our socio-economically sophisticated societies. The social problems we face today may supersede those of Jesus' day in "rural Palestine," yet Moltmann was and is able to sustain the potency of his political, cosmic, and transformative dimensions of eschatology by linking it with Jesus' work, particularly his crucifixion and resurrection. Moltmann's approach provides resources for both prophetic and politically engaged Christian eschatology and, by extension, Christology.

Finally, Moltmann's departure from his contemporaries is intrinsically linked to his face-to-face encounter with violence. That is why Moltmann's theology of hope is centered on the cross. And he goes even further, arguing that "the theological foundation for Christian *hope* is the *raising* of the crucified Christ. Anyone who develops a 'theology of hope' from this center will be inescapably reminded of the other side of that foundation: the *cross* of the risen Christ." In summary, World War II dashed human hope to the ground. As a cloud of despair hovered over the future of humanity, Moltmann attempted to gather the shattered pieces of hope. He was able to realize that there is yet hope in spite of what seems to be the reality of the world. Perhaps the question was, "Is there yet hope left for this life or must we wait for the end of time?" Moltmann answers with an emphatic, "Yes!" Hope remains because of God's promise confirmed by the raising of Christ from the dead. Hope does not mean burying our heads in the sand. Rather it means opening our eyes wide to the possibilities. God is "eternally present" and actively involved and in control.[28]

Last Days: Pentecostal Eschatology in Conversation with Jürgen Moltmann," eschatology faces the modern Christian community with a variety of challenges. Millennialist interpretations of the end time, with threats of apocalyptic catastrophe and ominous political implications, especially in the Middle East, grip the popular imagination of certain sectors of the evangelical subculture. Liberation movements recognize a theology of the kingdom that impels Christian engagement and even radical transformative action in the world.

28. Bauckham, *The Theology of Jürgen Moltmann*, 12.

1.4 Developing Creative Love Creates an Alternative to Violence: Dialogue

The significance of dialogue in a society where injustice, exploitation, oppression, marginalization, domination, and gross inequality are embedded cannot be overemphasized. Dialogue enables Christian love to be creative. Put another way, dialogue makes it possible for Christians to concretely embody the love of God as Christ epitomizes God's love. As Moltmann argues, "Faith in the God who raised the assailed and crucified Christ from among the victims of violence must of inner necessity, be active in *creative love.*"[29] Can Christians living in contemporary Northern Nigeria, with its spiral of violence and social fragmentation, embody this sort of love? Violence has produced a much-desired Christology in Moltmann. It is a Christology that matters in a world like ours. It challenges us to ask questions about our role in times of violence and about the identity of Christ and his relevance to our political, ethnic, and religious situations.

Moltmann does not only "understand love as the power of suffering through time with persistent passion for justice in the face of death and evil,"[30] but also that "Christian theology is fundamentally a theology of dialogue." That is, "It has and reveals its truth first of all in dialogue with other people and other religions and ideologies. Its center lies on their boundaries."[31]

The pursuit of justice necessitates dialogue between the different communities and religious traditions in Northern Nigeria. If Christians' intent in Northern Nigeria is "not to drive out one devil by another, but aim to minister to justice on every side," dialogue is the way to go.[32] Indeed, "Dialogue between the world religions and the ideologies of the modern world [postmodern] is necessary for the survival of mankind [humanity]."[33] It is the responsibility of the Christian community to seek to create the

---

29. Moltmann, *The Experiences of Hope*, 58.
30. Moltmann, *The Experiment of Hope*, xvii.
31. Moltmann, *The Experiment of Hope*, 12.
32. Moltmann, *The Experiences of Hope*, 59.
33. Moltmann, *The Experiment of Hope*, 13.

necessary atmosphere whereby "theology should strive to have dialogue everywhere."[34]

In Northern Nigeria Christian theology needs to dialogue with African Traditional Religion and Islamic ideologies with the view of understanding crucial issues of justice is that ultimately creates peace. Dialogue encourages openness to those who differ from us. It engenders a willingness to talk with the "other" in order to win him/her to the side of justice and peace. The target of dialogue is the dislodgement of unjust structures or systemic injustice, rather than the individuals who are in bondage to the system.

It is true that the church in Nigeria, particularly in Northern Nigeria, faces a crisis of faith in the midst of political, economic, ethnic, and religious violence. But Nigeria, or even Africa at large, is not alone in these situations, as Moltmann's work and others demonstrate. For example, from the European point of view, Colin Brown points out that two crises of faith "in particular overshadowed all the rest, for in them the issue at stake is that which sets Christianity apart from other religions and beliefs—the identity of Jesus Christ."[35] This identity of Christ cannot be separated from Jesus' overwhelming inclusive sense of human existence. As Glen Stassen rightly points out, "Jesus was crucified for his peacemaking, his inclusion of outcasts, "enemies of the law." He repeatedly angered the self-righteous, legalistic religious leaders by welcoming outcasts, lepers, prostitutes, the poor, women, tax collectors, and even hated Romans into fellowship."[36]

This issue of the identity of Jesus Christ as a peacemaker stresses the significance of dialogue. As Moltmann maintains, "A theology without relationships is a dead theology."[37] In light of this, I shall explore how dialogue creates religious freedom, and by extension peace, as well as how dialogue is understood by Moltmann and African theologians.

In his forward to *Jesus of Africa*, Robert J. Schreiter described in great detail the African context. Schreiter writes:

---

34. Moltmann, *The Experiment of Hope*, 13.
35. Brown, *Jesus in European Protestant Thought*, 1778–1860: Studies in Historical Theology 1 (Durham, N.C.: The Labyrinth Press, 1985), xv.
36. Jürgen Moltmann and Glen Stassen, *Justice Creates Peace*, Baptist Peacemakers International Spirituality Pamphlet No. 13, 1988, 19.
37. Moltmann, *The Experiment of Hope*, 13.

How to name Jesus, by Africans and for Africans, was placed on the agenda early in attempts to create a genuinely African theology. . . . But African theology, and its presentation of Jesus within that theology, faces new challenges. Dealing with the colonial heritage still remains. Economic dependence, being excluded by fast-moving globalization and the enduring legacy of the colonization of the mind (the most insidious aspect of colonialism) raise high hurdles. The social and political crisis in so many African countries, the devastating epidemic of HIV/AIDS, and the persistence of malaria are enervating two generations of Africans, depleting the possibility of their moving forward as they would wish. If Christ is to be relevant for Africa today, this hydra-headed challenge will have to be met.[38]

Schreiter has x-rayed the African context, which is similar to what Moltmann has been grappling with since the Second World War. These socio-political and socioeconomic issues have overwhelmed most Evangelical theologians of African decent. This is either because they think that there is nothing we can do about them or that they do not know how to develop a responsible political Christology and political philosophy which are grounded in the belief that Christ is the hope of Africa. African Christians and their theologians no doubt "stress Jesus' central place within African Christianity and the critical need to articulate the reality and significance of Christ in relation to the lives of African Christians."[39] This means that it is not only Europeans who have concern for Jesus' identity, as Brown reminds us, but the whole of Africa. But any discussion of African Christology vis-à-vis Christian identity must include the history of Euro-American missionaries' activities in the continent.

In the next section I shall attempt to look at insights from other sources that help us to grasp the inner logic of Moltmann's Christology, particularly,

---

38. Robert J. Schreiter, "Foreword" in Diane B. Stinton *Jesus of Africa: Voices of Contemporary African Christology* (Maryknoll, New York: Obis Books, 2004), xi.
39. Stinton, *Jesus of Africa*, 3.

his conception of theodicy: God voluntarily entering suffering with victims of violence.

2. Insights from Moltmann's Theme of God Entering into Suffering

Moltmann's theme of God entering into suffering has occupied the theological and Christological discussions of Moltmann's students. Among them, are two who I find very insightful: M. Douglas Meeks and Richard Bauckham.

2.1 M. Douglas Meeks

Meeks' take on Moltmann begins with an assessment of the central thrust of his theological enterprise. According to Meeks, to understand Moltmann's Christology or theology we must situate it in his overarching argument: "One cannot gain a future unless one is prepared to search one's past and to acknowledge and accept one's present, however distasteful that may be."[40] Moltmann is able to accept his past and present because he believes that hope liberates us from the shackles of our circumstances. This is "a deeper, liberating hope which works through love."[41] This mighty wave of hope plays out in all of his writings.

Simply stated, no analysis of the effect of violence on Moltmann's Christology can ignore the fundamental fact that Moltmann had a deeper encounter with Christ as he grappled with his experiences and those of others during the war and post-war era in Germany. Meeks aptly demonstrates that Moltmann is Christocentricly disposed because he has "learned the origin of the Christian faith in the suffering of him who was crucified and in the liberating power of the risen Christ."[42] Meeks further notes,

---

40. Meeks, *Origins of the Theology of Hope* (Philadelphia: Fortress Press, 1974), ix.
41. Meeks, *Origins of The Theology of Hope*, ix.
42. Meeks, *Origins of the Theology of Hope*, ix.

From the beginning Moltmann was influenced by the impetus of his Göttingen teachers. He followed their intention of articulating the lordship of God in terms of his act in the resurrection. Under their stimulation, he sought to create a view of history, which would not debilitate but rather facilitate Christians' mission in the world. In order to carry out this task, hope theology had to enter into the postwar debate on the recalcitrant, omnipresent problems of revelation and history. . . . [As a way of departure from his teachers and contemporaries] Moltmann's attempt to develop a view of revelation that describes the God of the exodus and the resurrection rather than the God of the "epiphany of the eternal present" is distinctly new in comparison with modern theology. The framework for dealing with these issues was provided by reflection on the God-question, as prompted especially by Iwand's reading of Hegel. Moltmann [thereafter] viewed the problems of modern theology as centering in the question of God.[43]

This sudden discovery is due in part to the effect of the war on the Church, on one hand, and the fruits of the Enlightenment, on the other. Thus Meeks set out to distinguish and examine the sources of Moltmann's theology, which make these projects theologically authentic new breakthroughs in contemporary theology. Meeks argues that "the genesis of the theology of hope was Moltmann's creation of the *dialectic of reconciliation*" [out of the following sources]: a genuinely futuristic eschatology, a theology of the kingdom of God as a reality within world history, a theology of the resurrection as a 'history making' event, and a theology of the cross as an irreducible criterion of Christian truth. . . ." These "were all theological projects which seemingly had been dismissed on various counts as impossible in the modern world."[44] They were the shattered pieces of hope that Moltmann gathered. For example, Moltmann's creation of the

---

43. Meeks, *Origins of the Theology of Hope*, 54–5.
44. Meeks, *Origins of the Theology of Hope*, 1–2.

144
The Impact of Ethnic, Political, and Religious Violence on
Northern Nigeria, and a Theological Reflection on Its Healing

dialectic of reconciliation is not unconnected with the fact that "it is in this contradiction that hope must prove its power."[45] But which contradiction is Moltmann talking about? It is the alleged "contradiction to our present experience of suffering, evil, and death."[46] The cross and resurrection stand in need of reconciliation, so to speak.

The idea of the cross in juxtaposition with resurrection reminds us that faith cannot escape the reality of suffering "into a heavenly utopia."[47] As Meeks points out, Moltmann uses Iwand's criticism of existent theologies to question Bultmann's program of demythologizing biblical apocalyptic and Greek cosmology so that Christian faith can be interpreted existentially.[48] Moltmann realizes that humanity is held in bondage by two questions: the question of theodicy and the identity question.[49]

Finally, as Meeks points out, Moltmann is able to unite "the biblical question of God, which becomes focused ultimately in the resurrection"[50] with "the questions of *righteousness* asked out of the suffering from injustice, of *identity* asked out of guilt and self-alienation, and of *life* asked out of the threat of death in all things."[51] Indeed it is this understanding of the God-question that enables Moltmann to propose a framework for a new concept of revelation. It seems Moltmann wants any society plagued by violence to find help by turning to his shared understanding of the question of theodicy and identity.

2.2 Richard Bauckham

Moltmann has influenced a whole generation of theologians. Richard Bauckham is one of the many who have been deeply impacted by Moltmann's acute analysis of theology in the face of a world turned against itself. Bauckham has also been able to move beyond Moltmann by carefully analyzing Moltmann's theology. He maintains that Moltmann's willingness

---

45. Meeks, *Origins of the Theology of Hope*, 19.
46. Meeks, *Origins of the Theology of Hope*, 19.
47. Meeks, *Origins of the Theology of Hope*, 19.
48. Meeks, *Origins of the Theology of Hope*, 57.
49. Meeks, *Origins of the Theology of Hope*, 58.
50. Meeks, *Origins of the Theology of Hope*, 58.
51. Meeks, *Origins of the Theology of Hope*, 59.

to dialogue and to listen to other voices in the field of theology and in the humanities enables him to "demonstrate an outstanding ability to appreciate and to integrate insights from the most varied sources, theological and otherwise."[52] Bauckham's purpose is to demonstrate that Moltmann has contributed positively to a theological understanding of suffering. He shows how Moltmann chose to pit his theology against those who, because of their socio-political circumstances, "become insolent and protest against God." Moltmann is aware that they do so because they do not grasp the significance of the cross and resurrection—what God the Father was doing in them. Bauckham started by teasing out the fundamental content of Moltmann's theology which includes, among other things, the cross and resurrection as eschatological promise.

2.2.1 The Cross and the Resurrection as Eschatological Promise

Moltmann sees the cross and the resurrection as eschatological promise. I have noted that Moltmann sets the cross and resurrection in dialectical tension. This gives his theology a methodological twist.[53] Bauckham contends that Moltmann's earlier work was controlled by his "dialectical interpretation of the cross and the resurrection of Jesus, which is then subsumed into the particular form of trinitarianism, which becomes the over-arching theological principle of his later work."[54] In other words, Moltmann employs a methodology that helped him to open "theology not only to the church but also to the whole world and its future."[55] I will add that this dialogic theology holds hope for any nation that might find itself divided along religious, political, economic, cultural, and ethnic divides. It does not pretend to know all the answers, but rather it is willing to learn from others about what God is doing in their history and experiences.

---

52. Bauckham, *The Theology of Jürgen Moltmann*, x.
53. Bauckham, *The Theology of Jürgen Moltmann*, 5.
54. Bauckham, *The Theology of Jürgen Moltmann*, 4.
55. Bauckham, *The Theology of Jürgen Moltmann*, 5.

The Impact of Ethnic, Political, and Religious Violence on
Northern Nigeria, and a Theological Reflection on Its Healing

146

2.2.2 The Key issues in Moltmann's Theology

Everything about Moltmann's theology revolves around eschatology. His eschatological enterprise has been generally extrapolated into seven characteristics: "(1) Christological, (2) integrative, (3) redemptive, (4) processive, (5) theocentric, (6) contextual, and (7) politically and pastorally responsible." Two things are significant to note:

(1) Eschatological hope for Moltmann does not mean waiting for the next world after the present world has ended. Rather eschatology is tied to God's promise of a change that is presently feasible and realistic. The resurrection of Jesus is a stamp of approval, which demonstrates that what God promised is already coming to fruition and will surely reach its acme. In this sense Moltmann is deliberately departing from his German contemporaries—Schweitzer, Dodd, Bultmann, and many other 1960s theologians—who thought that eschatological hope was no longer credible to a modern world.[56] In other words, in spite of the present violence, evil, sufferings, and resulting darkness, there is light at the end of the tunnel: we are actually standing at the threshold of God's rock of promised possibilities because Christ's "resurrection set in motion an historical process in which the promise already affects the world and moves it in the direction of future transformation."[57]

(2) Theodicy preoccupied Moltmann's theology because of the problem of those who worry about the enormous suffering of alleged innocent victims. "Many people who were overwhelmed by the horror of the Holocaust became insolent and protested against God. Moltmann situates both his theology of hope and the crucified God in such a way that it responds to this situation. Moltmann proposes an eschatological theodicy in *Theology of Hope*."[58] Moltmann does not in any way try to defend God. Rather he points to the implicit promise that God endorsed by the resurrection of Christ. The resurrection provides a window to the final triumph of God over all evil and suffering.[59]

56. Bauckham, *The Theology of Jürgen Moltmann*, 8.
57. Bauckham, *The Theology of Jürgen Moltmann*, 10.
58. Bauckham, *The Theology of Jürgen Moltmann*, 10.
59. Bauckham, *The Theology of Jürgen Moltmann*, 11.

Bauckham's fundamental argument that goes beyond Moltmann's is that "God suffers, but as the one who transcends all finite suffering. We may say that there is something analogous to human suffering in the divine experience, but we may not thereby claim that we know what it is like for God to suffer," as Moltmann perhaps implies.[60] So Bauckham is trying to provide a critique of Moltmann's view of God suffering in solidarity with us. I worry about a concept of suffering that confuses God's picture of suffering on the cross with a human picture of suffering. In other words, can God suffer outside the incarnation? Moltmann is very clear about what God's suffering in solidarity with us entails. It entails God voluntarily opening himself to the possibility of being affected by our suffering. Moltmann basically argues that if we believe that "God is capable of love we can equally believe that God is capable of suffering."[61]

In summary, Moltmann's work originated from one of the darkest moments in human history. He has grappled with how it could produce the fruits that God intended, particularly in the Church and its mission to the world. I will therefore attempt to show how Moltmann's experience might bring living hope and peace to Northern Nigeria's sense of despair and desperation, caused by decades of ethnic, political, and religious violence.

2.2.3 Missionary Context of the Discussion

The system of human violence is multifaceted. In order to grasp the sources of the misery violence creates, "we must understand the reasons for it, and analyze the system of violence"[62] involved. Moltmann has aptly noted that the concept of the kingdom of God bears witness to the fact that theology is *a missionary* project. That is true.

However, all of Africa, particularly Nigeria, has had both positive and negative experiences with this missiological project. In retrospect, this *missionary* enterprise of theology has led to cultural uprooting. In the past, Euro-American missionaries literally taught Africans to hate their culture.

---

60. Bauckham, *The Theology of Jürgen Moltmann*, 69.
61. Moltmann, *The Crucified God*, 230.
62. Moltmann, *Experiences in Theology*, 59.

With the benefit of hindsight, both missionaries and their colonial counterparts had one shared assumption: "the superiority of Western cultural values to those they found in African countries." Moreover, they usually assumed that they had, in one form or another, what the French liked to call a "civilizing mission," which always meant a Westernizing mission. This was no passing mood. It was the fundamental ideological justification of the whole colonial enterprise. And it was a justification that Europeans sought to have accepted by the African educated elite. Consequently this project birthed hierarchical communities that have continually sought to dominate others, both in the church and in society. As a result, people who look down on others because of their ethnic, religious, economic, and political placement in society characterize African societies.

Therefore I can say that, to some degree, this policy of cultural denigration of African society was successful. The African intellectuals did at first reject their own culture—not only its religion and its technology, but also its dress and its music, and most importantly, its link with the past. "These intellectuals very largely accepted the notion that Africa had no history [and] that the future lay [sic] in adopting a Western style of life."[63] Today, members of a new generation of African theologians are outraged at this past handling of the Christian mission in Africa. They are agitating for a cultural revival both in society and in the Church.

Yet in efforts to revive their culture, African theologians still face the challenge of confronting the marred perspectives within that culture. The task has not been easy. And causes pain because their theological approach is very reactionary and to some extent employs not only social engineering theories but also Euro-American methodology to make their books marketable. Furthermore cultural revival has caused pains because it both abets and hurts the process of theological transformation and sociopolitical modernization.[64] Yet there is an interesting prevailing paradigm that must be addressed.

---

63. Immanuel Wallerstein, *Africa: The Politics of Independence: An Interpretation of Modern African History, Vintage Books*, Vol. 206 (New York: Random House, 1961), 121.
64. Wallerstein, *Africa: The Politics of Independence*, 134–135.

3. The Prevailing Paradigm: Enculturation and Liberation

Some African theologians claim that the Church is the hope of Africa. By this it is meant that Jesus is the key to Africa's morality and by extension, African Christological method. How then can we help Africa embody the concept of the crucified Christ so that African culture (politics, economy, social, and customs) is transformed into an instrument of His glory? This is one of the questions that have occupied the Church in Africa for several decades. As Diane Stinton notes,

> African theology is commonly introduced according to two main trends that emerged from the late 1950s to the late 1980s: African or inculturation theology, and black or liberation theology. The former category entails theological exploration of African indigenous cultures in an attempt to integrate the African pre-Christian religious heritage with the Christian faith so as to "ensure the integrity of African Christian identity and selfhood." The latter category has been further subdivided into South African black theology, arising out of the particular context of apartheid in that country, and African liberation theology, found throughout independent sub-Saharan Africa and broader in scope. Its intention is to integrate the theme of liberation in the rest of the African cultural background. Liberation is not confined to modern socioeconomic and political levels but includes emancipation from other forms of oppression such as disease, poverty, hunger, ignorance, and the subjugation of women.[65]

The struggle is within two worlds: liberation theology and inculturation. But what is striking here is that liberation does not concern itself with the liberation from both structural and personal violence. People see violence

---

65. Stinton, *Jesus of Africa*, 49.

as a problem that needs help, but it seems to me that they seldom see the possibility of using Jesus' experience on the cross and resurrection as a starting point.

3.1 Contrasting Liberation Theology in Africa with Those of Latin America and the U.S.

Moltmann has consistently tried "to explore the dimensions of the Christian hope, especially the political dimension on the one hand, and the Trinitarian dimension on the other." Moltmann's attempt to interpret God's promise, out of which the awakened hope makes men and women creatively alive in the possibilities of history, provides significant insights. This is an effort to interpret Christology first within his social milieu and later within the global milieu. This puts Moltmann in a position for other theological discourses to be juxtaposed with his work.

In juxtaposing Moltmann's work with African Christology, we ought to remember that "African theology emerged in the post-missionary context of the 1950s and 1960s when African theologians started to reflect deeply on their own context of being Christian and being African." As I noted above, the impetus behind this movement was outrage about the negative attitude of the missionaries towards African cultures and religions. This means that it has been a reactionary theology and Christology. I would argue that this is connected to an awareness that the African traditional religion was "not far from the kingdom of God" (Mark 12:34).

Mercy Amba Oduyoye argues that there is what could be called "intra-Africa." That is, "Even thought West Africa differs from East and both differ from Southern," Oduyoye points out that Africa has certain shared experiences:

(1) All of Africa is one in the experiences of neocolonial economies. The skillful machinery of exploitation set up by world monetary systems is like a rainbow that begins in the Mediterranean and ends where South Africa ends.

(2) All African countries are in the throes of social crises created by modern technology, modernization of traditional societal

structures, and the multinational culture generated and promoted by the modern mass media.

(3) The crises created by certain legal structures, especially on the level of "personal law," have reached a distressing pitch where women's rights are concerned.[66]

(4) Having three main religions all vying for the soul of African has only added to the social crises. The most devastating to my mind is the type of Christianity being promoted by certain Western countries. It can be substantiated that the very people who own the wealth of the multinationals also sponsor this type of Christianity that orientates Africans toward buying into the capitalist system so that they may serve as its labor force and cannon fodder for its militarism. This religion is nothing short of the demonic.[67]

Thus I argue that what African Christology needs is to focus on the impact of a form of Christianity that uprooted African Christians from their cultural and social settings and left them dangling in midair. Our Christology needs to come to terms with this reality as well as other realities in the continent. As Oduyoye rightly points out,

As theologians we are concerned with the impact of Christianity, for it claims 28 percent of Africa's population. We do Christian theology in a context that has 41 percent Muslims and 31 percent practitioners of Africa's own indigenous religions. We cannot ignore the Islamic revival that is spreading in Africa; neither can we close our eyes to the inseparability of Africa's religion from African culture and its impact on Christianity and Islam alike. Theology in Africa has to be dialogical.[68]

---

66. Mercy Amba Oduyoye, "Commonalities: An African Perspective" K.C. Abraham, ed., *Third World Theologies: Commonalities & Divergences* (New York: Orbis Books, 1986), 101.
67. Oduyoye, "Commonalities: An African Perspective" in *Third World Theologies*, 100
68. Oduyoye, "Commonalities: An African Perspective" in *Third World Theologies*, 101.

African Christology cannot afford to be in isolation. It must be a Christology that is willing to stay in touch with what God is doing not only in its own context but also in other contexts. In his article "Divergences: A Latin American Perspective" *Third World Theologies,* Sergio Torres looks at Latin America's 'relation with and dependency upon the West.' He contends,

> People from Latin America are the most Westernized in the Third World. It is true that Latin American races and cultures were the outcome of an ethnic and racial mixture of Spanish and Portuguese people with the pre-Colombian indigenous peoples, but it is also true that this mixed race has been always dominated by the white minorities of the traditional classes and emerging bourgeoisie. . . . Racial and cultural context has also made its mark on the theology of liberation. This theology has affirmed its Latin American identity, becoming independent from European theology. However, only recently it has rediscovered its mestizo roots, and it has enriched its view about the poor—the starting point of this theology— incorporating the racial and ethnic components.[69]

The focus of Latin American Christology/liberation therefore is "social, cultural, ecclesial, and theological." This situation distinguishes Latin American Christo-liberation from those of not only Africa, but also U.S. and Asia. Generally speaking, "The Third World is emerging with a new face and with different cultures which challenge the traditional white supremacy. For the Latin American theology of liberation this indeed is a true challenge."[70] Latin Christology worries about the white supremacy but they often tend not to recognize that their own cousins collaborate with the whites. Thus is not a matter of White or Latin or African, but of violence

---

69. Sergio Torres, "Divergences: A Latin American Perspective" *Third World Theologies,* 121.
70. Torres, "Divergences: A Latin American Perspective" *Third World Theologies,* 121.

and abuse of power, whoever may be wielding it. Those who collaborate with the status quo are often more dangerous.

In a global community no nation can desire isolation. Hence Africa Christology must be willing to listen to those of Asian countries. Tissa Balasuriya has helped us with that perspective. He recognizes that our "divergences are due mainly to the context in which theologizing is done."[71] According to Balasuriya, "One key element that sets the Asian situation aside is its historical and socio-cultural background." Balasuriya tells us that

> The difference is in the large populations of some of the Asian countries and the consequent enormity of the problems of development and liberation. In Asia the religio-cultural traditions come down from ancient times and are experiencing a revival and modernization, which give them a new vigor. Politically and socially, the ideologies of capitalism and Marxism are dominant influences in some Asian countries. The largest secular democracy as well as the largest country under a Marxist regime is in Asia. Concerning theology in relation to poverty, there are more similarities than divergences among the theologies of Asia, Africa, and Latin America. The attitude toward Marxist analysis is of a critical nature, and other factors, such as sex, ethnicity, and religious communalism, are also important influences on society. Further, the influence of both popular religion and the more developed world religions brings in a dimension that is not adequately explained by Marxism.[72]

Despite the divergences much of these continents have a shared experience; that is, "the poverty of the masses of the people is common to Africa, U.S. Latin America, and Asia."[73] The truth is Asian Christology faces

---

71. Balasuriya, "Divergences: An Asian Perspectives" *Third World Theologies*, 113.
72. Balasuriya, "Divergences: An Asian Perspectives" *Third World Theologies*, 113.
73. Balasuriya, "Divergences: An Asian Perspectives" *Third World Theologies*, 113.

many challenges like any other continent. As Balasuriya explains Asian Christology and liberation's primary commitment is:

(1) A response to God and a source of empathetic understanding responding to the exigencies of reality; and contemplation as a union with God that leads to and is nurtured by commitment.

(2) An approach toward spirituality of action that is holistic, unitive, and mystical. This spirituality takes place prior to the elaboration of theological concepts. It seeks God in the other, in the situation, and in creation.

(3) An influence of the meditational and contemplative traditions of the Asian religions Hinduism and Buddhism, including Zen, the mystical tradition of Islam and the general Oriental temperament that seeks interiority and harmony.

(4) Emphasizes . . . and . . . develops methodologies of personal liberation through reflection, meditation, and deeper consciousness of the transience of being, and escape from delusion concerning the nature of temporal reality.[74]

Liberation theology in the United States is different from that of Africa, Latin America, and Asia. James H. Cone's liberation theology is a response to his people's (the African Americans) situation of servitude in North America. Cone tries to investigate "the meaning of black existence, and how blacks could reconcile black servitude and oppression with the biblical claim that 'God is our refuge and strength, a very present help in times of trouble.'"[75] Liberation to Cone is Christo-Liberation. Thus the question is: "How have black people understood their history and culture, and how is that understanding related to their faith in Jesus Christ?"[76] Cone equally insists that because Christian theology is theology of liberation, it entails a rational study of the being of God in the world in the light of the existential situation of an oppressed community.

---

74. Balasuriya, "Divergences: An Asian Perspectives" *Third World Theologies*, 114.
75. James H. Cone, *Risks of Faith: The Emergence of a Black Theology of Liberation*, 1968–1998 (Boston: Beacon Press 1999), 170.
76. James H. Cone, *God of the Oppressed* (New York: Orbis Books, 1975), 9.

Hence the forces of liberation ought to be related to the essence of the Gospel, which is Jesus Christ.[77] This demonstrates that Cone pays attention to what God does through his Son Jesus Christ and what that means to the oppressed in America and elsewhere. For example, Cone argues that "On the cross, God's identity with the suffering of the world was complete . . . the cross of Jesus reveals the extent of God's involvement in the suffering of the weak" ['the little ones'].[78] Cone contends that "the divine involvement in suffering, radically revealed in Jesus' cross, counts decisively against any suggestion that God is indifferent to human pain."[79] African American liberation Christology is a theology construed from the larger context of white's claim of supremacy in America. It is thus closely linked to other oppressed people in the world who suffer infamous social and political structures. Finally, Cone's careful analysis of the concept of "the little ones" in Matthew 25:45 yields three conclusions:

(1) That without struggle, the vision of a new heaven becomes a sedative that makes the victims of injustice content with servitude.

(2) That without struggle, the negative suffering inflicted by oppressors becomes positive and thus leads to passivity and submission

(3) That without struggle, the idea of redemption becomes a human creation of the oppressors that is designed to numb the pain and forestall challenges to the structures of injustice.[80]

3.2 African Liberation Defined

Africa has an interesting scenario in that Catholic theologians have done more reflection on the African context of Christology than Evangelical and Pentecostal theologians. One of the Catholic theologians, Charles Nyamiti, holds that liberation seen from the perspective of Christologies in Africa is an effort to incarnate the Gospel message in the African cultures on the theological level. For example, he tries to show how Christology examined from the standpoint of African Traditional Religions has a concept of God

---

77. James H. Cone, *A Black Theology of Liberation* (Philadelphia and New York: J.B. Lippincot Company, 1970), 17.
78. Cone, *God of the Oppressed*, 161.
79. Cone, *God of the Oppressed*, 163.
80. Cone, *God of the Oppressed*, 168.

156

The Impact of Ethnic, Political, and Religious Violence on
Northern Nigeria, and a Theological Reflection on Its Healing

that is closer to the concept of the biblical God.[81] Generally, for Nyamiti these Christologies are "on the whole, more numerous and in many cases relatively more profound than those of liberation Christologies."[82] Other scholars in Africa have disagreed with his take on this. For example, Mugambi criticized Nyamiti's categorization for being too sharp, contending that commitment to one approach does not necessitate inattention or opposition toward the other approach.[83]

I suspect some African theologians are thinking that oppression is limited to what the elite do to the poor. While there are some who do think that oppression is what the poor do to themselves, the number of those who think otherwise is greater. For example, Stinton cites Ela who decries "the traps of Africanization," in the proliferation of research on the confrontation between the Gospel and African authenticity, and "the dead-end of ethnotheology." Against such a one-sided approach, Ela protests with his central thesis that *"liberation of the oppressed must be the primary condition for any authentic inculturation of the Christian message."*[84]

Ela is not alone in this view. For instance, Stinton tells us that "Bujo strongly concurs, and these two theologians express mutual acknowledgment in this regard." Bujo argues that genuine African deliverance is impossible "without rediscovering deeply rooted traditional cultural values." Bujo denounces any theology of inculturation that focuses on "anthropological poverty" without adequately addressing the ills of the post-colonial context, which inculturation alone cannot remedy. He charges that the theology of inculturation is too academic and "a pompous irrelevance, truly an ideological superstructure at the service of the bourgeoisie."[85]

These charges are incisive. But I worry about a theology that tends to ignore the larger issues and also neglect what God is doing in other contexts. The controlling thesis has the tendency to ignore some issues. Muzorewa argues that "when we speak of the sources of African traditional theology

---

81. Charles Nyamiti, *African Theology: Its Problems and Methods* (Uganda: Gaba Publications, 1977), 1.
82. See Stinton, *Jesus of Africa*, 49.
83. Stinton, *Jesus of Africa*, 49.
84. Stinton, *Jesus of Africa*, 49.
85. Stinton, *Jesus of Africa*, 50.

a key word is *experience*.[86] The word *experience* can be vague. What sort of experience is it? John Agbeti says it is "the African traditional experience of the Supreme Being."[87] Similarly Muzorewa points out that "This experience, interpreted by Africans, is the essential *content* of African traditional theology."[88] This is pointing to a built-in-weakness in African Christology. That is, some African theologians by dwelling on the African experience of the Supreme Being largely obscure the African experience of violence and war. Thus when they discuss violence the discussion is theologically and ethically bankrupt.

African Christology therefore can function well with Moltmann's theology because the content is the same—experience. But that will happen only if African Christology pays attention to the African experience of violence and war, and how they impact and shape the African theological and ethical outlook. Muzorewa asked an important question: "Since we have maintained that experience is essentially the content of African traditional theology, what is its nature?" John S. Mbiti answers that question by observing that, "In the African culture, 'experience' is a way of life."[89] Thus Muzorewa writes, "Since experience and theology are two sides of the same coin, the African's daily activities could be interpreted as a manifestation of African theology."[90] Experience that is theological has some bearing on the God who is worshipped. It is not very clear whether this experience includes the violence and wars of African countries. What is explicit however is African theology and Christology is "the interpretation of a people's experience of God, the Supreme Being or the ultimate reality, and his dealings with them in history."[91] This statement explicitly explains that the experience is limited to what goes on in worship. But it seems to me that violence

---

86. Gwinyai H. Muzorewa, *The Origins and Development of African Theology* (New York: Orbis Books, 1985), 82.
87. John K. Agbeti "African Theology: What it is." *Presence* 5:5–8. 1972, 6, as cited by Muzorewa, *The Origins and Development of African Theology*, 82; and John S. Pobee, "Theology" *The Ghana Bulletin of Theology*, June 4: 1–13, 1973, 5.
88. Muzorewa, *The Origins and Development of African Theology*, 82.
89. John S. Mbiti, *Concepts of God in Africa* (London: S.P.C.K, 1979), 75, as cited by Muzorewa, *The Origin and Development of African Theology*, 82.
90. Muzorewa, *The Origins and Development of African Theology*, 82–83.
91. John K. Agbeti "African Theology: What it is." *Presence* 5:5–8. 1972, 6, as cited by Muzorewa, *The Origin*, 84.

is not fashioned into that experience. Therefore this question remains unanswered: "In what way does this experience include war and violence?"

Nevertheless, it would be naïve to just conclude that all African theologians pay little or no attention to the situation of violence and war in the continent. In essence, it is not all African theologians who ignore the African experience of violence and war. For example, Desmond Tutu describes how his environment impacts what he writes: "Liberation theology more than any other kind of theology issues out of the crucible of human suffering and anguish. It happens because people cry out, 'Oh, God, how long?' 'Oh, God, but why?'" These questions fit nicely with Moltmann's questions during World War II: "My God where are you? Why am I alive?" It is the cry of the victims of human wickedness, rebellion and sin. It is the cry of those who experience their lives as being God-forsaken. Therefore, for Tutu, ". . . liberation theology is in a sense really a theodicy. It seeks to justify God and the ways of God to a downtrodden and perplexed people so that they can be inspired to do something about their lot. They have not even doubted that such a God was a living God, a powerful God, and a God of righteousness and goodness."[92] Tutu further explains,

> All liberation theology stems from trying to make sense of human suffering when those who suffer are the victims of organized oppression and exploitation, when they are emasculated and treated as less than what they are: human persons created in the image of the Triune God, redeemed by the one Savior Jesus Christ and sanctified by the Holy Paraclete.[93]

The African concept of the Trinity is challenged by violence and its resultant misery.[94] This is why Tutu believes that liberation theology faces a challenge in Africa and elsewhere. Thus he writes, "Liberation theology is

---

92. Bishop Desmond Tutu, "The Theology of Liberation in Africa" Kofi Appiah-Kubi and Sergio Torres, eds., *African Theology En Route* (New York: Orbis Books, 1979), 163.
93. Appiah-Kubi, et al., *African Theology En Route*, 163.
94. Appiah-Kubi, et al., *African Theology En Route*, 163.

no mere intellectual exercise, no mere cerebral enterprise, for it deals with matters of life and death for those on whose behalf it is being done" Given that it is done on behalf of the voiceless, the downtrodden, and victims of injustice and infamous policies, "liberation theology must enable the victims of oppression to assert their God-given personhood and humanity and must help exorcise from them the awful sense of self-hatred and self-disgust which are the ghastly consequences of oppression."[95] As Dryness rightly points out, "A major contribution of liberation theology has been the introduction and use of the social sciences as a means of better comprehending the setting in which theology is done."[96] In Africa the sources of liberation theology and Christology include the African traditional experience, as I have noted above.

African liberation theology and Christology seek to relate Jesus to the unique African situation: power. This drama necessitates unpacking Jesus' significance to the African experience.[97] For example, Nyamiti's theological intent is to "introduce into the African church the traditional piety [based on his Catholic tradition], adapting it and Christianizing it from within."[98]

Nyamiti sees Jesus and the ancestors on an equal level of authority.[99] According to Dyrness, this features the common African tendency to celebrate death, not as an ending, but as the passing to a new level of existence.[100] Nyamiti also sees the salvation, which Jesus brings primarily as freedom from sin and death. Here unlike James Cone and other liberation theologians in Latin America who put a premium on socio-political liberation, Nyamiti gives priority to spiritual liberation and secondary status to socio-political liberation. Nyamiti contends, "It is sufficiently clear that the salvation brought by Jesus is not in the first place a revolutionary social

---

95. Appiah-Kubi, et al., *African Theology En Route*, 163, 167.
96. William A. Dyrness, *Learning about Theology from the Third World* (Grand Rapid: Zondervan Publishing House, 1990), 111.
97. Charles Nyamiti, *Christ as Our Ancestor: Christology from an African Perspective* (Gweru, Zimbabwe: Mambo Press, 1984) as cited by Dyrness, *Learning about Theology from the Third World*, 116.
98. Dyrness, *Learning about Theology from the Third World*, 136, Nyamiti, *Christ as Our Ancestor*, 166.
99. Nyamiti, *Christ as Our Ancestor*, 19, cited in Dyrness, *Learning about Theology from the Third World*, 116.
100. Dyrness, *Learning about Theology from the Third World*, 167.

or political element."[101] As Dyrness relates, "Kwame Bediako is not happy identifying the role of Christ with that of the ancestors. . . . He believes one can too easily assume parallels that do not in fact exist. Nor should Christ simply replace the ancestors."[102] I argue that undue attention has been paid to the relationship between the ancestors and Christ to the extent that the impact of Christianity on the African concepts is hard realized. So this kind of argument ignores those who have been uprooted from their cultural base, resulting in the erosion of most of their African cultural past. They only live in Africa but they have been more or less influenced by a foreign-cultural outlook. The foregoing analysis yields the following conclusions:

(1) Moltmann's concept of Jesus Christ as a *brother* provides extraordinary insight into what the biblical text teaches. The nuance of ancestors distances Christ from us while the nuance of *brother* deeply unites us with Christ and reflects John 1:12: "Yet to all who received him, to those who believed in his name, he gave the right to become children of God [not ancestors of God]—children born not of natural descent, nor of human decision or a husband's will, but born of God." similarly the writer of Hebrews says, "So Jesus is not ashamed to call them brothers."[103] As Kwame Bediako has rightly observed "Jesus Christ surpasses our natural ancestors also by virtue of who he is in himself. Ancestors, even described as 'ancestral spirits,' remain essentially human spirits; whatever benefit they may be said to bestow is effectively contained by the fact of their being human. Jesus Christ, on the other hand, took on human nature without loss to his divine nature."[104]

(2) African theologians who pay attention to the doctrine of the Trinity are more relevant to the African context and fit nicely with Moltmann's Trinitarian stance. African Christologies that weigh in on the nuance of the Trinity are clearly Trinitarian Christologies. As Muzorewa states, "The Christian doctrine of the Trinity teaches that the Godhead consists of the

---

101. Charles Nyamiti, *African Tradition and the Christian God* (Kenya: Gaba Publications, 1975), 38.
102. Dyrness, *Learning about Theology from the Third World*, 168.
103. Hebrews 2:11a.
104. Kwame Bediako, *Jesus in Africa: The Christian Gospel in African History and Experience* (Malaysia: Regnum Africa, 2000), 31.

Father, Son, and the Holy Spirit, and that the three persons are simultane-ously one." He notes, "In traditional theology, a composition of the three in one was made, even prior to the historical event of the incarnation."[105] For example, Mbiti relates how, "The Shona believe that God's unity exists in multiplicity. 'A form of God's Trinity or Triads is reported among the Shona and Ndebele peoples. In one area of the Shona country, God is conceived of as "Father, Son, and Mother." Among the neighboring Ndebele, there is a similar belief "in a Trinity of spirits, the Father, the Mother, and the Son.' But the important point for the Shona is not the multiplicity of God, but what God does in these varying modes of being."[106]

(3) Trinitarian conception of Christology carries the sense of creation in community with God and with itself. I claim that it is a concept that situates Christ in the history of humanity: Christ has always been and will continue to be a brother. Indeed, Christ is the only brother that both the oppressor and the oppressed need.

4. Critiquing Moltmann's Work

Moltmann's alternative to injustice and violence is a profound gift to the world. Moltmann's revisiting Germany after World War II was to "create a new, different, more humane world."[107] He has succeeded in bringing out themes that are very significant as well as ahead of his generation and relevant to future generations. But like any other human being, Moltmann has weaknesses, of which two stand out. The first observation is mine, the second is from other scholars' perspectives.

(1) Moltmann believes it is only the rich that require conversion. The poor, Moltmann argues, do not need any condition to come to Jesus. "Jesus proclaims to the poor the kingdom of God without any condi-tions, and calls them blessed because the kingdom is already theirs. But the gospel of the kingdom meets the rich with the call to conversion

---

105. Muzorewa, *The Origins and Development of African Theology*, 85.
106. Mbiti, *Concepts*, 30, as cited by Muzorewa, *The Origin*, 85.
107. Jürgen Moltmann, *Experiences of God*, 6.

(Mark 1:15, paraphrase)."[108] Moltmann further maintains, "Those who are converted (the rich) become a single people, one with the poor, and welded into the new community."[109] Moltmann's presentation here is a bit problematic.

Apparently Moltmann eclipses the poor's need of repentance and forgiveness. He seems to make poverty a license to God's favor. I suppose this is because Moltmann's conception of sin is developed from a social vantage point. "Jesus brings good news of joy to the oppressed." Moltmann's treatment of the subject of sin is very critical to understanding his contrasting perspective between the poor and the rich. "Jesus proclaimed the kingdom of God to the poor" Moltmann writes, "and bestowed the power of God on the sick; and in the same way he brought 'sinners and tax-collectors' to the justice of God, which is the justice of grace."[110] Moltmann points out that in Jesus' day sin was defined in social terms. Thus Jesus' table fellowship was a clear sign that "Jesus was embarking in a social conflict which was religiously determined—the cleft between the just and the unjust, the good and the bad."[111] Moltmann sees an analogous similarity between Jesus' day and his day. Two theses of Moltmann unravel his overarching passion. The first thesis:

> Christian theology is faced today with a twofold crisis. Rapid social and cultural change has brought it to a crisis of its meaning for the world. And the more theology tries to be relevant to the social crises of its society, the more deeply it is itself drawn into the crisis of its own Christian identity.[112]

Equally, Moltmann's second thesis not only reveals his ardent concern, but also the way he does his theological reflection:

---

108. Moltmann, *The Way of Jesus*, 102.
109. Moltmann, *The Way of Jesus*, 103.
110. Moltmann, *The Way of Jesus*, 112.
111. Moltmann, *The Way of Jesus*, 113.
112. Moltmann, *The Experiment of Hope*, 4.

Christian theology is being confronted on various sides with false alternatives. In reality it has no alternative between evangelization and humanization, between interior conversion and improvement of conditions, or between the vertical dimension of faith and the horizontal dimension of love. Whoever separates and divides any of these, destroys the unity of God and man in the person and in the future of Christ.[113]

This second thesis seems to show that Moltmann is an advocate of evangelism and social action. But a careful reading of his entire argument demonstrates that his emphasis is more on social action than on evangelism. There is lack of consistency in his inner logic about evangelism. In Northern Nigeria, the Church cannot afford to preach social action to the detriment of evangelism and vice versa. The situation of the church in Europe is perhaps what it is because the distorting influences of violence have caught up with it. Some of their theologians emphasize social and political theology to the detriment of evangelism. In Germany, Jesus is not, in most spheres, a Savior of humanity.

African theology has its downside too. Many African churches go to either of two extremes: social gospel without evangelism or evangelism without social action. Evangelicals are divided into two extremes or more. Evangelicals who believe in human depravity see the world going downhill without hope of improvement. They place a premium on individual salvation. To this group "the question of social hope simply does not register."[114] This group believes that "salvation and deliverance from sin are purely personal positions, rooted exclusively in the hope that each individual who has received such things will live on after death."[115] The downside of this perspective is, "The ancient Jewish messianic narrative is completely transformed in view of its fulfillment in the Christ event, and any elements of social, political, or global hope that marked the Jewish tradition are thereby

---

113. Moltmann, *The Experiment of Hope*, 6.
114. Miroslav Volf and William Katerberg, eds., *The Future of Hope: Christian Tradition amid Modernity and Postmodernity* (Grand Rapids: Wm. B. Eerdmans Publishing Company, 2004), 33.
115. Volf and Katerberg, *The Future of Hope*, 33.

excised from it."[116] The individual believer's hope has little or no relevance for the present world that is going downhill.

The second group of evangelicals, however, emphasizes social and political action to the detriment of an individual's need for salvation. This group "projects their hopes onto more levels than just the personal."[117] They hold and hope for the redemption of all things humanly possible, both individual and social.[118] "They hope and also anticipate the healing of the natural world and the reestablishment of healthy relations between humanity and nature."[119] Based on the above charge, Moltmann could be situated in this group of evangelicals.

My point is that in a world full of injustice, violence, and bloodshed, Christians need both evangelism and social action. Therefore, not to hold evangelism and social concerns in balance "is to raise the suspicion that one is placing faith in what humans can achieve on their own."[120] Moltmann aptly argues that "By accepting 'sinners and tax-collectors' and prostitutes, Jesus is not justifying the sin, the corruption, or the prostitution." Yet, I recognize that in Jesus' day sin was defined socially. Thus Moltmann is using the term 'sin' in that context. That is to say, Moltmann's definition of sin stopped at the social level. In that case, he has fallen into the trap of many liberation theologians that define sin socially to the detriment of the human condition of sin that requires everyone, in spite of their social standing, to personally accept Jesus Christ as Lord and Savior. I believe both the perpetrators and the victims of violence—the poor—need to come to faith in God and receive his offer of salvation. Therefore, Ron Sider argues, Moltmann needs to balance his call for social and political action with equal emphasis on the human situation of sin: keep social action and evangelism in balance.

---

116. Volf and Katerberg, *The Future of Hope*, 33.
117. Volf and Katerberg, *The Future of Hope*, 33.
118. See David O. Moberg, *The Great Reversal: Evangelism and Social Concern* (Philadelphia: Lippincot, 1972; especially James Davison Hunter, *Evangelicalism: The Coming Generation* (Chicago: University of Chicago Press, 1987), 40–46.
119. Volf and Katerberg, *The Future of Hope*, 34.
120. Volf and Katerberg, *The Future of Hope*, 35.

(2) Although Moltmann's Christology is Trinitarian, it is not very clear where Moltmann fits Christ's resurrection into history. In his *Theology of Hope*, Moltmann contends that "the latencies of future pregnant in 'God's promises' and in the history of Israel pertain not to *Historie*, the objectified and dead past of facts, but only to *Geschichte*, the subjective presence and representation of the past open to possibilities for future."[121] Moltmann argues that the *Geschichte* of promise, in which all the elements of "Christian faith are sociologically reinterpreted (including God with future as his mode of being, humanity, the christological titles of Jesus, the resurrection and the Parousia), is an open process which can never be completed, lest it lose openness to the future."[122] Therefore in Moltmann's theology, "fulfillment can never come; eschatology merely serves as a heuristic to motivate revolutionary change in the present."[123]

This is why some scholars, particularly Jul Souletie, worry that "Moltmann cannot offer a satisfactory view of the relation between eschatology and history primarily because his eschatological perspective prevent him from giving due weight to history itself." Souletie's key question, then, is whether or not Moltmann's conception of history "gives us a proper view of God acting within history on our behalf or leads rather to the Hegelian idea that history is in God." Colin Brown is right that Souletie's comments raise the question of Moltmann's panentheism. Brown aptly suggests that the question emerges most openly at two points: (1) God's suffering in the world's suffering and (2) Moltmann's eschatology. Put another way, Souletie's concern raises the question of whether God's immanence necessarily entails panentheism.[124] This question is very interesting and important but it is beyond the scope of this study.

Souletie further weighs in on what Moltmann means by the Resurrection. He assumes that Moltmann argues that "the Resurrection cannot be seen as a fact but is understood on the basis of the disciple's experience as a

---

121. Moltmann, *Theology of Hope*, 206.
122. Jul Souletie, "The Shape of Things to Comes: Toward an Eschatology of Literature" in *Christianity and Literature*, January 1, 2004, 2.
123. Moltmann, *Theology of Hope*, 179–180.
124. Colin Brown's general observation after completing the reading of the first draft of this dissertation on January 2, 2007, 9.

The Impact of Ethnic, Political, and Religious Violence on
Northern Nigeria, and a Theological Reflection on Its Healing

166

vision, which has the prophetic meaning that God is seen to be at work eschatologically in the cross of Christ bringing justice to the impious and powerless." Simply put, Moltmann has been charged with being unable to maintain the traditional sense of the Resurrection as an event that took place in the life of Jesus on our behalf. Moltmann seems to confuse its objectivity with the disciples' vision experiences and thus falls into a version of the "Jesuology" he himself rejects.[125]

Perhaps some of these criticisms stem from a lack of attentiveness to Moltmann's social milieu. Moltmann's social situation includes, among other things, the holocaust. In general, a careful reading of Moltmann's theological works from the 1960s to date would reveal that there was a wide array of responses to the holocaust. To reiterate, Moltmann's theology was birthed during one of humanity's darkest chapters of violence ever—World War II. He knows firsthand what violence does to humanity and indeed creation itself. Moltmann's primary focus was not really history but how to respond to the confusion and the incredible sense of despair that the aftermath of the holocaust created.[126] Moltmann could grasp this reality because of his personal experience: four long years as a prisoner of war, from 1945–1948.[127]

As it is both Souletie's criticism and Moltmann's own explanation above turned out to buttress the impact of violence. However, Moltmann overcame the temptation to self-destruction by grappling with the theologies of post-war Germany and was able to depart from those who do not bring hope to the situation. As a matter of fact, Moltmann even departed from theologies of pre-war Germany in two basic ways:

First, Moltmann departed from Luther's Reformation theology of justification, which one-sidedly explained justification to mean salvation from sin only. Moltmann argues, "The resurrection of Christ has a saving significance of its own, which goes beyond the forgiveness of sins and is termed 'righteousness,' 'rebirth,' 'new creation,' and 'the outpouring of the

---

125. Jul Souletie, "The Shape of Things to Come: Toward an Eschatology of Literature" in *Christianity and Literature*, Jan. 1, 2004, 2.

126. Moltmann, *Experiences in Theology*, 201–202.

127. Moltmann, *Experiences in Theology*, 202.

Spirit.'"[128] That is to say, we are justified by God's mercy and set apart for the work of peacemakers.[129] There can't be a living hope devoid of peace with God and with oneself, with others and creation.

Second, Moltmann parted paths with the political theology of Carl Schmitt which endorsed dictatorship regimes. Moltmann's acute analysis reveals that theologically, Schmitt justified the need for a political dictatorship by way of a secularized doctrine of original sin: "In the face of the radically evil, there can only be a dictatorship."[130] Schmitt's assumption and inner logic were that human beings are 'evil' by nature; they need a strong hand to control them.

This negative anthropology has always served to justify the dictator's tyranny. Moltmann aptly concludes, "Schmitt's political theology was nothing other than a theologically legitimated doctrine of political sovereignty."[131] On the whole, this is the background against which I suppose Moltmann's theological paradigm shift is very significant to Northern Nigeria. It provides the impetus for a critical hermeneutic of violence and insights into the political dimension of Christ's crucifixion and the political relevance of God's kingdom in an environment of ethnic, political, and religious violence. I will next attempt to demonstrate that Moltmann embodies an alternative to the current cycle of violence that brings hope to a hopeless situation. That is to say, Moltmann's Christology analogously speaks to the situation of violence in Northern Nigeria. Below I encapsulate those insights.

---

128. Moltmann, *Experiences in Theology*, 107.
129. Moltmann, *Experiences in Theology*, 108.
130. Moltmann, *Experiences in Theology*, 115.
131. Moltmann, *Experiences in Theology*, 116.

5. Moltmann's Christological and Theological Contributions to Understanding Northern Nigeria's Culture of Violence: A Proposal for an Analogous Application

Moltmann's experience in World War II forced him to seek a brother who was beyond any earthly brother. God showed him that Jesus, whom Hebrews 2:10–11 says is not ashamed to call us His brothers and sisters, was a real brother to him.[132] It is against this backdrop that Moltmann is especially helpful to Northern Nigeria's chaotic situation of violence.

5.1 Moltmann's Contribution to an Understanding of the Way of Jesus

I have observed that Moltmann's theology develops into several basic components. These themes include, among other things, Trinitarian view of the cross, doctrine of salvation, eschatology (hope), ecclesiology, peneumatology, and ecology. All of these themes are critically needed in Northern Nigeria. But the analysis of all these themes is beyond the scope of this chapter. I attempt to delineate and articulate some specific ways in which some of these themes speak to Northern Nigeria's situation of violence.

Moltmann has enriched our grasp of the significance of the gospel. Any society confronting a situation of injustice and violence also faces many social, political, economic, and theological as well as moral challenges and temptations. Christians in such circumstances must be willing to ask hard questions: How does violence impact our conception of the gospel of Jesus Christ? According to the writer of Hebrews, the gospel is about God's provision of rest—shalom—peace. This rest is shalom which can only exist when there is justice and righteousness.

Violence tends to raise questions in the minds of its victims that can easily lead some to resent God or to not take God seriously because the answers to their questions are not forth coming; or when they view themselves as "innocent victims." The rich people deprive the poor not only of

---

132. Moltmann, *Experiences in Theology*, 4.

peace but also of justice.[133] Moltmann was able to see beyond shattered hopes to a living hope. Thus in what follows below, Moltmann concretely provides answers to my question, "How does the way of Jesus speak to the present-day violence occurring in Northern Nigeria?"

5.1.1 The Victims of Violence and the Gospel of the Reign of God

Moltmann's contribution to Christian understanding of the gospel in Northern Nigeria is fantastic. Generally, his work reveals that in an environment of violence the gospel faces the danger of being misconceived or misinterpreted. Violence can distort the message of the gospel. Moltmann helps Christians to realize that Jesus' "mission embraces his proclamation and his acts, his acts and his suffering, his life and his death."[134] These aspects of his mission are based on the prophecy in Isaiah 61:1f, which Jesus read in Luke 4:18–19. Moltmann notes that Jesus' concept of the gospel is from Isaiah 61:1, which "shows the proclaiming Jesus as God's messianic messenger of joy."[135]

That means that Moltmann correctly sees Jesus as the fulfillment of the prophet Isaiah's announcement of a second "exodus into the freedom of the direct lordship of God (Isa. 52:7)."[136] I contend "the Spirit of the Lord" that Isaiah talks about is the spirit of God's righteousness, which creates justice and by extension creates peace, as I shall show later. This is the reason why Moltmann argues, "The messianic message about the coming rule of God is not a reduction of human freedom." I would add that as Christians, in Northern Nigeria and elsewhere, we can only escape the distortion of violence when we understand the gospel in all its truth.

The gospel is not only about the lordship of Christ in all of life. But it is also about the kingdom of God in a new creation. It is about the already and not yet. This is why we have a hope that encourages faith and patience. As Moltmann puts it, it is "hope and anxiety." The gospel brings

---

133. Jürgen Moltmann, *Experiences of God* (Philadelphia: Fortress Press, 1980), 6.
134. Jürgen Moltmann, *The Way of Jesus: Christology in Messianic Dimensions* (New York: Harper Collins Publishers, 1990), 94.
135. Moltmann, *The Way of Jesus*, 95.
136. Moltmann, *The Way of Jesus*, 95, 96.

"a hope which can incite man for the future, embolden him for freedom, and inflame him for the possible, thereby subduing his depression and melancholy over the present state of his life and his society."[137] What has kept Moltmann going in the midst of all odds is his belief that:

> In history God rules through Spirit and Word, liberty and obedience. The lordship of God, to which the healings witness, restores sick creation to health. Jesus' healings are not supernatural miracles in a natural world. As parables of the kingdom, Jesus' parables are also parables of the new creation in the midst of the everyday life of this exhausted world.[138]

Moltmann shows how the gospel of God's reign gives the victims of violence back their dignity.[139] This brings us to a crucial theme in the whole history of God's dealing with human beings: Justice.

The gospel is about giving back humans their God-given dignity in a world that seeks to deny them their human dignity. The gospel also brings the rich face-to-face with the reality that what they call hope is false hope. What the rich call dignity is false dignity. It is only through God's righteousness and justice that human dignity can be realized in all its truth.

5.1.2 The Rich's Liberation is through Conversion

The gospel has a holistic approach to life. The rich are not left to their continuous acts of injustice and violence, doing as they wish. God calls them to repentance—turning away from their wickedness and dead works to the living God.[140] But if, as Moltmann insists, conversion enables "true life that begins here and now, the true life which will come for the whole of

---

137. Jürgen Moltmann, ed., *The Experiment of Hope*, translated with forward M. Douglas Meeks (Philadelphia: Fortress Press, 1975), 16.
138. Moltmann, *The Way of Jesus*, 99.
139. Moltmann, *The Way of Jesus*, 99. Moltmann writes, "The gospel of the kingdom of God is proclaimed to 'the poor' (Luke 4:18–19; Matt. 11:5)."
140. Moltmann, *The Way of Jesus*, 102.

creation with the kingdom of God,"[141] it means that both the poor and the rich need conversion.

5.1.3 Moltmann's Contribution to an Understanding of the Sermon on the Mount

The basis of Moltmann's anthropological and political theology is the way of Jesus Christ as it is found in the Sermon on the Mount. The Sermon on the Mount is a protest against socioeconomic and sociopolitical injustice and violence. "The center of the Sermon on the Mount,"[142] Moltmann argues, "is the liberation from violence."[143] The writer of Hebrews has this to say: Jesus "loved righteousness and hated wickedness; therefore, his God has set him above his companions."[144] In summary, Jesus loves righteousness, justice, and human rights. Consequently, God is speaking to the world today through Jesus, his Son. God is speaking to humanity through Jesus because God too loves righteousness, justice, and human rights. That equally means that God also hates injustice, wickedness, and violence. On the whole, Jesus loves peace.[145] I will take Moltmann's contribution to an understanding of the Sermon on the Mount as the Way of Jesus Christ in my chapter on "The Understanding of the Powers and Authorities in Northern Nigeria." But in passing I argue hat the thrust of the Sermon on the Mount is justice. It is therefore necessary to familiarize ourselves with the concept of justice.

5.2 Understanding the Concept of Righteousness-creating Justice

Moltmann brings a clear understanding to the concept of justice that I believe can be very helpful to Northern Nigeria. The question is, "What is justice?" From a Judeo-Christian perspective justice is God-given. That is, the definition of justice is incomplete without reference to God. God's righteousness enriches our understanding of justice and liberates justice

---

141. Moltmann, *The Way of Jesus*, 102.
142. Hebrews 1:2.
143. Moltmann, *The Way of Jesus*, 127.
144. Hebrews 1:9.
145. Moltmann, *The Way of Jesus*, 112.

from the shackles of the Greco-Roman-individualistic definition of justice, which the West has adopted: an individual meeting a defined standard or worth. Righteousness from the biblical standpoint is relational, communal not individualistic. Therefore God's justice is creative, justifying and it is itself creating justice. God is just because he brings justice to unjust men and women and makes them right. His justice is a saving justice (Ps. 31:2; 146:7). Through this justice God creates that peace which lasts: *shalom*. Peace does not bring justice, but justice brings peace. As Moltmann aptly observes, "Unjust systems can be kept alive only through violence. Where there is violence there is no peace, for where violence reigns, it is death that reigns and not life."[146] Moltmann compares the Jewish-Christian concept of justice to the concepts of justice in most legal systems. He delineates the meaning of justice as follows:

> (1) An earlier concept of European jurisprudence defined justice as justitia distributive suum cuique—to each his own. This brilliant formula combines equality in the eyes of the law with the real difference between human beings. (2) To each according to his or her capacity and in accordance with his or her needs (Marx), or as the Hutterite brethren say: "Everyone gives whatever he can and gets whatever he needs." However, this concept of justice is primarily related to objects, to achievements and goods: all men and women have a right to life, food, work and freedom. (3) The personal concept of judgment, through which human society is brought about, goes beyond this concept of justice, which is related to objects. The personal concept consists in the reciprocal recognition and acceptance of other people. Reciprocal recognition of human status and mutual acceptance creates a humane and just community. This personal concept of justice also underlies the modern federalist concepts of democratic society like covenant and constitution. (4) But the supreme form of justice is the

---

146. Jürgen Moltmann, *Creating a Just Future* (Philadelphia: Trinity Press International, London: SCM Press, 1989), 39.

law of mercy, through which those who are without rights receive justice. This is the justice of the God of widows and orphans.[147]

In summary, true peace is the presence of justice not the absence of violence. That is, it is the presence of justice, which creates peace—shalom—peace of God. Thus, "The positive definition of peace calls peace a state of social justice, the democratic settlement of conflict and equilibrium in a permanent development of all."[148]

5.2.1 God's Justice: The Significance of a Correct Concept of Justice

God's justice sets the tune for all human relationship. Thus the need to understand the concept of God's justice in Northern Nigeria cannot be overemphasized. Moltmann's work has concretely contributed to Northern Nigeria's grasp of the subject of justice. With injustice and violence, one thing is constant: *the cry for justice.* In Northern Nigeria, as in many societies, minorities are crying for justice. Moltmann has profoundly unraveled how this cry is caused by breaches of justice. What is the cry of justice about? The cry of justice can be categorized into two spheres.

(1) Individuals, victims, and perpetrators cry. The cry of justice is "the cry of the victims of injustice, violence and lies."[149] "The victims of injustice, violence, sickness, suffering, and death torment themselves with the question: 'is God just?'"[150] The phrase "innocent victims of violence" is a testimonial to this all-embracing cry for justice. Moltmann contrasts the two cries, "The victims cry to God out of their God-forsakenness, and the perpetrators cry out against God out of their godlessness: 'there dare not be a God, for there dare not be any justice to condemn what we have done.'"[151] Moltmann did well in recognizing that, as human beings, both victims

147. Moltmann, *Creating a Just Future*, 39–40.
148. Moltmann, *Creating a Just Future*, 41.
149. Jürgen Moltmann, *In the End—The Beginning: The Life of Hope* (Minneapolis: Fortress Press, 2004), 56.
150. Moltmann, *In the End—The Beginning*, 57.
151. Moltmann, *In the End—The Beginning*, 59.

and perpetrators are all faced with the challenge of the inclination toward evil. The rich have allowed the force of evil to choke them up to the extent that they have willingly become agents of death. They create structures and systems or institutions that enable them to continually hold the poor in check and maintain the status quo.

(2) Thus the cry for justice is a cry against structural violence: social, economic, political, and cultural structures or institutions that benefit from violence. As Moltmann says, "There are political systems in which good things, brought about with great personal commitment, minister only to the greater evil, because they stabilize the system of injustice and organized violence."[152] As we are aware, human beings can repent but structures cannot. However, according to Moltmann, human beings can change them, because it is human beings who have made them. In summary, "The cry for justice is directed against these experiences of history to which our lives are surrendered."[153] The point of contention is clear from Moltmann's concluding remarks: "God is just when he brings about justice."

Moltmann's grasp of God's justice corrects a whole lot of misconceptions about justice in its distributive or attributive dimensions. "If God brings about justice for those who suffer violence, then he also identifies himself with the victims of violence, putting himself on their side." In short, Jesus Christ is God's righteousness and justice in the world of victims and perpetrators.

God's righteousness creates justice and justice creates the dignity of the poor. God's righteousness creates justice that declares the unjust just. The justice of God enables the poor to have their deprived dignity rise to all its potentialities. Moltmann tells us that on the one hand, the justice of God is presented as the right to have pity on the most pitiable; on the other hand the future of the kingdom of God begins among the people who suffer most from acts of violence and injustice—and that is the poor. The gospel assures the poor of God's life giving, newly creating activity. The gospel is realistic, not idealistic. The poor are the subjected, oppressed, and humiliated people.

---

152. Moltmann, *In the End—The Beginning*, 59.
153. Moltmann, *In the End—The Beginning*, 60.

In summary, the poor are marginalized minorities in Northern Nigeria, people regarded as infidels, displaced persons: "the poor are 'non-persons;' 'sub-human,' 'dehumanized,' 'human fodder.'"[154] If there are those who are considered poor, there are those who are not poor who oftentimes are responsible for the poor being poor. Moltmann calls such a person (individually and corporately) "'the man of violence,' who makes someone else poor and enriches himself at the other's expenses. 'The God of the rich is 'Mammon,' and he is an unjust god. The rich therefore have to be exposed as the unjust and the men of violence."[155]

The gospel opens the eyes of the victims of violence to the reality that, on the one hand, there is hope for the poor in this life and in the future. On the other hand, the gospel points the rich to their need of conversion—turning them away from their violent activities to embrace the lordship of God. By pointing the poor to reality, the gospel brings the poor face to face with a new definition of their humanity, "a new dignity."

Violence makes poverty self-destructive and produces self-hate in the poor themselves.[156] But "The gospel about the kingdom of God which belongs to the poor, vanquishes this self-hate, and gives the poor courage, so that they can live with 'their heads held high' and can 'walk erect.'"[157] They can do so because they grasp the fact that "God is on their side and God's future belongs to them. The men of violence have shut them out of the pleasures of the present." Because Moltmann is carefully pointing out that the gospel is not the opium of the poor, he notes that "through them (the poor) the future of God comes into the present, because this future is already theirs. The poor become God's children in this world of violence and injustice."[158] Moltmann shows his departure from earlier theologies that misunderstood the future reign of God as having nothing to do with the present by pointing out, "It is only in community with the poor that the kingdom of God is thrown open to the others [the rich]. . . . Jesus brings the gospel to the poor, and discovers the kingdom of God among the

---

154. Moltmann, *The Way of Jesus*, 99.
155. Moltmann, *The Way of Jesus*, 100.
156. Moltmann, *The Way of Jesus*, 101.
157. Moltmann, *The Way of Jesus*, 101.
158. Moltmann, *The Way of Jesus*, 101.

poor. The poor are his family, his people, for they are the people of God's
coming kingdom."[159]

5.2.2 Human Rights

Moltmann brings richness to Christian understanding of the concept of
human rights in Northern Nigeria. Moltmann rightly points out, "In the
conflict of human history, people always live with a disturbed balance in
their human rights." Moltmann's conception of human rights is rich: "The
human rights to life, freedom, community, and self-determination mir-
ror God's right to the rights of human being because the human being is
destined to be God's image in all conditions and relationship of life."[160]
Since the concept of human rights has various understandings, we have
to know what we are talking about. Moltmann suggests how Christians
uphold and shape human rights in the way they relate to each other, God
and the systems surrounding them:

> (1) In the struggle for human rights and political priorities
> they [Christians] will represent the unassailable dignity of
> human beings and thus also the indivisible unity of their
> human rights and duties. Both are constituted through the
> claim of the one God upon persons in all of their relationships
> of life. (2) They will overcome their own egoism in order to
> overcome the egoism of individual, social, and human rights
> over against nature and the egoism of the present generation
> over against the coming generations, in order to serve the
> humanity of each and every person in the interest of God their
> Creator and Redeemer. (3) Through public proclamation and
> education they will sharpen the duties of the individual which
> are inexorably bound up with the rights of human beings with
> regard to their God-given dignity, to other people, to nature,
> and to the future. (4) For the sake of God they will stand up

159. Moltmann, *The Way of Jesus*, 102.
160. Jürgen Moltmann, *Man: Christian Anthropology in the Conflicts of the Present*
(Philadelphia: Fortress Press, 1974), 17.

with all means at their disposal, acting as well as suffering, for the dignity of human beings and their rights as the image of God. For their service to the humanity of persons they need the right to religious freedom, the right to form a community, and the right to public speech and action.[161]

The aim of living in peace is so that human beings have every opportunity to achieve their calling: glory to God. Human rights are about human relationship with God, one another and creation.[162] Righteousness is impossible without relationship with others. This is why dialogue is crucial to human relationship. As Moltmann notes, "Life is exchange. . . . Human life is necessarily life in community. Human life is what happens *between* individuals"[163] and between individuals and their community and the larger society.

6. Conclusion

Moltmann grasps the fact that in any circumstance of violence, theology cannot remain as it was. It must be relational. This relational dimension is what makes theology relevant to people who are hardest-hit—the poor. Violence impacts the poor more than anybody else.[164] The issue at stake here is how to create a just society and thus a favorable environment for both human beings and the earth at large. In order to have a healthy nation, the issues of justice, human rights, responsible government, and responsible theological ethics must be addressed. Therefore in the next chapter I will analyze the role of power and authority in perpetrating injustice and violence in Northern Nigeria. This approach will reveal the misery that violence causes its victims and its perpetrators.

---

161. Jürgen Moltmann, *On Human Dignity: Political Theology and Ethics* (Philadelphia: Fortress Press, 1984), 35.
162. Jürgen Moltmann, *God in Creation: A New Theology of Creation and the Spirit of God* (Minneapolis: Fortress Press, 1993), 70.
163. Moltmann, *God in Creation*, 266.
164. Moltmann, *The Crucified God*, 22.

CHAPTER 6

Understanding the Language of the Powers in Northern Nigeria: The Contribution of Walter Wink

Human beings are capable of using power justly and rightly. In Scripture we have numerous examples of good kings in Israel who used power justly and rightly. David is a classic example of such kings.[1] In Northern Nigeria we also have redemptive examples of kings who ruled rightly and justly. For example, the current chief of Kagoro, Dr. Gwamna Awan, who was on the throne for over sixty years, is known as one of the chiefs who have ruled their communities rightly and justly.[2] In his discussion of the question of whether there is a redemptive example of democracy in African traditional communities, Bénézet Bujo contends,

> A very good model of a council of elders can be found among the Barundi, the people of Burundi. It was called *Ubushingantahe*. According to their tradition, a single *Ubushingantahe* was appointed by the people as advisor to the King in order to represent them and lay all their problems before him. He had

---

1. It was because David administered his people justly and rightly that the Lord promised him eternal dynasty (see 2 Sam. 7; 1 Chron. 17; Ps. 132).
2. Dr. S.A. Yabaya, "Congratulation Your Royal Highness" in *New Impression*, June 30, 2005, 17. Yabaya writes, "I wish to heartily and warmly felicitate with His Royal Highness, the Chief of Kagoro, Mallam Gwamna Awan *OON MBE* on your sixty (60) solid years on the throne as Oegwam Oegworok."

The Impact of Ethnic, Political, and Religious Violence on
Northern Nigeria, and a Theological Reflection on Its Healing

180

the duty to act as a just referee in controversial matters. If a conflict arose, he had to ensure that reconciliation took place. The *Ubushingantahe* institution was not supposed to merely assume a temporary social function. Hence, introduction into the office had a religious character as well, which gave the *Ubushingantahe* the right and the duty to moderate the political power, which itself was unimaginable outside of the religious sphere. After the inauguration into office, which sealed the pact between the people and the *Ubushingantahe,* the latter was related to every member of the community. He had to care for everyone's well being, both in favorable and unfavorable times, even in cases where this was not a legally binding obligation. His duty was to be at the service of all people and to ensure that the socio-economic and political community served the humanity of everyone."[3]

Although not all African communities are like the people of Burundi, our politicians and elite—if they mean business—can find redemptive examples of how to work for the interest of those who elected them to be their voice. Therefore I am concerned about the misapplication of power in Northern Nigeria and, indeed, elsewhere. That is, despite the fact that human beings are capable of using power justly and rightly, violence emanates from the wrongful application of power. Thus, my primary aim in this chapter is to answer the question, "Why is power not used justly and rightly?" Specifically, "Why is power an instrument of violence in Northern Nigeria?" I recognize that the issues surrounding the use of power are complex. Hence, like any scholar of social, religious, or political engineering, I realize, as Walter Wink aptly notes, "No social struggle can hope to be effective if it only changes structural arrangements without altering their spirituality."[4]

---

3. Bénézet Bujo, *The Ethical Dimension of Community: The African Model and the Dialogue Between North and South* (Nairo, Kenya: Paulines Publications Africa, 1998), 158.
4. Walter Wink, *Engaging the Powers: Discernment, and Resistance in a World of Domination* (Minneapolis: Fortress Press, 1992), 165.

Human beings have made unprecedented progress in science and technology in the twenty-first century. Ironically, the violent and fierce application of power has tended to overshadow this incredible progress resulting in the unhealthy control of human beings against their consent. Wink rightly contends, "We do not freely surrender our authenticity; it is stolen from us by the Powers."[5] No wonder even at the turn of the twenty-first century, a heightened fear of domination continues to spread terror all over the globe. Scientific and technological advancement have become the symbol of power and have decreased our reliance on and accountability to the God who gives power. Patrick Chabal observes,

> The Present condition of Africa has engendered despondency because we seem to have lost the capacity to understand it. . . . Disenchantment with African studies is not only the result of despair in the face of human suffering but also of our inability to account, historically and conceptually, for what is happening.[6]

The situation Chabal is describing is not disconnected from the brutal use of power by African leaders and their elite. But must power devour forever? Why has humanity not realized that power is behind almost all forms of human-inflicted pain and suffering? These questions are crucial to an understanding of the sources of the violent exercise of power. Therefore, I shall

(1) attempt to define power,[7]

(2) compare Jesus and Paul's conceptions of power,

(3) compare Paul and Peter's conceptions of power,

(4) explore Wink's contribution to an understanding of the language of *the powers* in the New Testament, and

(5) conclude with lessons learned from Northern Nigeria.

---

5. Wink, *Engaging the Powers*, 150.
6. Patrick Chabal, ed., *Political Domination in African: Reflections on the Limit of Power* (London, New York: Cambridge University Press, 1986), 3.
7. I shall be using "power" to mean power generally and "the Powers" to mean supernatural beings that influence the use of this general power.

I shall interchangeably use the term "power," "the powers," or "authorities." Generally humans tend to see power as a means of domination.

1. Seeing Power as Domination

Domination is a key issue. That is to say, power is not the problem; power is God-given and thus good. As Marcus J. Borg notes, "Jesus' healings were the result of 'power.' Indeed, the favorite word for the mighty deeds of Jesus in the synoptic gospels is, in Greek, *dunamis,* which translates as 'power.' It is most frequently used in the plural—the mighty deeds of Jesus' 'powers.'"[8] That is a clear indication that the gospel writers and indeed Jesus himself understood his deeds as an embodiment of not only good use of power but the goodness of power.

However, like many other things God created and declared good, human power has been distorted by a fallen world. Yet there is still a remnant of God's goodness in human power. Hence power is redeemable.[9] As Borg notes, "In the Book of Acts, written by Luke . . . this power is directly associated with the Spirit of God: 'but you shall receive *power* when the Holy Spirit has come upon you.'"[10] Luke further makes the connection in his gospel: "And Jesus came in the power of the Spirit into Galilee."[11] But why is power a threat to human survival? Is the fear of domination real or imagined? Clearly, the fear of domination is real. Two factors contribute to this fear in Northern Nigeria.

(1) The lie that human beings believe about power: "domination gives me the chance to move ahead of and above my fellow men and women." Hence people seek power to gain control of the resources that enable

---

8. Marcus Borg, *Jesus: A New Vision: Spirit, Culture and the Life of Discipleship* (San Francisco: HarperSanFrancisco, 1987), 66.
9. See Walter Wink's trilogy where he tells us that the New Testament language categorically declares "the Powers are good, the Powers are fallen; the Powers must be redeemed" (Wink, *Engaging the Powers,* 10).
10. Acts 1:8.
11. Luke 4:14.

them to hold onto and wield that power unhindered. This is the fear of being powerless.

(2) This creates unnecessary suffering—particularly, but not exclusively—in Northern Nigeria. This suffering has largely resulted from the social boundaries and walls that human beings have created against each other. This is the fear of those who are different and the fear of suffering. Generally, for the sake of power, humanity is being destroyed. Besides destroying people and property, these conflicts further depress already fragile economies.

Suffering encourages a sort of silent tension, which often births future violence. As a study conducted by United Nations High Commissioner for Refugees (UNHCR) in 1993 noted,

> For the past several years ethnic conflict has been the world's most common form of collective violence and a major cause of the steadily increasing refugee problem. . . . We should not ignore the many non-violent conflicts that are the seedbeds of future violence. Non-violent ethnic conflict often takes the form of political, economic, or cultural repression of ethnic minorities and includes restrictions on voting, burdensome taxes, exclusion from certain professions, residential isolation, educational quotas, prohibitions on the use of the ethnic language, and restrictions on religious worship.[12]

Although this study is outdated, the situation has not changed. It is striking to realize that the aim of the powers in perpetrating violent domination—silencing their subjects in order to keep hold of power unchallenged—is gaining ground.[13] The consequence of violence knows neither church nor mosque. Desmond Tutu is right, "The Church is constantly tempted to be conformed to the world, to want influence that comes from

---

12. UNHCR *Focus:* "Ethnic Conflict: Refugees," October 1993, 4. Many economies in the so-called Third World are fragile because of the destructive economic policies of transnational corporations, World Bank and IMF.
13. Wink, *Engaging the Powers*, 144.

power, prestige, and privilege, and it forgets all the while . . . Jesus' solidarity was with the poor, the downtrodden, the sinners, the despised ones, the outcasts, the prostitutes, the very scum of society."[14] Given that power is dynamic, we need to understand its dynamic nature. People need to grasp the best option available. As Jacques Marquet writes,

> The relation of *social inequality* is found between two actors of superior and inferior status, whereas the relation of *equality* is found between two actors of the same status. The relationship of *dependence* unites a protector and a dependent on the basis of an agreement between the two actors (the feudal relationship is a variant of this). In an *economic* relationship, goods and/or services are exchanged between two actors, who, for want of a better word, we shall call dealers. *Kinship* relations link the descendents of a common ancestor, while those of *alliance* (family) bind together two actors in matrimony, either directly or through a group. Finally, the *association* relationship binds actors who voluntarily unite in order to reach a common goal.[15]

The real challenge is not only knowing what options there are, but also realizing that much of Africa is accustomed to a hierarchical and patriarchal system that trickles down to the way democracy is run. It is both the pursuit of and the desire to monopolize happiness that makes it difficult for leaders to give up power once they have acquired it. I argue that power in Africa and elsewhere is wrongly used because of the assumptions attached to status. For as Marquet maintains, "In Africa, as elsewhere, power is a value of prime importance for the individual or the group—a universal value, for it gives access to the 'good things of life,'"[16] [He noted that] Max Weber defined power as the probability that an actor within a social relationship

---

14. Desmond Tutu, *Hope and Suffering* (Grand Rapids: Wm. B. Eerdmans Publishing Company, 1985), 85.
15. Jacques Marquet, *Power and Society in Africa*, trans., Jeannette Kupfermann (London: World University Library, 1971), 25.
16. Marquet, *Power and Society in Africa*, 27.

will be able to carry out his own will despite resistance.[17] Violence, which is the clearest manifestation of the evil use of power, has gradually taught Christians how to abandon the teachings of Jesus. In their startling study of current trends in Christian ethics, Stassen and Gushee assert,

> Christian churches across the theological and confessional spectrum, and Christian ethics as an academic discipline that serves the churches, are often guilty of evading Jesus, the cornerstone and center of the Christian faith. This evasion of the concrete teachings of Jesus has seriously malformed Christian moral practices, moral beliefs and moral witness.[18]

This is intrinsically connected to the impact of war and violence over the centuries. I resonate with this assertion because of what I know about the social problems that power struggles create. For example, America's acclaimed political theorist and theologian, Reinhold Niebuhr, changed from being a pacifist to a just war theorist because of the social conditions created by the violent use of power that his congregation encountered during his pastoral years in Detroit.[19]

Niebuhr was overwhelmed by the social evil perpetuated against the weak by the powerful, to the extent that he concluded that Christ's ethical teaching in the Sermon on the Mount could not adequately deal with a sophisticated modern society like America because it was meant for a local context, Palestine. Niebuhr's theological anthropology combined with his social interpretation led him to the conclusion that human nature is such that the use of force is inevitable. Niebuhr writes, "All political positions are morally ambiguous because, in the realm of politics and economics, self-interest and power must be harnessed and beguiled rather than eliminated.

---

17. Max Weber, *The Theory of Social and Economic Organization*, ed., Talcott Parsons, (Glencoe, IL; London: Hodge, 1957), 3 as cited by Marquet, *Power and Society*, 33.
18. Stassen and Gushee, *Kingdom Ethics*, xi.
19. See Richard Hays, *The Moral Vision of the New Testament: Community, Cross, New Creation: A Contemporary Introduction to New Testament Ethics* (Edinburgh: T & T Clark, 1997), 340. W. Kegley and Robert W. Bretall, eds., *Reinhold Niebuhr: His Religious, Social, and Political Thought* (New York: The Macmillan Company, 1956), 8, where Niebuhr tells of how he changed his position.

In other words, forces which are morally dangerous must be used despite their peril."[20] Since then Niebuhr's teaching has influenced many generations of Christian churches, ethicists, pastors, and theologians worldwide.

Consequently, the continuous erosion of the Christian moral vision has resulted in the evasion of Jesus' teaching and practice as Stassen and Gushee propose. With them, I call the church in Northern Nigeria to bring Jesus back to the center of its teaching and practice, where He belongs.[21] In an age when the global community is obsessed with the fear of violent terrorism, it will be disastrous not to bring Jesus to the center. Undoubtedly, violence is shaping and impacting people's perspectives and values. In my own context, Northern Nigeria, where there have been decades of religious, ethnic, and political violence, evading Jesus is a grave danger. Christians and non-Christians alike need to recognize that evil and deception are concrete manifestations of power in Northern Nigeria.

1.1 Evil and Deception as the Concrete Manifestations of Power

I have noticed that many New Testament scholars have identified evil as the source of violence. But what is this evil about? Walter Wink calls it "the Domination System." A host of other scholars have conclusively argued that behind the matter of violence stands a colossal issue—*the powers and authorities*. But why are the powers and authorities using violence? As Cornel West noted, "the powers use violence to cause the subjected people to hate themselves."[22] From the standpoint of the New Testament, many people are uninformed about the other face of violence because, as Wink tells us, they have been "caught in a powerful delusion."[23] That is why they evade Jesus. As Miroslav Volf also notes, "oppression needs deceit as a prop."[24]

---

20. Reinhold Niebuhr, *Love & Justice: Selections from the Shorter Writings of Reinhold Niebuhr*, D. B. Robertson, ed. (Cleveland and New York: Meridian Books, 1967), 59.
21. Stassen and Gushee, *Kingdom Ethics*, xi.
22. Cornel West, *Race Matters* (Boston: Beacon Press, 1993), 18.
23. Walter Wink, *Engaging the Powers*, 88. Wink notes that "the delusion system is a game being played on us by the Powers That Be" (*Engaging the Powers*, 89).
24. Miroslav Volf, *Exclusion and Embrace*, 182. Volf's thesis is that we live in a world of three evils: injustice, deception, and violence (see *Exclusion and Embrace*, 10).

Since the aftermath of 9/11, it has become extremely clear that the world is obsessed with the fear of domination. Fear is extraordinarily dangerous because, as I have argued in chapter 4, people who are afraid rarely have compassion. They only recovery compassion after they have overcome their fears. So Richard Rohr is right, "Unless we observe and surrender our small, daily anxieties, we won't recognize the really big fears, in all their disguises, that control our politics, our denominations, our bank accounts, and the world's future."[25] I will add that unraveling the deception behind the powers and authorities requires a careful definition of the language of the powers and authorities in Scripture.

The powers and authorities get themselves off the hook because they employ deception: "The thief comes only to steal, kill and destroy."[26] In John's Gospel, Satan is called the "father of lies."[27] By implication this means that the powers and authorities feed on deception. But what do we really mean by the term *power*? I recognize that defining the term is not an easy task. Yet I believe it is a task that must be squarely faced if one wishes to grasp the larger picture of its connection to ethnic, political, and religious violence in Northern Nigeria.

1.2 Defining Power

The term *power* is part and parcel of everyday reality. It includes, among other terms, authority, control, influence, rule, dominance, force, capacity, nation, or sovereign state and so on.[28] Still, *power* is very elusive, and many people are uninformed about its complicity in the affairs of human life. This is because often when scholars talk of power, they pay little attention to its oppressive use. On the other hand there are some scholars who see power as one thing only: satanic.

However, power is multifaceted. In spite of its destructive use by human beings God does overrule the plans of the powers. Power can mean the ability to influence others to do what they would otherwise not have done.

25. Richard Rohr, "Fear Itself" in *Sojourners* magazine, October 2004, 13.
26. John 10:10.
27. John 8:44.
28. Sinclair B. Ferguson, "Power" in *New Dictionary of Theology* edited by Sinclair B. Ferguson and David F. Wright (Downers Grove, IL: InterVarsity Press, 1988), 524.

An effective teacher can influence her or his students to achieve heights of knowledge that they would otherwise not have achieved. But I am using the term *the powers* in the fallen sense. Because of humans' greed for power, domination, and control of their fellow men and women, they make themselves vulnerable to the forces of evil; that take advantage of their vulnerability, influencing them and using them as agents of destruction and death. This subverts the true administration of power through those who possess it: to become agents of life, delivering justice, compassionate love, just peace, embracing hope and just freedom. Sydney H.T. Page points out, "Modern Christians are confronted by a bewildering array of conflicting ideas and claims"[29] about the powers.

The West and other Christian-influenced parts of the world cannot always fathom the concept of forces of power in the cosmic systems and structures. In Scripture, it seems clear that the term the *powers,* or *authorities,* are used interchangeably. In the Old Testament they both refer to strength, power, and might. The main idea therefore is that "all human powers must be measured, not against other human beings, but against the overwhelming power and strength of God."[30]

In the New Testament, the terms *powers* and *authorities* are the currency of Pauline theological ethics. The concept of power is expressed by the following Greek words: *ischys, kratos, exousia, and dynamis.* These words are generally used to express varying degrees of power, strength, might, and freedom of action. These ideas are not only grounded in the Greco-Roman influence on Paul's theological ethics but they are also indicative of the inherent problem of human society—evil and its attendant violence. As Wink notes, we live in a violence-infested world to the extent that it is naturally assumed that "violence is the ethos of our times. . . . Violence simply appears to be the nature of things."[31]

---

29. Sydney H. T. Page, *Powers of Evil: A Biblical Study of Satan & Demons* (Grand Rapids: Baker House, 1996), 9. Page also argues, "The Old Testament accepts the reality of demonic powers while insisting that their power is insignificant in comparison with the power of God" (68).
30. See Lawrence O. Richards, *Expository Dictionary of Bible Words* (Grand Rapids: Zondervan Publishing House, 1985), 582.
31. Wink, *Engaging the Powers,* 13.

I have noted above that the word *power* or *powers* is among the ethical currency which characterizes Paul's writings on theological ethics. I shall turn to Paul for a definition of what these terms mean. Paul's focus is not the powers and authorities per se. Rather the powers and authorities come into the discussion because of their opposition to the Lord of lords and Kings of kings, Jesus Christ.[32] These words—*ischys, kratos, exousia, and dynamis*—are terms that enable Paul to articulate not only the experience of Jesus but more importantly human experience. In Wink's sharp critique of the powers, which he calls *the Domination System*, he surveys the whole range of Paul's usage of these terms. His conclusion is that based on ancient sources and biblical data the language of the powers was part of the experience and everyday vocabulary of the ancients and the Hebrews because of the problem of evil and its attendant suffering.

Against this backdrop Wink concludes that Paul's primary purpose in employing the imprecise and interchangeable language of the powers was to refer simultaneously to the "inner and outer aspects of any given manifestation of power."[33] The discussion of the powers has considerably been within the confines of a hermeneutical horizon shaped by political and social concerns.[34] Therefore I attempt to weigh in on the sociopolitical and socioeconomic context of first-century Christianity.

1.3 Understanding the Sociopolitical and Socioeconomic Structures of Injustice in the Greco-Roman World

The Greco-Roman World was an embodiment of how a powerful minority can dominate the majority. That is to say, the Romans, a small minority, were the colonizing powers of the then majority of the world. Imperial Rome epitomized the corrupted use of power to terrorize fellow human beings. In Jesus' time Israel was an occupied territory, subject to imperial, often brutal, Roman rule. As Ian Hunter rightly notes, "But then, as now,

---

32. Lawrence O. Richards, *Expository Dictionary of Bible Words*, 583.
33. Walter Wink, *Naming the Powers: The Language of the Powers in the New Testament* (Philadelphia: Fortress Press, 1984), 3, 5.
34. Gerald F. Hawthorne, Ralph P. Martin, and Daniel G. Reid, eds., *Dictionary of Paul and His Letters* (Downers Grove, IL: InterVarsity Press, 1993), 747.

the line between good and evil did not run between Rome and Jerusalem, or between nationalities, not even between ruler and the ruled. The line between good and evil ran down the center of each and every human heart."[35] For instance, the abusive exercise of power and authority was not just limited to unbelieving Roman occupiers but it was also from the Pharisaic religious establishment within the Jewish-cum-Roman system. Ironically, even today, the church is not immune to the ways of the powers.[36] Thus Myers suggests,

> Genuine revolution demands a radical break with all the accepted canons of power politics, with every expression of violence, exploitation, and dehumanization. . . . The means of the old order cannot bring about the ends of the new. Anything less than a politics of militant, nonviolent resistance is counterrevolutionary, a recycling of the old world. Mark's Jesus calls for a more radical (driving-to-roots) social transformation, a unity between means and ends.[37]

Society is dynamic. Therefore each Christian generation must realize its need of continuous repentance, forgiveness and transformation.

1.4 Summary

Human beings are capable of using power justly and rightly. That is why God gives humans the opportunity and the privilege to exercise power for the interest of their fellow men and women and for the whole ecosystem. Yet, because of economic greed, humans rarely use power for the intended purpose of God. It is this lack of exercising power for fulfilling God's purpose that endangers the contemporary application of power. As I

---

35. Ian Hunter, *Catholic Insight*, Dec. 1, 2000, 1.
36. Luke tells of how Paul warned the church about this danger: "I know that after I leave, savage wolves will come in among you and will not spare the flock. Even from your own number men will arise and distort the truth in order to draw away disciples after them." Conflicting interests are endangering the proper use of power both in the church and in society (Acts 20:29–30).
37. Ched Myers, *Binding the Strong Man: A Political Reading of Mark's Story of Jesus* (Maryknoll New York: Orbis Books, 1988), 438.

have attempted to argue, money and power corrupt the perspective of the elite and political leaders in that the elite become arrogant, overfed, and unconcerned about the plight of the poor and needy masses. Put another way, money and power not only cause the corruption of religion but also encourage the elite or political class to invent all kinds of injustice and violence in order to perpetuate the status quo. Thus pride, self-sufficiency, and neglect of the poor and the unemployed characterize their use of power in Northern Nigeria.

Human greed has led to the corruption of God-given power and authority. Yet corrupted power or authority goes beyond human greed. Power saturates all spheres of human life. Hence in order for power to be judiciously used it must take its bearing from the central fact of salvation—Jesus' crucifixion and recognition of the divine vocation of every person who has power entrusted to him or her. From the standpoint of Christianity, power resides in the freedom that Jesus gives to his disciples, to let go of all that hinders and to embrace a life centered on love, compassion, and justice.[38] I recognize that the problem of suffering, which is directly connected to the powers and authorities mentioned in Scripture, does not only concern Christians. Particularly, the suffering inflicted by the struggle for domination does not know separation of mosque, church, Temple, and state.

2. The New Testament's Context of the Language of the Powers and Authorities: Walter Wink's and other Scholars' Contribution

The language of the powers is generally understood within the confines of Jesus' ministry, death, and resurrection. Wink presents astounding insights in the climactic volume of his trilogy, *Engaging the Powers*. According to Wink, the "irreducible fact about Jesus is that he was executed" because "not only did he and his followers repudiate the androcratic values of

---

38. See Mark 10:42–45; John 10:17–18; 13:1; Philippians 2:5f.

192

The Impact of Ethnic, Political, and Religious Violence on
Northern Nigeria, and a Theological Reflection on Its Healing

power and wealth, but [also] the institutions and systems that authorized and supported these values . . . indeed, every conceivable prop of domination, division, and supremacy." Therefore, "the powers that executed Jesus did so under a necessity dictated by the Domination System itself" since Jesus, living out "God's domination-free order, poses the most intolerable threat ever placed against the spirituality, values, and arrangements of the Domination System."[39]

Wink's ability to connecting the dots between power and wealth makes his work very relevant to Northern Nigeria's situation of violence, particularly the causes of violence. For as Sylvester Asoya points out, the Biafran civil war in Nigeria, which was master minded by the Northern elite, was fought for the sake of economic gain. Sylvester writes, "Plainly speaking, the federal troops fought the civil war because of the rich crude oil found in the coastal areas." But "those who fought were never told the truth," he revealed.[40] The powers are adept at concealing the truth.

Wink's interpretation of Paul's concept of the powers is lucid and revealing. Wink detected an error that modernity has created, which the church then—as now—could not comprehend. Wink writes, "It is a modern bias to single out just the supernatural Powers as if they alone were of significance."[41] The reason for this problem is because the concept of the powers has been distorted. In his careful exegesis of the New Testament, Wink observed a shift in the use of the Greek term *dynamis*. "In the Jewish sources of the period," Wink writes, "dynamis is most often used of military or political power or forces (a 'host' or army, military might, or political clout) . . . By extension it was applied to the angelic 'army' or 'host' of God."[42] At that time, "God was 'Lord of the 'powers' (*dynameōn*). As 'heavenly hosts,' the

---

39. Walter Wink, *Engaging the Powers: Discernment and Resistance in a World of Domination* (Minneapolis: Fortress, 1992), 109–110.
40. Sylvester Asoya, "A Soldier's Story" *The News* (Lagos) Book Review, September 27, 2004, posted to the web September 20, 2004, htt://allfrica.com/stories/printable/20049200960.html, 1. Asoya noted that "the usual Nigerian ethnic politics played itself out even on the battled field" (2).
41. Walter Wink, *Naming the Powers: The Language of Power in the New Testament* (Philadelphia: Fortress Press, 1984), 16.
42. Wink, *Naming the Powers*, 17.

powers were identified in the LXX with angels (Ps. 29:1; 89:5–8)."[43] But with time, the New Testament, "with the exception of Revelation 13:2 and 17:12–13, ignores the military, political, and economic uses of the term, so frequent in the LXX and Josephus, focusing instead on the spiritual dimension of power in its capacity to determine terrestrial existence for weal or for woe from above."[44]

The resultant impact of the shift was that the term, *the powers*, lost both its explicit and implicit meanings.

> Consequently, we encounter the term as denoting evil spirits, the spirits of the dead, stars, spiritual powers, Godhead, and delegated authority. . . . In the New Testament, and increasingly in later Christian writers, both orthodox and Gnostic, the "powers" are no longer so much God's agents as God's enemies. The "Lord *of* the powers" now is engaged in a cosmic struggle to assert lordship *over* the powers.[45]

In summary, if the powers are only recognized as evil spirits two or more things will happen: Whenever the powers appear as "angel of light" Christians will find it difficult to detect them; whenever God decides to use them (as he still does) as his agents Christians may not recognize it; and, Christians will mistakenly assign a sphere of influence to the powers to the detriment of the Christians' view of Jesus Christ as Lord of all of life.

It is against this backdrop that Wink weighs in on debated texts found in Paul's epistles. Wink argues that Paul's usage of the term *thrones* in Colossians 1:16 refers not to personalized beings but to their structures.[46]

In Ephesians 6:10–24 Paul's intent is to explain in simple terms that we are facing "formidable enemies." The whole exhortation refers to the present duty of believers. Paul points to the fact that righteousness should be in place as the breastplate. Paul declares that "our struggle is not with men but

---

43. Wink, *Naming the Powers*, 17.
44. Wink, *Naming the Powers*, 17.
45. Wink, *Naming the Powers*, 17.
46. Wink, *Naming the Powers*, 17.

against the rulers, against the authorities, against the powers of this dark
world and against the spiritual forces of evil in the heavenly realms."

According to Charles Hodge, the "reference is to evil spirits. In Scripture
they are called 'demons,' who are declared to be fallen angels (2 Peter 2:4;
Jude 6) and who are now subject to Satan, their prince. They are called
rulers, those who are first or high in rank, and authorities, those invested
with authority."[47] Given that the authorities are associated with Satan they
are naturally linked with evil and its attendant suffering. I shall now turn
to this very matter—the problem of evil—in light of Wink's hypothetical
concept of the Powers.

2.1 Walter Wink's Hypothesis

Both Western Christians and non-Christians alike have questioned Satan's
existence as a person. In a world where scientific proof is what matters,
Satan's existence as a person is not an issue. Wink argues that our contemporary materialistic worldview has blurred our concept and interpretation
of the term *the powers*. In our contemporary world, we tend to limit their
influence to the material sphere. This is in stark contrast to the ancients who
often "understood power as the confluence of both spiritual and material
factors."[48] Modern minds find it difficult to grasp the reality of the powers
and authorities because of the Enlightenment, which ushered in a scientific
and technological age. Wink's primary concern is the interpretation of the
powers and authorities.

Based on his careful analysis of ancient and contemporary data, Wink
conclusively believes that the concept of the powers is influenced by the
question of theodicy.[49] It is a combination of the Greco-Roman attribution
of every calamity to the gods and the Jewish belief in angels. Wink argues
that the powers and authorities, depending on the context, can be human
or angelic. Wink's logic goes like this:

---

47. Charles Hodge, *Ephesians: Crossway Classic Commentaries* (Wheaton: Crossway Books,
1994), 213.
48. Wink, *Naming the Powers*, 3.
49. Wink, *Naming the Powers*, 23.

The "principalities and powers" are the inner and outer aspects of any given manifestation of power. As the inner aspect they are the spirituality of institutions, the "within" of corporate structures and system, the inner essence of outer organizations of power. As the outer aspect they are political systems, appointed officials, the "chair" of an organization, laws—in short, all the tangible manifestations which power takes. Every Power tends to have a visible pole, an outer form—be it a church, a nation, or an economy—and an invisible pole, an inner spirit or driving force that animates, legitimates, and regulates its physical manifestation in the world.[50]

This suggests that in the Epistles, Paul's primary concern is that both the human and angelic powers have been disarmed of their power and authority.[51] That is to say, "When a particular Power becomes idolatrous, placing itself above God's purposes for the good of the whole, then that Power becomes demonic."[52]

Wink, in discussing Romans 13:1–7, puts forth this question: "the chief controversy surrounds Romans 13:1—are the 'higher authorities' angels of the nations or merely human rulers?"[53] In as much as that is a critical issue, for Wink, Romans 13:1–7 shows how often the concept of power comes up in the New Testament. Wink sees a parallel between Romans 13:1–3 and 1 Peter 2:13–17.[54] Wink's believes this controversy centers on the controlling worldview of the then world. Wink claims, Paul "does subscribe to the broader Greco-Roman conception of spiritual forces behind all earthly institutions, of which the Jewish notion of angels of the nations was a

---

50. Wink, *Naming the Powers*, 5.

51. Walter Wink, *The Powers That Be: Theology for a New Millennium* (New York: Galilee Doubleday, 1998), 5.

52. Wink, *Naming the Powers*, 5. Therefore "The church's task is to unmask this idolatry and recall the Powers to their created purposes in the world—'so that the Sovereignties and Powers should learn only now, through the Church, how comprehensive God's wisdom really is' (Eph. 3:10, JB)."

53. Wink, *Naming the Powers*, 32; Wink predicated his analysis on the fact that "In biblical studies, word studies are the equivalent of field exploration and mineral classification in geology" (*Naming the Powers*, 35).

54. Wink, *Naming the Powers*, 46.

special adaptation."[55] But Paul's primary concern is "the way Christians should behave toward magistrates and tax collectors in the interim before the end."[56] Wink tells his readers that since the dawn of a technological and scientific epoch, the human race, particularly in the West, has been trying to get the idea of the powers off its social radar.[57]

In contrast, the Greco-Roman world was obsessed with the language of the powers. But why is it so? (1) It was as a result of the Greek Hellenization of the Roman Empire.[58] (2) It was a strategy employed by both the powerless and the powerful to expound theodicy—the reason for human evil and suffering.[59]

Generally, today's scientific and technological advancements have contributed to the assumption that demons and their prince, Satan, are beings that are not only floating in the air but also are responsible for all evil in the world. This presupposition, according to Wink, impinges upon our comprehension of what Scripture teaches about Satan.

I believe that this is why Satan traps Christians easily. If we are only accustomed to connecting Satan with evil, when he appears as an angel of light we cannot recognize him until he has finished destroying us. If God is Lord of all of life, I believe He can overrule Satan's intentions. Hence, as Wink contends, "Satan is God's holy sifter."[60] That is, God sometimes uses Satan to accomplish His purposes for our lives.

Wink believes that Satan is both an agent of God and an agent of evil. Since Satan is God's servant humans must be careful in relegating him to the realm of permanent evil. I think what Wink fundamentally wants Christians to recognize is the need to balance our view of Satan, so that we will not fall prey to Satan's deception. Wink wants the church to recognize that *the powers* can be construed "as institutions, social systems, and political structures."[61] Undoubtedly, Wink's New Testament work has

---

55. Wink, *Naming the Powers*, 47.
56. Wink, *Naming the Powers*, 47.
57. Walter Wink, *Unmasking the Powers: The Invisible Forces that Determine Human Existence* (Philadelphia: Fortress Press, 1986), 3.
58. Wink, *Unmasking the Powers*, 3.
59. Wink, *Unmasking the Powers*, 4.
60. Wink, *Unmasking the Powers*, 16.
61. Wink, *Naming the Powers*, 5.

brought the subject of the powers to the forefront. Its contribution to an understanding of contemporary situations of domination cannot be overstated. Yet Wink's work is packed with some built-in weaknesses for which scholars have critiqued him.

2.2 Critiquing Wink's Hypothesis?

Wink's primary concern is the interpretation of the powers and authorities. However, Wink's hypothesis that Satan is not a person but an experience and a structure can be confusing and problematic. That is why some scholars have charged that he denies the personal existence of Satan. Stating what Wink says might help us unravel what he actually means. Wink writes, "We are not dealing here with the 'literal person' of popular Christian fantasy, who materializes in human forms as a seducer and fiend."[62] Wink further suggests, "Perhaps in the final analysis Satan is not even a 'personality' at all, but rather a function in the divine process, a dialectical movement in God's purpose which becomes evil only when humanity breaks off the dialectic by refusing creative choice."[63] What does Wink mean by "literal person?" Is he denying the existence of Satan as a person?

It seems to me that the charge is basically from lack of understanding what Wink is arguing. But supposing that Wink is denying the personal existence of Satan, how can he account for the fact that Satan is a created angel? What is personality? Physiological features are not the only things that make a person a person; their personality includes emotions, intellect, and will. Satan possesses all these. Thus the question of Satan's personality cannot be ignored because experience alone cannot satisfactorily explain the activities of Satan. Jesus describes Satan as a thief who comes to "steal, to kill and to destroy."[64] This is not just an experience or structure but a personality. As Charles Ryrie argues, Satan is not just some "mythical tale of heathen origin."[65] Yet Wink's point is that Satan comes into the discussion

---

62. Wink, *Unmasking the Powers*, 25.
63. Wink, *Unmasking the Powers*, 173.
64. John 10:10.
65. Charles Ryrie has argued correctly that "Satan is a real personality." Ryrie arrived at this conclusion because of what the Bible teaches about Satan. According to him, "The Bible teaches that he possesses intelligence (2 Cor. 11:3), has emotions (Rev. 12:17) and

because of our experience of evil structures. Systemic injustice ensures that the experience of suffering and its attendant pains are alive and well in the world. Without them, no one would care about the existence of Satan.

Therefore it seems to me that Wink's argument is basically that Satan cannot be reduced to only a material being or only an experience because Satan possesses "inner and outer" realities. It is against this understanding that Wink argues, "Satan is an archetypal image of the universal human experience of evil, and is capable of an infinite variety of representations. The archetype itself is unfathomable; the primordial power of evil is as much more than our images of it as God is more than our images of God."[66]

As Colin Brown aptly suggests, "Wink is seeking a middle way between a traditionalism, which sees Satan and the powers as objective personal beings and a Bultmannianism that demythologizes them."[67] Brown's suggestion is congruent with the fact that Wink believes the powers are real but are generated by oppressive social structures.[68] For Wink, then, the material existence of a "personality" called Satan does not give us the larger picture of his activities! Thus Wink's primary interest is not to prove the existence of Satan as a person per se. He is primarily arguing that Satan is not limited to a spirit being or a material being as we often assumed.[69] This is not to say there are no challenges to Wink's theorizing. Stassen once said, "[A] weakness of Wink is that he does not talk about justice and checks and balances much. Or human rights and democracy."[70] It is surprising that with all his eloquent discussion of the problem of injustice in society Wink does not discuss the role of justice in dislodging unjust structures.

Undoubtedly, we live in an age when the world seems permanently dichotomized between the "good guys" and the "bad guys." That is a "We" and "They" kind of logic. Thus the reverential fear that is due to God[71] has now

---

has a will (2 Tim. 2:26)" [Ryrie, *A Survey of Bible Doctrine* (Chicago: Moody Press, 1972)], 92, 93.

66. Wink, *Unmasking the Powers*, 25.

67. Colin Brown's general comments after reading my first draft on January 2, 2007, 10.

68. Colin Brown's general comments, 10.

69. Wink, *Unmasking the Powers*, 28.

70. Glen Stassen's reaction to my appreciation of Walter Wink's contribution, during a personal interaction in 2006.

71. Deuteronomy 10:20.

become "fear and serve regionalism, religious, and political communities, nationalism, individualism, and transnational corporations."[72] Finally, Wink has contributed to our understanding of the forces at work in the world. He has shown us why it is important to unmask them. He writes, "We unmask them only in order to engage them, in the spirit and power of the One in whom and through whom and for whom they were created: the truly Human Being incarnated by Jesus."[73] Clearly, Jesus, Paul and Wink call us to active involvement in society with the view of dislodging the unsanctified use of power, which results in deformed devotion, and destruction of human and nonhuman life on planet earth.

The starting point is dislodging the lie and deception that the powers use to keep us in perpetual bondage to fear. Wink points out that "exposing the delusional system is the central ascetic task in our discernment of the powers. For the powers are never more powerful than when they can act from concealment."[74] How do we respond to the powers in a world of Domination? Wink suggests the following:

(1) We have to realize that the powers are good, fallen, and redeemable.

(2) We must expose the lies and delusions that camouflage them.

Wink is referring to a democratic society. But what about the case where democracy is in place but overshadowed by patriarchal or hierarchical understandings of human relations? How much can the Christian achieve in such circumstances? 1 Peter addresses this situation better. Peter suggests that Christians are to live by example. That is Christians are to demonstrate their confidence in God by obediently doing what is right even to the point of suffering in defense of the truth they proclaim in a non-Christian environment.

Eschatological hope is one of the outstanding themes of 1 Peter because of the situation of Peter's audience (1 Peter 1:1–12). This hope is the foundation of Christian ethics in the present (1 Peter 1:13–2:3). It makes us desire to live a holy life, showing compassion and love to both Christians

---

72. Glen Stassen's reaction to my appreciation of Walter Wink's contribution, during a personal interaction in 2006.
73. Wink, *Unmasking the Powers*, 88.
74. Wink, *Engaging the Powers*, 88.

and non-Christians alike. This hope is the knowledge of Jesus as Savior and
Lord through whom we are now called God's children (1 Peter 2:4–12).
As Moltmann says, "Jesus has become the brother to the God-forsaken of
this earth."

It is important to recognize that the heart of the gospel is righteousness,
or right standing with God, for humankind attained by the death of Christ
not by our work. "For Christ died for sins once for all, the righteous for the
unrighteous to bring you to God." As God's people, Christians are called
to live in society and in community with God's creation (1 Peter 2:13–25).
Peter places a premium on the home or family because his ethics (and the
ethics of Jesus and Paul) is based on community. That is to say, as the adage
goes, "Charity begins at home"; ethics develop from the context of the
home (1 Peter 3:1–7). Therefore, Peter teaches on the ethics of the family.
We see in 1 Peter what it means to live a holy life at home.[75] As Whitman
points out, Peter encapsulates five things that take place in the context of
the family and result in preparing healthy Christians for life in society:

(1) Love is homegrown and developed; i.e., love is best developed in the
context of the family before it can be expressed in public (cf 1 Peter 1:22;
2:17). Christians are able to love other Christians and non-Christians as
brothers and sisters only if they have learned how to love in the context of
the family (1 Peter 3:8).

(2) Christians are to "be compassionate." While compassion is vital for
Christians who minister to fellow Christians who are experiencing difficul-
ties, it can only be effective when it is experienced in the context of the
family (1 Peter 3:8).

(3) Christians are called to be humble; that is, the humility so despised
by the Greeks was to be prized by Christians (1 Peter 5:6).

(4) Christians need to be aware that living with other Christians does
not always mean heaven on earth. But as the family encounters conflicting
interests, issues must be resolved before they create roots of bitterness.

---

75. Peter's emphasis on the necessity of family ethic is crucial to the situation of Northern
Nigeria where children hear the stories of past mistreatment meted out to their great grand
and grand parents by the Muslims. These stories create tensions.

(5) Interaction with a hostile world requires patience that is learned in a family context.[76] But the Christian life is not only meant for the family but also for the public sphere.[77] Peter is addressing the age-old question of "How can human beings respond to the problem of theodicy?"[78] This resonates with the purpose of 1 Peter: when believers live in such a way, they indicate that they are placing their hope in God rather than in the joys and comforts of this world. When believers set their hope on the future, they reveal that their salvation comes from the cross of Christ, who bore their sins (1 Peter 2:24; 3:18). The Christ who suffered is also the Christ who is now exalted (1 Peter 3:19–22). Those who resist the Church of Jesus Christ now will be judged on the last day (1 Peter 4:1–6). Since the end is coming soon, believers should imitate Jesus Christ and follow his example of suffering, for all those who suffer will also experience a great reward."[79] In our age, however, passivity is dangerous. Jesus nonviolently confronted the powers in his own day. Jesus taught his disciples of all ages not only to avoid the vicious cycle but also to take "transforming initiatives" that will bring about deliverance and justice and provide a community of hope for the future.[80] I seek to compare Jesus and Paul's conceptions of the powers so as to see the bigger picture of the powers' influence on violence in human community.

3. Comparing Jesus' and Paul's Ideas of the Powers

Paul's idea of the powers and authorizes has a direct connection with that of Jesus. Paul does not preach another gospel than that of Jesus Christ. Yet

---

76. Andrew Whitman, *1 Peter: Free to Hope* (Grand Rapids: Baker Books, 1994), 199–120.

77. Whitman, *1 Peter: Free to Hope*, 120.

78. P. J. Achtemeier, "Newborn Babes and Living Stones: Literal & Figurative Usage of 1 Peter" in *To Touch the Text: Biblical and Related Studies in Honor of Joseph A. Fitzmyer, S.J.* (New York: Crossroad, 1989), 235. Achtemeier argues that the controlling metaphor in the letter is the new people of God [222–231] as cited by Schreiner, 45.

79. Schreiner, *The New American Commentary*, 45–46.

80. For a detailed treatment of this vital subject, see Glen Stassen and David Gushee's acute discussion of this in their book, *Kingdom Ethics*.

202
The Impact of Ethnic, Political, and Religious Violence on
Northern Nigeria, and a Theological Reflection on Its Healing

Paul and Jesus are two different people. It is therefore important to attempt to grasp their individual conceptions of the powers and authorities.

3.1 Jesus' Attitude toward Power and Authority

Jesus' attitude toward power and authority revealed that power and authority are not necessarily evil. From the Gospel account of Jesus' ministry, it is clear that his attitude toward *the powers* was unique. He was an embodiment of how power or authority was meant to be exercised by humans. Jesus exercised his authority and power in a generally nonviolent way. Jesus' attitude toward the powers is seen early on from His humble incarnational birth. Simply put, His teachings and practice embody the ushering in of the Kingdom of God. Generally, Jesus faced crucifixion because He was encountering the powers.[81]

Power is necessary because it keeps the world from chaos. As John H. Yoder has demonstrated, the world cannot do without structures that ensure order. These structures include, among other things, moral structures, religious structures, political structures, economic structures, and social structures. These structures fall under the term *the powers*. They are not human or Satan's creations but God's. These structures, according to Yoder, were created good for the benefit of not only humanity but also for the whole ecosystem. That is why these structures are intrinsically connected to both human and nature's survival.

Yoder stresses their importance thus: "Society and history, even nature, would be impossible without regularity, system; order—and this need God provided for."[82] But there is more; the plain truth is:

---

81. James A. and John C. John, *A Dictionary of Christ and the Gospels* (Honolulu Hawaii: University Press of the Pacific, 2004), 147.
82. John Howard Yoder, *The Politics of Jesus* (Grand Rapids: Wm. B. Eerdmans Publishing Company, 1972), 143. "The universe is not sustained arbitrarily, immediately, and erratically by an unbroken succession of new divine interventions. It was made in an ordered form and 'it was good.' The creative power worked in a mediated form, by means of the Powers that regularized all visible reality." Yoder recognizes that most of the references to the Powers consider them as fallen. Therefore he seeks to make it categorically clear that in the beginning God created angels for good works. Hence even though they are now fallen, God still uses them to achieve a greater good.

Man (sic) and his world are fallen, and in this the powers have their own share. They are no longer active only as mediators of the saving creative purpose of God; now we find them seeking to separate us from the love of God (Rom. 8:38); we find them ruling over the lives of those who live far from the love of God (Eph. 2:2); we find them holding man in servitude to their rules (Col. 2:20); we find them holding men subject under their tutelage (Gal. 4:3). These structures, which were supposed to be our servants, have become our masters and our guardians.[83]

Second, the powers are redeemable. The powers are not completely relegated to an evil sphere. In other words, "the working of the powers is not simply something limitlessly evil."[84] They are still capable of performing God's original intent—continuing "to exercise an ordering function." Paul grasped this reality. That is why, as Yoder maintains, "even tyranny (which according to Romans 13:1 is to be counted among the powers) is still better than chaos and we should be subject to it."[85] Consequently, Yoder makes three conclusions about structures of the powers and by extension stresses the necessity of power:

> (1) All these structures can be conceived of in their general essence as parts of a good creation. (2) But these structures fail to serve man as they should. They have absolutized themselves and they demand from the individual and society an unconditional loyalty. They harm and enslave man. *We cannot live with them.* . . . (3) Man is lost in the world, in its structures, and in the current of its development. But nonetheless it is in this world that man has been preserved,

---

83. Yoder, *The Politics of Jesus*, 143.
84. Yoder, *The Politics of Jesus*, 143.
85. Yoder, *The Politics of Jesus*, 143–4.

204

The Impact of Ethnic, Political, and Religious Violence on
Northern Nigeria, and a Theological Reflection on Its Healing

that he has been able to be himself and thereby to await the redeeming work of God.[86]

The existence of these rebellious powers necessitated a Savior, and a new Lord. In the words of Ched Myers, this new Lord must be able to bind the strong person or the powers. This strong person(s) in Jesus' day created unbearable conditions for the Jews. Donald B. Kraybill's New Testament study shows that "The Jews suffered political, economic as well as religious oppressions during the time of Jesus because of the Roman supremacy," on the one hand; and "the chief Priests, the Sadducees, merchants, rich land-lords, and tax-collectors" who "collaborated with the Roman authorities" on the other hand. Kraybill notes that "These rich people would oppress the poor and take away 40% to 70% of the peasants' annual income."[87] These together formed what was known as the structures of the powers in Jesus' day. Hence Yoder is right, "Their sovereignty must be broken." In Philippians 2:6 Paul shows how Jesus cleverly and willingly subjected himself to these powers, resulting in the dismantling of their hold on power. Jesus' crucifixion becomes center stage for the breaking of the sovereignty of the powers. The cross exposes their deception! Yoder writes,

> His very obedience unto death is in itself not only the sign but also the first fruits of an authentic restored humanity. . . . This authentic humanity included his free acceptance of death at their hands. Thus it is his death that provides his victory: "Wherefore God exalted him to the highest place and gave him the name that is above every name . . . that every tongue might confess that Jesus Christ is Lord" (Phil. 2:9–11).[88]

Despite Jesus' negative experiences with the Powers, Jesus used his authority and power justly and rightly. Hence the authority and power

---

86. Yoder, *The Politics of Jesus*, 145–6.
87. Donald B. Kraybill, *The Upside-Down Kingdom* (Pennsylvania: Herald Press, 1978, Basingstoke Hants: Marshall Morgan & Scott, 1985), 82–3.
88. Yoder, *The Politics of Jesus*, 147.

of Jesus comes to us in the form of teaching and revelation of what God's kingdom is all about. Jesus concretely demonstrated how to use power justly and rightly. That is to say, unlike us greedy and self-centered human beings, Jesus recognized God as the source of his power: "All authority in heaven and on earth has been given to me."[89] This statement not only demonstrates that Jesus chose to receive power and authority from the source of power—God—but it also expresses Jesus' sense of absolute competence in his vocation: "he had everything given to him to accomplish the work he had to do, and he was conscious of being equal to his task."[90]

In short, Jesus is reminding his listeners that all authority including power comes from God. Jesus categorically rejected the domination system. In his study of the spiral of violence in Roman-occupied Palestine, Richard Horsley made this rejection abundantly clear in his description of Jesus' behavior:

> [He] consistently criticized and resisted the oppressive established political-economic-religious order of his own society. Moreover, he aggressively intervened to mitigate or undo the effects of institutionalized violence, whether in particular acts of forgiveness and exorcism or in the general opening of the kingdom of God to the poor. Jesus opposed violence, but not from a distance. . . . He rather entered actively into the situation of violence, and even exacerbated the conflict.[91]

Jesus was not a passive challenger of the powers and authorities. Rather he was a radical and active-nonviolent challenger of the powers and authorities of his day. No wonder the elite and the rich sought to steal, kill, and destroy his life. Horsley's point above confirms that it was this system of domination that eventually killed Jesus. Yet they were only able to steal

---

89. Matthew 28:16.
90. Hastings, et al., *Dictionary of Christ and the Gospels*, 147.
91. Richard Horsely, *Jesus and the Spiral of Violence: Popular Jewish Resistance in Roman Palestine* (San Francisco: Harper & Row, 1987), 319.

The Impact of Ethnic, Political, and Religious Violence on
Northern Nigeria, and a Theological Reflection on Its Healing

206

and kill him. They were not able to destroy his life. Kingsbury's conclusion on this matter:

> The issues Jesus and the authorities' debate are weighty and go to the heart of what it means to rule God's people. They have to do with matters of authority, tradition, and rules of purity, law, and one's relationship to God and to neighbor. The authorities [of Jesus' day] address these issues from their human, this-worldly point of view.[92]

Jesus addresses them from the standpoint of the Giver of all power, God. Jesus demonstrates how power is meant not to be used to deprive others of their right to life, to freedom, to community with peace, and to human dignity but to empower them to achieve their God-given potential. But how did Jesus resist using power to dominate?

(1) Jesus resisted Satan's offer of power. For example, after the forty days' fast in the desert, Satan tempted him to rule the world but Jesus resisted the temptation.

(2) He also resisted the temptations to exclude sinners, outcasts, and tax collectors in order to be accepted by the status quo.

(3) Jesus used His power to heal oppressive diseases, forgive sins, to give life, and to exorcise the powers that illegally inhabited humans.

Jesus used power for edification! Jesus' Apostles got the message. For example, Paul declared: "According to the power which the Lord hath given me for edification. . . ." In this statement, Paul demonstrates that power is meant to be used for the edification of people and for building their character. Paul's conception of "Character . . . means effectiveness, force, capacity for service, and Christian manhood [or humanhood] is not only life, but life at the full."[93] One of Jesus' apostles, Mark, presents a powerful insight into Jesus' radical departure from the status quo. Jesus' use of power is intentionally directed toward the deliverance of the socially, politically,

---

92. Kingsbury, *Conflict in Luke*, 84.
93. Archibald B. D. Alexander, *The Ethics of St. Paul* (Glasgow: James Maclehose and Sons, 1910), 355.

and religiously marginalized. For the Marcan Jesus what matters is the ability to use power for the benefit of those who have no voice.

3.2 Marcan Jesus: Compassion as Power

Mark breaks the silent violence that the common people in Palestine have been suffering under the powers and authorities, both from within and from without their society. As Ched Myers astutely pointed out, Mark is "a narrative for and about the common people. The Gospel reflects the daily realities of disease, poverty, and disenfranchisement that characterized the social existence of first-century Palestine's 'other 95%.'"[94] On the whole, Myers demonstrates that in Jesus' day, as in our contemporary societies, violence stems from a lack of compassion and a distorted pursuit of holiness. That is, holiness viewed by the Pharisees as separation and exclusion. Myers writes, "Jesus' compassion is always first directed toward the importunate masses and their overwhelming needs and demands. He responds to their desperate situation of hunger and hopelessness, and nurtures their dreams of liberation."[95] In choosing to emphasize compassion, Jesus illustrates that his opponents were mistakenly interpreting the Jewish holiness code in the Torah. Therefore the Marcan Jesus pays attention to compassion because it is the bottom line in the Old Testament holiness code as well as the basis of Christian ethics.

By choosing to stress compassion, the Marcan Jesus shows that the Church and its members are called to be merciful because God is merciful to all of us. Thus, as Borg aptly notes, "Jesus advocated a hermeneutic based on the conviction that God's primary attribute for human emulation was compassion." Therefore Borg succinctly concludes, "This was the paradigm in conformity with which the people of God were now to structure their existence."[96] The ethics of the Marcan Jesus is grounded on one of the communicable attributes of God: compassion. It is this nature of God that

---

94. Ched Myers, *Binding the Strong Man: A Political Reading of Mark's Story of Jesus* (Maryknoll, New York: Orbis Books, 1991), 39.
95. Myers, *Binding the Strong Man*, 39.
96. Borg, *Conflict, Holiness and Politics in the Teachings of Jesus*, 173.

The Impact of Ethnic, Political, and Religious Violence on
Northern Nigeria, and a Theological Reflection on Its Healing

208

causes him to gather a community of peace, a way that flowed intrinsically from the paradigm of inclusive compassion.

Yet in a world that has been reduced to violence, the hope of humanity resides not only in compassion but also in dialogue with the other, in forgiveness, in reconciliation, in embrace, in righteousness, in truth-telling as well as in delivering justice which enables the creation of checks and balances, free speech, free courts, and just economic structures and institutions. This is to say, although compassion is meant to prevent the cycle of violence, it is inadequate. As Stassen correctly noted, "It also requires justice that checks and balances power. Jesus did not show compassion to the poor and then leave the powers and authorities to do as they wanted."[97] Rather his practices of table-fellowships with sinners and tax collectors, touching and healing lepers or performing exorcism and miracles on the Sabbath, left no stone unturned. For example, as Myers puts it,

> From the moment he strides into a Capernaum synagogue,
> it becomes clear that Jesus' kingdom project is incompatible
> with the local public authorities and the social order they
> represent. . . . The risk of provoking official hostility does not
> deter Jesus from pressing his criticism of every social code that
> serves to institutionalize alienation.[98]

Jesus was deeply involved in community building, healing and exorcism as well as encountering local-political conflict with the religious leaders of his day (who were the Romans lieutenants in Palestine). As Myers further observes, Mark's campaign narratives focus on "Jesus' struggles to overturn the social codes upon which an oppressive caste system is based."[99] Jesus' life and ministry clearly present an extraordinary evidence of how human beings are capable of using power for the edification of their fellow men and women.

---

97. Glen Stassen's correction of my draft, Feb. 10, 2007.
98. Myers, *Binding the Strong Man*, 137.
99. Myers, *Binding the Strong Man*, 139.

In summary, compassion and mercy can actually transform a society of injustice and violence into a community of deliverance and hope when it embodies dialogue and other transforming initiatives that are available today. According to Stassen and Gushee, "Jesus gives us a powerful way of deliverance from the vicious cycles that lead to violent death and destruction."[100] Simply put, the way of compassion. But we must note that compassion is not one thing. It is, as Stassen and Gushee note, a package of the way of Jesus, which includes among other things, "peace, justice, and compassion." I suppose their conclusion is drawn from the prophet Isaiah. Based on Isaiah's prophecies, these communicable attribute "depend on each other because they are part and parcel of God's will and God's action of deliverance" (Isa. 54:10; 60:17–18; 52:7; 42:2; 53:7–9; 49:6).[101]

The Marcan Jesus has confrontations with the powers and authorities incarnated in demonic forces and the pharisaical establishment. This lends credence to Wink's conclusion that "Every power tends to have a visible pole, an outer form—be it a church, a nation, or an economy—and an invisible pole, an inner spirit or driving force that animates, legitimates, and regulates its physical manifestation in the world."[102] What this means is that "the Powers we are speaking about . . . are real"—not myth. "They work on us whether we acknowledge them or not."[103] Therefore we should not allow ourselves to be deceived by those who claim that these powers are myths. For as Wink tells us, "There is no question that the myths of power are used to legitimate, exploit, and oppress."[104] In short, every use of power must be judged by whether it fits the standard set by Scripture: the values that Jesus taught—love, forgiveness, reconciliation, and embrace; delivering justice and community that provides hope for the future through dialogue with the other.

Finally, Jesus' primary concern is the avoidance of the vicious cycle. Christ's disciple is able to break the cycle and even challenge the status

---

100. Stassen and Gushee, *Kingdom Ethics*, 150.
101. Stassen and Gushee, *Kingdom Ethics*, 150–151.
102. Walter Wink, *Naming the Powers: The Language of Power in the New Testament* (Philadelphia: Fortress Press, 1984), 5.
103. Wink, *Naming the Powers*, 136.
104. Wink, *Naming the Powers*, 136.

quo. Hans Küng points out that the Christian who takes the way of Jesus seriously and sees it as the standard and determining factor of his [or her] life "will not be a silent witness." He reminds us how deluded and blinded are "all who think that the use of power and violence, getting one's own way and exploiting others, whenever this is possible without risk to oneself, is the most advantageous, the shrewdest and even humanly speaking the most rational policy."[105]

The language of the powers in Romans 13:1–7 has been a point of contention. The question has been whether or not Paul sees the rulers as referring to the powers he describes elsewhere in his Epistles. An examination of the passage will shed light on what the tension is.

3.3 The Language of the Powers in Romans 13:1–7

Paul's understanding of the powers is shot through the import of the cross, and by extension the way of Jesus. The cross of Jesus is where the powers were publicly declared empty. Summarizing Wink's treatment of the powers in the New Testament, Neil Elliott notes, "The cross robs the powers of Death of their 'final sanction,' exposing the powers 'unable to make Jesus become what they wanted him to be, or to stop being who he was.'"[106] Wink himself states, "[W]ithout exception every structure of authority, role, office, incumbent, institution, system, and ruler, angel, in heaven and on earth and under the earth—all will be brought into subjection under his feet."[107] Over the centuries, theologians and ethicists have tried to expound Paul's conception of the state, particularly its connection to the subject of the powers. They wondered whether or not Paul's conception of the powers includes the state and its operators.

The Letter to the Romans, particularly 13:1–7, provides rich insights into the antecedents of Paul's notion of power as well as his political thoughts. It is a political thought that is influenced by Platonism and Aristotelianism.[108]

---

105. Hans Küng, *On Being a Christian*, trans. by Edward Quinn, (New York: Doubleday & Company, Inc., 1976), 592.
106. Neil Elliott, *Liberating Paul: Justice of God and the Politics of the Apostle* (New York: Orbis Books, 2001), 123.
107. Wink, *Naming the Powers*, 50–51.
108. Bruno Blumenfeld, *The Politics of Paul: Justice, Democracy and Kingship in a*

Greek political philosophy was still reigning in Paul's time. In his cultural-background study of Greco-Roman world, Blumenfeld writes, "Despite the ebbing of the *polis's* political power, and despite social erosion, the power of the *polis* to mobilize devotion and civic emotion was little altered. Political theorists continued to reflect on the *polis* with fervor and longing, and it was precisely this sentiment that Paul tapped into. . . . Political reflection is a major dimension of Paul's thought."[109] Paul worked and wrote within the confines of classical Greek political philosophy. The Roman Empire was intrinsically connected to its past.[110] Two types of philosophers existed: Classical philosophers and popular philosophers. The Classical philosophers wielded more power than the popular philosophers.[111] Paul belongs to the popular philosopher group.[112] Blumenfeld tells us that the methodology of the "popular philosopher was a mixture of poet, philosopher and prophet, a product of political disenfranchisement who delivered hymns, moral lectures and visions in the marketplace or at the city gates to an eager rabble pitching in their *obols*, or at a wealthy man's estate for a fee."[113]

The popular philosophers were closer to the masses than the professional philosophers who tended to maintain the status quo. Perhaps, like Jesus they were in solidarity with the poor, the downtrodden, the sinners, the despised ones, outcasts, the prostitutes, the very scum of society.[114]

Paul is aware of the threat the Roman Empire poses to Christianity. Paul also believes that it is only Christ's way of life that will bring the desired transformation of the Roman Empire. Paul is therefore careful not to upset

---

Hellenistic Framework (London and New York: Sheffield Academic Press, 2001), 33–34.
109. Blumenfeld, *The Politics of Paul*, 15.
110. Blumenfeld, *The Politics of Paul*, 16. Blumenfeld observes, "Hellenization is the continuation of the traditions of the *polis*. The Hellenistic socio-political system is binary: king and city, *basileia* and *polis*. Power rests with the king, who relentlessly gambles it: but the *polis* is the Hellenistic determinant; it signifies the age," 98.
111. Blumenfeld, *The Politics of Paul*, 18–19. Plato and Aristotle were considered the classical philosophers. Their students throughout the ages were considered more professional and powerful than the popular philosophers who were only itinerant lecturers. Blumenfeld observes, "The authority of the Classical philosophers was absolute, and it remained so even as their relevance was vanishing."
112. Blumenfeld, *The Politics of Paul*, 17.
113. Blumenfeld, *The Politics of Paul*, 18–19.
114. Desmond Tutu, *Hope and Suffering* (Grand Rapids: Wm. B. Eerdmans Publishing Company, 1983), 85.

the Roman officials. But how is he to avoid offending them if he is going to achieve his objective of injecting a sense of God's ownership of all of life in the Empire? Blumenfeld tells of how Paul goes about his task: "Paul's relation to the empire is paradoxical," Blumenfeld writes. He recognizes his indebtedness to the empire. That is to say, "Not only does Paul need the empire as the support infrastructure for his message, but he defends the power system with unabashed pride."[115] Blumenfeld believes that Paul pretended to defend the Roman Empire so that he could be accorded the opportunity to import the concept of power that does not only base justice with the state but transcends the state to the originator of justice—God.[116] Paul believes that it is only Christ's way of life that can bring the desired result in Rome. "Paul usurps the power system in two ways." Taking his cue from the example his Lord and Savior, Jesus Christ, Paul confronted the structures of injustice from within the system. As Blumenfeld right-ly maintains:

> First, he challenges the system from within: he forces on his hearers a new language, which, although it mirrors the concepts and categories of the existing system, subverts them either by occluding them with new idioms or by reinterpreting them while keeping the old terminology. This produces an unsettling intellectual space in which disorientation is mixed with a feeling of privilege, or having a claim to the prerogatives of power. The second mode of subversion is radically transgressive: Paul erases ethnic, social, and political binaries: Jew—Greek, Greek—barbarian, free—slave, wealthy—poor, ruler—ruled, and so on. Paul makes each individual body the image of the whole community, and transforms each and every member of the group into a Christ-type.[117]

---

115. Blumenfeld, *The Politics of Paul*, 391.
116. Blumenfeld, *The Politics of Paul*, 389–390.
117. Blumenfeld, *The Politics of Paul*, 291. Interestingly, Blumenfeld has left out scriptures allusion to their being no "male or female." What this means in relation to his politics is a point of interest.

However, recent studies are beginning to look at the salient truth of Paul's primary concern. For example, Stassen and Gushee have pointed out that "Romans 13:1–7 is about owing nothing but love to our enemies, including the Roman government, and making peace with them; it is not about approving of killing people."[118] Romans 13 constitutes a severe censure of arrogant and self-divinizing rulers. Paul strategically stresses the fact that God is the institutor of governing authorities. By implication, the governing powers are God's servants.[119] Thus if the powers, who are given the task of judging wicked people within their sphere of authority, misuse their God-given power by going beyond the bounds of compassion, justice, love and mercy, they will be judged by the God who set them up.[120]

In Romans 13:1–7 Paul implicitly calls the powers to their divine vocation. Besides, given the social and political atmosphere of the Roman Empire, Christians in Paul's day did not have many options. This means that they were left with only two choices: either they could obey or they could disobey and get crushed by the Roman soldiers.[121] In other words, they did not have as many choices as we have today in most democratic societies.

Therefore some scholars of Paul have noted that in Romans 13:1–7 he was articulating a standard Jewish and then Christian belief—that ruling authorities are what they are because God wants order in the present world. N.T. Wright tells us that the good news is: "God is not going to allow chaos to reign even in the present evil age. God desires that even in the present time; that is, even in the world that has not yet confessed Jesus as Lord, there should be a measure of justice and order."[122] Wright further observes

---

118. Stassen and Gushee, *Kingdom Ethics*, 207.
119. See Jeremiah 27:6, 17. Having realized that God has called the pagan king, Nebuchadnezzar Babylon, His servant, Jeremiah encouraged his audience to listen and obey Nebuchadnezzar.
120. Leander E. Keck, ed., *The New Interpreter's Bible*, Vol. 10 (Nashville: Abingdon Press, 2002), 719.
121. In Paul's case, unlike in our democratic society, "The right of public agitation was very limited in the Roman empire, and any attempt to rouse the people against the oppression of the government would not only have been relentlessly crushed, but would have sown widespread discontent and created useless revolution among a vast population." (Rauschenbusch, *Christianity and the Social Crisis*, 152 as cited by Archibald Browning Drysdael Alexander, *The Ethics of St. Paul* (Glasgow: James Maclehose, 1910), 318).
122. N.T. Wright, "The Letter to the Romans: Introduction, Commentary, and Reflection" in *The New Interpreter's Bible*, Vol. 10. Edited by Leander E. Keck, et al.,

that the mere fact that the authorities are there to look after such matters is strong incentive to forswear freelance attempts of "justice."[123] According to Paul (and Jewish tradition in which he stands) the rulers are not themselves divine; the one God sets them up, and they owe this God their allegiance. Blumenfeld points out, "The concept of power that Paul espouses here [Rom. 13:1–7] is Oriental and Hellenistic."[124]

Blumenfeld observes that "Paul's vocal approval of taxation (Rom. 13:6–7) is perhaps his most overt consent to the existing political regime. Paul understood the political advantages of Christianity and used them to strengthen the Roman political system, which he admired and endorsed."[125]

Paul's political genius is shown in his ability to link the concept of power back to its Originator—God. It was very intriguing and crucial in an age when the kings or the emperors saw themselves as gods.[126] Paul's move is also very significant in our own age when modernity has stripped us of the concept of a God who is involved in all spheres of life. The result is a decreasing reliance on and accountability to the God who gives human power by those who exercise that power. Paul brought God to the center of the concept of political power.

Paul's emphasis shows that the state and the church—as well as ethics and politics—are inseparable. Does Paul have a sense of the separation of church and state? Yes! But as Blumenfeld states, "Paul conceives the Christian community as a distinct social, economic, and political entity. Its constitution is not a democracy nor a polity nor the rule of a philosopher-king, but *to euangelion tou Christi*, the evangel of Christ."[127] For Paul, "Christ is the mean, the right principle, the being at the crossroads between

---

(Nashville: Abingdon Press, 2002), 718.

123. Wright, "The Letter to the Romans: Introduction, Commentary, and Reflection" in *The New Interpreter's Bible*, 718.

124. Blumenfeld, *The Politics of Paul*, 390. Blumenfeld also explains: In the two notorious passages in which Paul speaks about the established political powers (Rom. 13:3; 1 Cor. 2:6); *archontes* is a generic name for rulers, authorities or officials. To them is owed obedience as appointees of God and defenders of the laws (13:6), 391.

125. Blumenfeld, *The Politics of Paul*, 391. According to Blumenfeld, "Echoing the political dogma of imperial Rome, Paul declares that all political power is from God (13:1)." That is, Paul is "giving voice to a novel idea: the monarch as God's servant," 392.

126. Blumenfeld, *The Politics of Paul*, 37.

127. Blumenfeld, *The Politics of Paul*, 294.

humanity and divinity, error and truth. Paul's *euangelion* is the expression of this objectivity."[128] Christ is at the center of all of life.

Other scholars have argued that Paul was protecting his benefactors: the Roman authorities who protected him from the wrath of his people, the Jews.[129] While it is true that Paul enjoyed some level of protection from the Roman authorities, this argument has no basis. It runs counter to Paul's attitude to the powers in general. Paul's recognition of human government is twofold. On the one hand Paul sees the state as a divine institution and wants Christians to see it as such. On the other hand Paul recognizes that it was also an institution that was managed by fallen human beings. In short, Paul argues that the state is not a human initiative. I would argue that Paul's primary motivation was to encourage Christ's disciples "to pray for kings and for all that are in authority," in order that the kings and the rulers may use their power to protect the vulnerable in society; and that under their protection Christ's disciples "may live quiet and peaceable lives in all godliness and honesty." Consequently, that pleases God, our Lord and Savior.[130]

Paul's situation is analogous to the days of Jeremiah when the Jewish captives were encouraged to seek the peace of the city where they lived because in its prosperity they would have peace.[131] Perhaps, as Colin Brown suggested, Paul may have seen himself in the same position as Jeremiah (as Josephus did later).[132] Thus I claim that reading Romans in the light of Jeremiah gives not only the bigger context of the issue of the powers, but may also hold the key to Paul thoughts.[133]

---

128. Blumenfeld, *The Politics of Paul*, 61–62.
129. See Elliott, *Liberating Paul*, 93. Elliott's book has a catalogue of scholars who think Paul's approach to the Roman Empire was nothing short of blatant betrayal of Jesus' mission. Elliott cited J. Christiaan Beker as one of the critics of Paul's political stance.
130. 1 Timothy 2:2.
131. Jeremiah 29:7 "Also, seek the peace and prosperity of the city to which I have carried you into exile. Pray to the Lord for it, because if it prospers, you too will prosper."
132. Colin Brown's general comments in my first draft, 11.
133. See Jeremiah 29:7 cf 1 Timothy 2:1–3.

The Impact of Ethnic, Political, and Religious Violence on
Northern Nigeria, and a Theological Reflection on Its Healing

216

3.4 Paul's and Peter's Ethics in the Context of the Powers

Many lessons can be extrapolated from the materials that I have so far covered in an attempt to grasp the concept of the powers in my context, Northern Nigeria. These lessons include, among other things, the following:

(1) God rules over suffering. This is why Peter, like Jesus, Paul, and Moltmann, places a premium on hope. As Schreimer's analysis indicates, Peter's audience lacks a certain privilege that contemporary Christians in the West have: democracy. Schreiner analyzes the letter with the understanding that "Peter wanted his readers to conceive of themselves as the people of God. They had become part of Israel by virtue of their belief in Jesus Christ. They were God's holy nation and special people (1 Peter 2:9–10). The encouragement to live as sojourners and set their hope only on God is also matched by the threat that they will be judged if they turn away from the gospel."[134] By His patient suffering and glorious future destiny, Jesus Christ has given them the pattern to follow and also a living hope." Life in a non-Christian society "is difficult and requires humility and submission" (1 Peter 4:7–18).[135]

(2) Shame and honor can be symbols of the oppressive use of power. Thus there are issues that must be addressed if we want to dislodge the lie and delusion of the powers. In short, underlying violence in the days of Jesus, Paul, and Peter was the issue of shame and honor. Today, just as then, this is still one of the clearest manifestations of the powers' strategy to keep us silent. Shame and honor make nonviolence unattractive in most cases. Violence is perpetuated because of the concept of shame and honor. No wonder Jesus was killed by a traditional society that valued shame and honor. Gilbert I. Bond argues, "The cultural complex of Paul was governed by the codes of honor and shame."[136]

---

134. Schreiner, *The New American Commentary*, 46.
135. Frank E. Gaebelein and J. D. Douglas, *The Expositor's Bible Commentary*, Vol. 12 (Grand Rapid: Zondervan Publishing House, 1981), 213.
136. Gilbert I. Bond, *Paul and the Religious Experiences of Reconciliation: Diasporic Community and Creole Consciousness* (Louisville, KY: John Knox Press, 2005), 90; "Shame—that sudden or anticipated rupture of this relational matrix—fragments this imago by severing the relational suspensions that uphold the self. The rupture in relationship is experienced as exposure or uncovering of one's most vulnerable core and

(3) Shame, honor, and holiness can be weapons of violence used for the sole purpose of concealing the evil of the powers. Generally the effect of violence is nuanced by the social situation of shame, honor, and holiness. This is why it requires careful analysis to unravel their secrets. Bond notes,

> Paul's location in the Jewish Diaspora of the Greco-Roman world adds a crucial dimension to the role of shame and honor in his experience; that is, in the Greco-Roman culture, honor would directly depend upon one's status, gender, and power. One's birth, intelligence, virtue, physical appearance, oratorical skills, virility, and other expressions of status located one within a hierarchy of values based upon the manifestation of various forms of power.[137]

In this case, violence embodied the culture's understanding of the dynamics of honor and shame. But shame and honor are not the only dimensions that the powers use to terrorize the weak. In Jesus' day, as Borg reminds us, holiness was the center of conflict with the Pharisaic establishment. Thus shame, honor, and holiness became the basis of domination. The drive for purity and holiness in first-century Palestine became the tool for social definition. Jesus' nonviolent reaction was his table fellowship with those who had been sidelined as sinners.[138]

Paul and Peter were very familiar with this Jewish holiness code, which, as Borg explained, had consciously or unconsciously forced these categories of people to place themselves or allow others to place them outside the holiness code of Israel, which the Pharisees and certain circles in Palestine were mistakenly interpreting. The "powers that be" then had succeeded in convincing many a populace, as Wink notes, that "to include outcasts such as these in the kingdom of God was to reject the postexilic self-interpretation of Judaism as separation from the uncleanness of the world.

---

the global, inextricable sense that the painfully overwhelming detestable core of oneself is unacceptable and indelibly stained. The self becomes individualized," 92.

137. Bond, *Paul and the Religious Experiences of Reconciliation*, 92.

138. Wink, *Engaging the Powers*, 115.

The Impact of Ethnic, Political, and Religious Violence on
Northern Nigeria, and a Theological Reflection on Its Healing

218

Jesus distinguishes between those falsely called sinners—who are in fact the victims of an oppressive system of exclusion—and true sinners, whose evil is not ascribed to them by others, but who have sinned from the heart (Mark 7:21–23)."[139]

(4) The *Domination System* depends on social classification and structural stratification. Today the concept of "bad guys" vs. "good guys" serves the same purpose. Shame, honor, and holiness were used and are still being used by the powers in many societies to create social classifications that are then used to their advantage.[140] In short, Wink is arguing that "Domination depends on ranking. Without such distinctions, how can one know whom to dominate"[141] others? Peter and Paul declare that we are born anew to a living hope. Thus our Christian ethics need to be based on the character of God, which Jesus clearly demonstrated on the cross: God's deep love, mercy, and compassion was evidenced by his sacrifice, but also by his introduction of a counter reality to the domination system, the kingdom, He birthed an enduring community with hope for the future, as Stassen and Gushee remind us.[142]

In the next section, I shall argue that this system of social classification is embodied in the Muslim culture of Northern Nigeria. The Muslim North is a society of shame, honor, and holiness/purity. The Shari'ah law finds its impetus in these codes. According to Berkow Usman Dan Fodio jihad was fought in the name of "purity."[143] Therefore it is important to articulate their connection to violence in Northern Nigeria.

---

139. Wink, *Engaging the Powers*, 115–116.

140. Wink maintains, "Rules of ritual purity are what keep the various people and parts of society in their 'proper' place. Without purity regulations, there would be a crisis of distinction in which everyone, and everything, was the same: women equal to men, outsiders equal to insiders, the sacred no different from the profane. There would be no holy place or holy priest or holy people. Gentile would be no different from Jew [Muslim would be no different from Christian]. 'Clean' people would sit at table with 'unclean'; [infidels with believers]; no one would be better in God's sight. Socially imposed shame about body keeps people submissive to societal authority by weakening in them the immediacy of their own sense of what is right. Without such shame, what becomes of societal authority?" (*Engaging the Powers*, 116).

141. Wink, *Engaging the Powers*, 116.

142. Stassen and Gushee, *Kingdom Ethics*, 22.

143. Berkow, "Hausa" *Muslim People*, 152. The *jihad* was as a result of a Fulani Islamic scholar, Dan Fodio questioning the purity of the Islam the Hausa people practice in

4. Analyzing the Power Structure of Northern Nigeria

The study of the powers and authorities requires a contemporary context. Northern Nigeria provides such a contemporary context. In other words, the situation of Northern Nigeria helps us put the sorry stories of the endangered use of power and authority in a modern perspective. I therefore attempt to analyze the scenario of the use of power and authority in Northern Nigeria.

4.1 Sociopolitical and Socioeconomic Matters in Northern Nigeria

Reconstructing the social, political, and economic experiences of minorities in Northern Nigeria as they encounter violence is crucial; but it is not my primary focus. My cardinal concern is to explore the functions and meaning of violence from the standpoint of political power and authority in the context of Northern Nigerian. In this case, I attempt to go beyond Matthew Hassan Kukah's interpretation of the powers in Northern Nigeria (1993). My focus maximizes the importance of ethnic minorities' issues within Northern Nigeria and argues that their marginalization is heightened by the fear of domination. This fear can only be understood through a demonstration of ethnic social dynamics in relation to matters usually regarded as more central to Northern Nigerian society: kingship, feudalism, shame, honor, and purity. These social codes are interrelated. They are the clearest manifestation of power not only in Nigeria but also in many African societies.

I recognize that many studies (Falola, 1998; Kukah, 1993; and Turaki, 1997, to name a few) on Northern Nigeria have focused on the political and social dynamics of the region. Some of these studies have stressed the dominance of Hausa-Fulani over other ethnic groups within the geographical North. The contribution of these studies cannot be underestimated. Yet they have left so much to be desired and have been somewhat detrimental

---

Northern Nigeria. Thereafter in 1802 he launched an onslaught on the aristocracy and replaced them with his followers.

220

The Impact of Ethnic, Political, and Religious Violence on
Northern Nigeria, and a Theological Reflection on Its Healing

to the understanding of other areas that reveal a bigger picture of the sociopolitical, socioeconomic, and socioreligious dynamics that conceal the
source and impact of violent use of power.

I claim that the ideological concepts of kingship, honor, shame, and
purity are intrinsically connected to the oppressive use of power. Therefore
I would attempt to define them in the context of the powers in the North.
I will take the trajectory of royal slaves to interpret these social and political
phenomena. How can we best understand the Powers in Northern Nigeria?
How is the issue of power causing or impacting violence in the region?
These are questions that I attempt to unravel as I analyze kingship, honor,
shame, and purity.

Kingship: because it is a hierarchical system, kingship creates conflict
with democratic principles. As Peter Beinart notes, "Northern Nigeria, since
its conversion to Islam in the fifteenth century, had been divided into vast,
centralized emirates—governed through strict, pyramid-like hierarchies led
by an emir or sultan."[144] The Sokoto Caliphate and the established emirate
system have since been seen as the loci of control not only in the Northern
region but in the country at large.[145] But we have to remember that like
every system of domination, the Sokoto Caliphate was good, is fallen, and
can be redeemable. God always demonstrates that God is sovereign, King
over all. This is why, in Northern Nigeria, as Sean Stillwell points out, a
category of slaves known as "royal slaves" gained access to the kingship.

Ironically, the narrative of how they gained access to the throne is linked
with their heroic performance in civil war. For as Stilwell pertinently notes,
"In 1893 in one of the Northern cities, Kano, civil war broke out between
two rival claimants for the throne—the rebel Yusufu and the newly appointed emir, Tukur—which devastated the Kano emirate."[146] According to

---

144. Peter Beinart, *The New Republic*, July 6, 1998, 2.
145. In "Sokoto Caliphate and its Legacies" *Sunday Tribune*, February 25, 2007, Prof.
John N. Paden writes that "The [Sokoto] caliphate stretched from present-day Burkina
Faso in the west, to Cameroun [sic] in the East." Paden also tells of how "the Influence of
Ahmadu Bello, (a direct descendant of Usman Dan Fodio), as the first and only premier
of Northern Region cannot be over-emphasized. The First Republic (1960–1966), set the
basic pattern of regionally based federalism in Nigeria."
146. Sean Stilwell, "Power, Honor and Shame: The Ideology of Royal Slavery in the
Sokoto Caliphate" in *Africa Magazine*, June 22, 2000, 1.

Stilwell, "The victory of the rebel forces was in part made possible by the astute leadership of a number of powerful royal slaves. All of these royal slaves used the opportunity provided by the civil war to accumulate power, influence and wealth."[147] This set the scene not only for the slaves' liberation and ascendancy to the throne, but also for power coming to be seen as a symbol of honor.

Hence as noted by Wakilin Panshekera and Alhaji Abba Sadauki, in an interview on March 30, 1998, the blowing of triumph during coronation or turbanning in the North signifies "the assumption of 'honor' by a slave." Stilwell tells us that "the roles of these elite slaves in the Kano civil war points to the emergence and consolidation of a royal slave office-holding elite by the end of the nineteenth century." These royal slave elite immediately created "codes of conduct" which included, among other things, "a system of honor" that gave them social claims to influence, offices, and wealth."[148] In short, it is crucial to unpack the connection between kingship-cum-honor and shame in the context of the powers.

In his acute analysis of West Africa, Martin Klein suggested that in West Africa, particularly the French part, honor "defined not only the boundary between slave and non-slave, but also the identity of the non-slave."[149] This conception of honor is not limited to French West Africa. It is the reigning ideology in Northern Nigeria. It is ingrained and embedded in the culture of elitism in the region. Therefore, it is the key that unravels the sources and deep roots of violence in Northern Nigeria. Klein claims that "The social distinction between 'those who are honorable and those who are not' was [and still is] crucial to a hegemonic ideology, which enabled the ruling elite to control both agricultural slaves and the more privileged slave warriors."[150]

---

147. Stilwell, "Power, Honor and Shame: The Ideology of Royal Slavery in the Sokoto Caliphate" in *Africa Magazine*, 1.
148. Stilwell, "Power, Honor and Shame: The Ideology of Royal Slavery in the Sokoto Caliphate" in *Africa Magazine*, 1.
149. Martin Klein as cited by Stilwell, "Power, Honor and Shame: The Ideology of Royal Slavery in the Sokoto Caliphate" in *Africa Magazine*, 1. Stilwell points out that the question of honor and Klein first suggested shame to him (1998: 249). See also Bazin (1982).
150. This is clear, as Stilwell argues: "the ideology of Islam further reinforced the importance of honor and kinship in defining both who was slave and who was free. In this regard, the Sokoto Caliphate and the states of the western Sudan shared much

Since the Usman Dan Fodio jihad, which led to the conquering of many pagan tribes in the region, the non-Muslim ethnic groups in the region have often been seen as conquered communities that are only free as long as they bow to the system of honor and shame put in place by the ruling elite. Thus they may have their own chiefdoms today, but the assumption is that that does not guarantee complete freedom. In the olden days the emir could give royal slaves their titles only because they were slaves and therefore could not claim to be honorable; similarly, today the ethnic groups who have been granted their chiefdoms, particularly in Southern Kaduna state are still seen as people without real freedom, particularly political, cultural, and religious freedom.[151] I suppose this is why ethnic, political, and religious violence has prevailed in the region.

But the history of Northern Nigeria is not unilateral. It is a combination of factors. Religious homologations are deeply embedded in the culture.[152] The Islamic-religious establishments have sanctioned kingship, honor, shame, and purity in Northern Nigeria. As we are aware, religious cultures generally ascribe spiritual significance to all parts of their worlds. All of life—including food, work, suffering, human relations, sexuality and marriage, education, the arts, and government—are given religious significance. Islam, Christianity, and paganism all have detailed rules of purity that affect every aspect of behavior.[153] These rules are often used as tools of domination through the process of separation and differentiation.

The situation is complex. We have people who were free and those who were freed at the risk of their lives.[154] This situation is best illustrated in Stilwell's description of the social dynamics in Northern Nigeria. Stilwell

---

in common. In Kano royal slaves stood outside the systems of honor and shame that governed the behavior of the free elite. This was indeed the central reason why royal slaves were able to attain positions of power and authority in Kano" (Stilwell, "Power, Honor and Shame" in *Africa Magazine*, 3).

151. See Yusufu Turaki, *Socio-Political Role and Status of Non-Muslim Groups of Northern Nigeria: Analysis of a Colonial Legacy* (Ph.D. thesis Boston University, 1982).

152. See Matthew Hassan Kukah, *Religion, Politics and Power in Northern Nigeria* (Kaduna: Spectrum Books Limited, 1993), 1–2.

153. William E. Paden, "Religion" in *Religious Worlds: The Comparative Study and Interpreting the Sacred: Ways of Viewing Religion* (Boston: Beacon Press, 2006), 4.

154. Jared Diamond, *Guns, Germs, and Steel: The Fates of Human Societies* (New York: W.W. Norton & Company, 1999), 281–283.

points out that "the position royal slaves occupied as 'outsiders' was the primary source of their power and, in the end, the assumption of 'honor' by royal slaves was limited to, and governed by, what the free aristocracy would accept and allow of all their slaves." Furthermore, Stilwell claims that "the ability of royal slaves to operate outside the system of honor and shame that regulated the behavior of free individuals offered individual slave officials opportunities to contravene and transgress social and political norms and codes of behavior."[155] Thus the concept of honor is not simply related to a person's conduct or behavior but to a person's ability to claim a rightful position and place in the dominant culture. In this social environment, the powerless are left to fill the needed air of honor and shame.[156] Stilwell explains that

> The social status of freeborn and slaves, as well as the opportunities opened to them, varied dramatically in most cases. In the case of the Sokoto Caliphate, as in many highly stratified African societies, slavery and kingship were mutually exclusive. As dishonored outsiders, royal slaves were used and valued in a manner that was very different from free clients and kin. As slaves, they were more readily subject to control and coercion. They were thus brought within the fold of Islam and used to enhance the position of the ruler and facilitate the centralization of power in his hands. In a political system divided between family and household loyalties, royal slaves served as the perfect solution to ensure that the emir would retain his position and expand his power.[157]

---

155. Stilwell, "Power, Honor and Shame" *Africa Magazine*, 3. Generally, however, "both slaves and freeborn represented 'wealth in people' and were valued by the elite as result. No wonder today, as then, African political leaders and household heads strive to increase the number of dependents they control not only in order to secure access to labor power and to increase their own prestige and authority, but also to exploit them as a means of clinging to power."

156. See Bill Berkeley, *The Graves Are Not Yet Full: Race, Tribe and Power in the Heart of Africa* (New York: Basic Books, 2001), 16–17.

157. Stilwell, "Power, Honor and Shame" *Africa Magazine*, 3–4.

In short, Northern Nigeria today reveals not only the structure of violence and injustice in a society impacted by kingship-cum-colonialism[158] but also "the myth of redemptive violence."[159] It is a vivid illumination of how the Domination System operates. They know what society values and they use that to their advantage.

Like much of Africa, Nigeria is a culture of shame. In the North, this shame is baptized with religious connotations and thus it is used by the powers to dominate the weak. Shame is an instrument of violence and control. As Dr. Wayne W. Dyer says, "Low energy thoughts that weaken us fall in the realm of shame, anger, hatred, judgment, and fear. Each of these inner thoughts weakens us and inhibits us from attracting into our lives what we desire."[160] Many communities in the North have been left poor because poverty is a shameful thing and a tool to silence the masses.[161] The oppressed need to be reminded that shame is not necessarily bad; yet I argue that using shame as an instrument of oppression of the weak is evil and unjust.

Feudalism: The Northern elite practice a system of economic, political, and social organization resembling medieval European feudalism. However, in the core-North it may be accurate to say that the system has been modeled after the Arabic culture of domination. For the British, who conquered Nigeria early in the twentieth century, the emirate system, which was feudal, was a godsend. This sociopolitical posture was necessitated by the assumption that "A fragile political consensus underlay Britain's bid for an African empire, and that consensus depended upon keeping that empire cheap. The way to do so, colonial authorities decided, was to keep traditional African political systems in place and sprinkle a few British administrators on top. The less African society changed, the less it would cost to rule." It was in Northern Nigeria, with its clear lines of indigenous authority, that this policy

---

158. See Yusufu Turaki, *British Colonial Legacy in Northern Nigeria: A Social Ethical Analysis of the Colonial and Post-Colonial Society and Politics in Nigeria* (Jos, Nigeria: ECWA Challenge Printing Press, 1993, 1997).
159. See Wink, *Engaging the Powers*.
160. Wayne W. Dyer, *The Power of Intention: Learning to Co-Create Your World Your Way* (Carlsbad, California: Hay House, Inc., 2004), 44.
161. See Allen H. Barton, *Communities in Disaster: A Sociological Analysis of Collective Stress Situations* (New York: Doubleday & Company, 1970), 23.

of "indirect rule" reached its apogee. British administrators discouraged missionaries from traveling to the region, fearing that Christianity would undermine the authority of the emirs, and the British refused to introduce Western education.[162] Today, we usually associate colonialism with cultural supremacy and invasion, but indirect rule was actually a grand experiment in coercive cultural relativism.

Purity: The idea of purity has led to the implication of Shari'ah law in much of the Northern states. Shari'ah is the Muslim's law code, which guides and regulates their morality and ethics. But immediately after Nigeria's return to democracy in 1999 the Muslims decided to implement full Shari'ah law in the Northern region. They insisted that Shari'ah must be considered as having equal power over the citizenry as the constitution of the land: Shari'ah law should govern all Muslim-dominated states in the North. Since the Northern region is not all Muslims, the non-Muslims nonviolently protested the demand for the public implementation of Shari'ah law. Consequently, from February 21–25, 2000, the Muslims in the Northern city of Kaduna attacked the protesters, and the fighting and counter-fighting that ensued left over 2,000 people dead. Since then the experience of Shari'ah propaganda and the resultant violence has left over 10,000 people dead. Purity, as Richard Horsley points out, is one of the human acts that the Powers use as a tool to impair another person's dignity or integrity, with the sole intent of demeaning them.[163]

My intention in naming these social-cum-religious and political codes is to point out the deep deception of the Domination System in Northern Nigeria. In *Cracking the Gnostic Code: The Powers in Gnosticism*, Wink rightly argues that the message of John 8:44 is clearly that the God of "the religious authorities is not the God whom they believe they worship, but Satan himself; that is the spirit of the Domination System."[164] Equally true, the system of kingship in most cases is corrupt.

---

162. Berkow, "Hausa" *Muslim People*, 152. See also Johnson, et al., *Operation World*, 192.
163. Horsley, *Jesus and the Spiral of Violence*, 25.
164. Wink, *Cracking the Gnostic Code: The Powers in Gnosticism* (Atlanta, Georgia: Scholars Press, 1993), 27.

226

The Impact of Ethnic, Political, and Religious Violence on
Northern Nigeria, and a Theological Reflection on Its Healing

This is why I insist that Northern Nigeria needs the way of Jesus as an alternative to violence. Since Nigeria's Muslims are estimated to number over seventy million, this will not be simple, easy, or without challenges. We must find redemptive examples within Africa that will gradually point to an analogous application of the way of Jesus. Such redemptive examples are not far fetched.

The Niger Republic's political experience provides a window of understanding to the problem. Undoubtedly, two political-power structures, democracy and hierarchical aristocracy, are at war in Northern Nigeria, resulting in deception and violence year-in-and-year-out. It is generally assumed that "The political structure of Northern Nigeria is more inextricably bound up with its past than that of any other West African territory."[165] John N. Paden's article on "Sokoto Caliphate and Its Legacies" has made this point abundantly clear.[166] The British believed this lie. Consequently, in the style of the Roman Empire, Lord Lugard introduced indirect rule in Northern Nigeria in 1903. The introduction of indirect rule not only endorsed the domination of the ethnic groups but it also left the job undone. "The Dan Fodio Jihad of the eighteen century had succeeded in establishing Islam not only as the religion of Northern Nigeria but [also] as its political system."[167]

I claim the British thought that they would let a sleeping dog lie by introducing indirect rule in the North. In contrast, the French in Nigeria's neighboring country, Niger, which incidentally had a Muslim Hausa population with emirs and chiefs like Northern Nigeria, recognized that leaving the system—aristocracy [rule of the minority] and democracy [rule of the majority]—to coexist would only create conflict of interests and thereby hamper political development. Therefore, for administrative convenience "they removed all the traditional chiefs and replaced them with old soldiers and clerks."[168] At first, the masses who were already used to the system and the chiefs who enjoyed the dividends of such a structure did not like the move. However, as time went on, everyone started appreciating

---

165. Michael Crowder, *Pagans & Politicians* (London: Hutchinson, 1959), 109.
166. J. N. Paden, "Sokoto Caliphate and Its Legacies" *Sunday Tribune*, Feb. 25, 2007.
167. Crowder, *Pagans & Politicians*, 110.
168. Crowder, *Pagans & Politicians*, 107.

the wisdom of the French. Hence, as Crowder noted, "In Niger today a full-scale parliamentary democracy with universal suffrage including votes for women is at work."[169]

Nigeria's democracy cannot boast of any full-scale democracy with universal suffrage, even though women are voted into political position. The reason is simply put: the existence of a structure that runs counter to democratic principles—aristocracy/oligarchy. That means that one of the causes of social, political, and religious anarchy in Northern Nigeria is the political structure. As Kwambe A. Appiah points out,

> Rigidly stratified, Hausa society is based on class and official rank. Most important official positions are reserved for the aristocracy. An emir rules each of the many Hausa states, and the political structure is essentially feudal. These relationship were held over by British rule, ensuring a continuity of ten disrupted elsewhere by volatilization.[170]

The tension between an aristocratic system and a democratic system of government is not only a problem in Northern Nigeria but also in other parts of the country. The British later discovered that "like so many traditionalist Islamic states, Northern Nigeria is confused by this new notion [indirect rule]." As a result, "latent tensions which were largely concealed by the presence of the British administration, the power of the traditional chiefs, the lack of education and the conservative character of Islam, are now becoming apparent."[171] Yet the British were afraid to do something about the ugly situation. Consequently, after Nigeria gained its independence in 1960 an African friend told Crowder that, "The struggle for power is on. It's a struggle between the old forces of aristocracy represented by the chiefs and their native authorities and the new forces of democracy at Kaduna, [the capital of the political North], with its Ministers and democratically

169. Crowder, *Pagans & Politicians*, 107.
170. Kwame Anthony Appiah, Henry Louis Gates Jr. and Michael Colin Vazquez, eds., *The Dictionary of Global Culture* (New York: Vintage Books, 1999), 283.
171. Crowder, *Pagans & Politicians*, 110–111.

elected assemblies."[172] Crowder's friend was right because after barely six years the premier of the Northern Region, Sir Ahmadu Bello, was assassinated, as I have noted above.

The situation Crowder's friend predicted above has not changed because the system is still left intact. As a solution to violence in Nigeria, I propose the proscription of the traditional system, which is aristocratic in nature because of the following reasons:

(1) The mixture of two conflicting systems is problematic. Although we are in a democratic regime, our politicians behave like aristocrats. Perhaps this is because it is the system they know best or because it gives them more power than democracy. To some extent, one cannot blame them because they grew up with the system. They think and act as if they were kings, chiefs, or emirs instead of being their people's representative. That is to say, our politicians are confusing democracy with aristocracy. The former means, "giving the majority of the people what they want."[173] The later usually is the minority dominating the majority through deception and violence. As John H. Hallowell observes, "As a form of government, democracy rests upon the consent of the governed." The consent is often based on the realization of the significance "of community of values and interests."[174]

(2) The traditional institution, aristocracy, is a hierarchical system that makes democracy confusing. It is hard to think democratically when one is an amateur in democratic governance and principles. The cost of maintaining the structure could be plowed back and redirected toward providing work for our unemployed youth—Nigeria's unemployment rate is sixty percent. Niger did it, and it worked! North America, consisting of Canada and America, has no kings and lords though they too were former British colonies.

(3) Our political system will reach maturity when we are willing to take the bull by the horns. Many conflicting interests are impeding democracy in

---

172. Crowder, *Pagans & Politicians*, 111.
173. John H. Hallowell, *The Moral Foundation of Democracy* (Chicago and London: The University of Chicago Press, 1973), 21.
174. Hallowell, *The Moral Foundation of Democracy*, 35.

Nigeria. Woodrow Wilson's observation is true: "Interests never unite men; interests can only divide."[175] In a country of diverse ethnic groups, one can only imagine the level of such conflicting interests when coupled with those caused by the mixture of a hierarchical traditional institution—aristocracy; and a nonhierarchical system—democracy. Although the political party system in America, which Nigeria has adopted, has had its ups and downs, for the most part it has stood the test of time. As Hallowell pointed out, it "has worked reasonably well in integrating conflicting sectional, economic, and other group interests in terms at least of a national program."[176]

In summary, from the ongoing analysis in this section I posit the following conclusions: first, tension exists between aristocracy, incarnated in the traditional institution, and democracy. This tension would have been unnecessary today had the British followed the example of the French in Niger.

Second, those with traditional, non-Muslim, non-Christian beliefs, who were dominated by the Hausas and their cousins, the Fulanis, have been unwilling to accept either Islam or its adherents, because Muslims institutionalized slavery in Africa. The traditionalists were sold to rich Muslims in the North before the coming of the Europeans. When the Europeans arrived and the institution of slavery was globalized, the Muslims, as middlemen, in turn sold them to the Europeans.

Third, most of the tribes, especially in the immediate southernmost part of the North, the Middle-Belt, have grown in population and in education. They are now questioning Hausa-Fulani hegemony in Northern Nigeria.

However, it is not enough to ask for independence from the Northern emirs or to have their own chiefs. This is not bringing the desired result because it is still the same hierarchical system that runs counter to modern democracy. What they need to ask is the cancellation of the traditional titled institution. I propose the nullification of the traditional institution which only worked before we had adopted a modern democracy. This will allow for solid checks and balances of power. It will also enable robust civil society and rich public dialogue. This move is a key that will unlock the

---

175. Woodrow Wilson cited in Hallowell, *The Moral Foundation of Democracy*, 55.
176. Hallowell, *The Moral Foundation of Democracy*, 60.

impasse of violence in Northern Nigeria and the country at large. Finally, there is an extraordinary need to examine the applicability of the way of Jesus in Northern Nigeria via Moltmann's and Wink's trajectories.

4.2 Practicing the Way of Jesus in Northern Nigeria's Context

The way of Jesus, as suggested by Moltmann's experience and work, holds hope for delivering justice in a violence-embedded society such as Northern Nigeria. The question that must be answered, however, is how does one talk about the way of Jesus in a society where the powers seem to rule without concern for justice? What has this way of Jesus got to do with a dominant ethnic group exercising political, economic, social, religious, and ethnic power in order to control who gets the biggest piece of the 'national pie'? Where can we even find the way of Jesus in such a system?

These are crucial questions that require careful response. For as Paul A. Germond has observed, "To treat violence as an isolated issue, divorced from the full matrix of human relations out of which it comes, leads to a reification of violence and a distortion of the issues."[177] These questions need to be responded to if we want to find a path to "a just and a humanized society."[178] I will begin with the last question by noting that Jesus' way is found in the Sermon on the Mount. It is in the Sermon on the Mount where humans, for the first time, are shown how to live with those who differ with you or with those you may consider enemies—humans are shown how to encounter the powers nonviolently.

It is in the Sermon on the Mount that we have the vision of the possibility of overcoming violence with nonviolent actions, which include, but not exclusively, dialogue with the enemy. As Moltmann correctly noted, "From the politics of loving one's enemy (which is found in the Sermon on the Mount) there follows the politics of overcoming the rule of violence by non-violence."[179] I resonate with Moltmann that to talk about nonviolence

177. Paul A. Germond, "Liberation Theology: Theology in the Service of Justice" in Charles Villa-Vicencio, ed., *Theology & Violence: The South African Debate* (Grand Rapids: Wm. B. Eerdmans Publishing Company, 1987), 216.
178. Germond, "Liberation Theology: Theology in the Service of Justice," 216.
179. Jürgen Moltmann, *Creating a Just Future* (London: SCM Press; Philadelphia: Trinity

does not mean, "Depoliticising and renunciation of power," in Northern Nigeria. We need power to create order which is God's desire for humanity and the entire ecosystem. This study has shown that power is being used nakedly, brutally, tyrannically, and illogically. In summary, power in Northern Nigeria is used in a manner that runs counter to God's intention and is detrimental to human rights.

The way of Jesus, as shown in the Sermon on the Mount, if analogously applied, is an alternative-transforming antidote that has the capability to unseat systems of violence nonviolently and create an enabling environment for humans, animals, and nature to flourish. The possibility of creating an alternative community in Northern Nigeria is predicated on Christians' willingness to pay attention to the Sermon on the Mount. For "The Sermon on the Mount," writes Moltmann "is precisely and essentially not an individual ethic." That means that it is a communal ethic. Hence its goal for justice is a "corporate justice." Therefore, "The community of Jesus which lives and acts messianically in the sense described, practices the alternative to the world's present system."[180] That is to say, the world system uses violence in order to dominate fellow humans. This is what Wink calls, "the Domination System," which runs counter to God's "Domination-Free society."[181]

Wink calls the powers "a total system, extending into the global economy and world political system. This overarching network of powers is what we are calling the *Domination System*. It is characterized by unjust economic relations, oppressive political relations, biased race relations, patriarchal gender relations, hierarchical power relations, and the use of violence to maintain them all."[182] That is, violence becomes the instrument of keeping the status quo. Moltmann contrasts this with God's domination free system, connecting it logically to Jesus and ultimately to humankind:, "[A] domain freed from the ravage of war . . . reached its greatest clarity in Jesus. He gave it profound programmatic shape in his teaching of nonviolence. In

Press International, 1989), 44.
180. Jürgen Moltmann, *The Way of Jesus Christ: Christology in Messianic Dimensions* (San Francisco: Harper San Francisco, 1990), 122.
181. Wink, *The Powers That Be*, 11, 27.
182. Wink, *The Powers That Be*, 38.

his Beatitudes, in his extraordinary concern for the outcasts and marginalized, in his wholly unconventional relationship of master slave, teacher, and student."[183] Thus, "The Sermon on the Mount," writes Moltmann, "is popular preaching, not instruction for an elite. It is addressed to everyone, not to a chosen few."[184]

The Sermon on the Mount is addressed to the people[185]—"people who are poor, oppressed, lost,"[186] needy, and marginalized. Therefore the way of Jesus as found in the Sermon on the Mount, is the way of the good news of the dawning of the reign of God's peace—nonviolent-direct action. This is great news! As Stassen points out, "The good news of Christian peacemaking is a transforming initiative, loving, acting, and redeeming in the midst of enmity."[187] Similarly, Moltmann maintains, "The center of the Sermon on the Mount is the liberation from violence; enmity is to be surmounted through the creation of peace. The presupposition here is that humanity's real sin is the violence that leads to death and that consequently humanity's salvation is to be found in the peace that serves our common life."[188] This peace comes through dialogue, free press, free speech, and providing checks and balances of power.

But why must we be concerned about checks and balances of power? Because humanity has limitations and evil inclinations. Reinhold Niebuhr writes, "Man's capacity for justice makes democracy possible; but man's inclination to injustice makes democracy necessary."[189] Niebuhr's logic is clear; humans' greed causes humans to desire to get ahead, disregarding the needs and rights of others. One immediate way to get ahead is to acquire power. Niebuhr writes, "If men are inclined to deal unjustly with their fellows, the possession of power aggravates this inclination."[190] In order to

---

183. Wink, *The Powers That Be*, 65–66.
184. Moltmann, *The Way of Jesus Christ*, 124.
185. Moltmann, *The Way of Jesus Christ*, 125.
186. Moltmann, *The Way of Jesus Christ*, 124.
187. Stassen, *Journey into Peacemaking*, 11.
188. Moltmann, *The Way of Jesus Christ*, 127.
189. Reinhold Niebuhr, *The Children of Light and the Children of Darkness: A Vindication of Democracy and a Critique of Its Traditional Defense* (New York: Charles Scribner's Sons, 1960), xiii.
190. Niebuhr, *The Children of Light and the Children of Darkness*, xiii-xiv.

prevent that from happening there must be checks and balances. Niebuhr wants us to recognize the power of self-interest in all humans so that we will stop being naïve or taking things for granted.[191] Niebuhr's prescribes, "Every society needs working principles of justice, as criteria for its positive law and system of restraints."[192]

Niebuhr's work brings awareness of what is required in Northern Nigeria. As Dennis McCann notes, "Niebuhr's interpretation of the structures of justice is contingent upon his understanding of the nature of political power, which in turn is derived from his theological anthropology."[193] Niebuhr is aware that human nature "is a paradox of finiteness and freedom, and so human capacities to act are limited in various ways; the exercise of power therefore is always a synthesis of "vitality and reason" involving elements of both persuasion and coercion."[194] McCann observes that "this anthropological reflection suggests two things: first, since no one is omnipotent and no one is utterly powerless, the exercise of power inevitably occurs within human community; Second, the kinds of power are as various as the forms of human activity, and likewise irreducible to one another."[195]

Niebuhr's weakness, however, is that he thinks that Jesus' way is not relevant to the social situation of contemporary society. Niebuhr argued, "There is indeed a very vigorous ethical ideal in the gospel of Jesus, but there is no social ethic in the ordinary sense of the word in it, precisely because the ethical ideal is too vigorous and perfect to lend itself to application in the economic and political problems of our day."[196] In other words, the ethic of Jesus cannot work because it underrates human nature, particularly human self-seeking or self-interest by virtue of its proposal of perfect "disinterestedness."

The way of Jesus (that is the way of life) is a powerful antidote to the naked use of power;[197] it is capable of redeeming its brutal, tyrannical, and

---

191. Niebuhr, *The Children of Light and the Children of Darkness*, 10–11.
192. Niebuhr, *The Children of Light and the Children of Darkness*, 71.
193. Dennis P. McCann, *Christian Realism and Liberation Theology: Practical Theologies in Creative Conflict* (Maryknoll, New York: Orbis Books, 1982), 98.
194. McCann, *Christian Realism and Liberation Theology*, 98.
195. McCann, *Christian Realism and Liberation Theology*, 98.
196. Niebuhr, *Love & Justice: Selections form the Shorter Writings of Reinhold*, 30.
197. See also Wink, *Engaging the Powers*, 48.

illegal use. The way of Jesus is a character virtue.[198] Since the powers are not only good[199] but also fallen, the situation calls for setting up structures that check and balance power in the region and the country at large. The existence of such structures is not enough. Christians must pay attention to their vocation. Moltmann suggests some profound principles that those who suffer violence under a brutal regime or a religious establishment such as Northern Nigeria can adopt.

(1) The first principle is to realize that, "The first form of overcoming violence is to tie every exercise of power to the law. From that follows the duty of resistance to any unjust use of power, whether this is illegal, illegitimate, or directed against human rights."

(2) The second principle is to understand that "The principle of 'non-violence' does not exclude the struggle for power when this struggle is involved in binding power to justice."

(3) The third principle is to recognize that "The power of the peoples who suffer under a violent regime is not terrorism but solidarity. Terrorism disqualifies the goals of liberation and justifies only the rule of violence. Violent rule has a weak footing when it is rejected from within the people and is also isolated in foreign affairs by other peoples, and so is beyond both anxiety and trust."

(4) The fourth principle is the need to recognize that "It is possible to overcome violence non-violently. But it can also call for martyrdom. We think of Gandhi and Martin Luther King Jr. We think above all of Christ himself."[200]

The way of Jesus is the way of love, justice, and peace. The Sermon on the Mount calls Christians into a path which responds to evil through a departure from the use of violence. "Christianity," Moltmann writes, "was not able to make Jesus' Sermon on the Mount the basis for abolishing 'the

---

198. Marc H. Tanenbaum, *Religious Values in an Age of Violence* (Milwaukee Wisconsin: Marquette University, 1976), 12. Character virtue produces fruits that yield liberty, socioeconomic and sociopolitical prosperity, and socioreligious happiness for a given society or community. But corruption and obsession with luxury bears fruits, which produce political tyranny, economic poverty, social, and religious misery for a given society or a community.

199. Niebuhr, *Love & Justice*, 32.

200. Moltmann, *Creating a Just Future*, 45.

culture of violence' in the societies in which it spreads. But it did require justification for every application of power—especially by the state."[201] In Northern Nigeria two systems are in tension with each other: aristocracy and democracy. These political systems codify justice differently. For democracy justice is equality; while for oligarchy/aristocracy, justice is what one can produce. Thus justice is inequality.[202]

In a society of ethnic, political, and religious divide like Northern Nigeria, one needs to pay careful attention to the concept of love, justice, and peace. In many senses, these are character virtues which must not be seen as a simple solution to complex-communal problems. In other words, as Niebuhr noted, "Justice requires discriminate judgments between conflicting claims. A Christian justice will be particularly critical of the claims of the self as against the claims of the other. Without this criticism all justice becomes corrupted into a refined form of self-seeking."[203]

In essence, for justice to be genuine and comprehensive, it must embody love. Put another way, justice is more than mere abstention from injuring our fellow human beings. Rather as Isaiah the prophet says, "The fruit of righteousness will be peace, the effect of righteousness will be quietness and confidence forever."[204] The word *righteousness* in some translations uses *justice* and *righteousness* interchangeably. That is righteousness and justice. James D.G. Dunn's study has shown us a richer concept of righteousness and justice.[205] Dunn noted that in the Old Testament righteousness and justice carry a deeper and a thicker meaning than we have realized. In the Old Testament thinking righteousness is a relational concept.[206] He contrasts this with the Graeco Roman understanding where

'[R]ighteousness' and 'justice' were ideal concepts or absolute ethical norms against which particular claims and duties could

---

201. Moltmann, *The Way of Jesus Christ*, 130.
202. Blumenfeld, *The Politics of Paul*, 80.
203. Niebuhr, *Love & Justice*, 28.
204. Isaiah 32:17.
205. See Blumenfeld's detailed discussion of justice in *The Politics of Paul*, 79–80.
206. James D.G. Dunn, *The New Perspective on Paul: Collected Essay* (Germany: Mohr Siebeck, 2005), 200.

be measured. Failure to measure up to this standard involved ethical or criminal liability. Justice functioned as a quasi-divine principle, which had to be sustained and appeased lest disorder and anarchy prevail. We today still echo such a view when we say things like, 'the demands of justice must be satisfied.'[207]

I suppose it is this kind of conception of justice that has influenced some ethicists (for example, Reinhold Niebuhr), who are unwilling to recognize that Jesus' way of life is not "unattainable-high-moral ideals." It is like saying God gives us instructions that He knows cannot work in real life.[208]

Righteousness is not something that an individual has on his or her own, independent of anyone else, as could be the case in the Graeco-Roman concept: "'righteousness' as meeting the standard set by the ideal of 'justice.'" In other words, "in Hebrew thought . . . people are righteous when they meet the claims which others have on them by virtue of their relationship."[209] There are no untouchables when it comes to the matter of righteousness and justice. Israel's judges were therefore expected to act with justice. As Dunn noted, "the responsibility of the judge is to recognize what these various obligations are within the people and to judge them accordingly, clearing the innocent and not deferring to the great (e.g. Ex. 23:7; Lev. 19:15; Isa. 5:23)."

Righteousness and justice have the same connotation—relationship. This is best illustrated in the relationship of Saul and David. Dunn writes, "And Saul confesses that David is more righteous then [sic] he, because David had remained faithful to his responsibility towards Saul as God's anointed, whereas Saul had abused the responsibility of his superior status and power (1 Sam. 24:17)."[210]

In summary, the vertical dimension of righteousness (the obligation of covenant members towards God) was closely bound up with the horizontal dimension of righteousness (the obligation of covenant members

---

207. Dunn, *The New Perspective on Paul*, 200.
208. See Moltmann, *The Way of Jesus Christ*, 127.
209. Dunn, *The New Perspective on Paul*, 200.
210. Dunn, *The New Perspective on Paul*, 201.

toward each other). Responsibility towards one's neighbor arose directly out of Israel's covenant relation with God. That is to say, "one could not be righteous towards God without also being righteous towards one's neighbor; obligation toward God was incomplete when obligation towards the neighbor was deficient."[211] Justice, love, and peace are rich concepts. Rabbi Marc Tanenbaum tells us, justice's "positive conception" includes "economic well-being, intellectual and spiritual growth, philanthropy, and every endeavor that will enable human beings to realize the highest and best in their natures."[212] As Stassen and Moltmann rightly pointed out "justice creates peace." I will also add that justice grounded in genuine love necessitates peace that overcomes ethnic, political, and religious hatreds and tyrannical use of power.

5. Conclusion

Power is good because a good Creator gives it. Therefore it can be rightly and justly exercised. But human greed and its resultant craving for domination have led to the wrong use of power. The evil use of power has heightened human social and economic injustice, particularly in Northern Nigeria. Consequently, violence has become our lot. Violence is a human spirit of evil that has plagued our society. Thus, the search for the roots of Northern Nigeria's contemporary evil has led me to ask the question, "When did Northern Nigeria go wrong?" The New Testament provides a method that allows us to grasp the sources of Northern Nigeria's social and economic injustice, which result in violence.[213]

---

211. Dunn, *The New Perspective on Paul*, 202–3.
212. Rabbi Marc Tanenbaum, *Religious Values in an Age of Violence* (Milwaukee Wis: Marquette, 1976), 5.
213. As quoted by Horsley, *Jesus and the Spiral of Violence*, 22.

CHAPTER 7

An Ethical Framework For Giving Up Violence in Northern Nigeria

We have it in our power to begin the world over again.
—Thomas Paine, 1776

Generally, this research has demonstrated that violence has become part of the culture of Northern Nigeria,[1] that ethnic, political, and religious violence is eroding people's hope and stripping them of their human dignity and honor.[2] But since, as Thomas Paine once said, "We have it in our power to begin the world over again," the culture of violence in Northern can be altered.

The reality is that most individuals or groups in Northern Nigeria want to be able to experience life without fear of molestation or domination. Their cry—like the Psalmist—is "Protect me from men of violence, who devise evil plans in their hearts and stir up war every day."[3] This realization necessitates an examination of the concrete ethical problems of religious, ethnic, and political violence today in Nigeria. From chapter 1 to chapter 6, I sketched the long-term societal experiences in which the problems

---

1. Michael Crowder, *A Short History of Nigeria* (New York, Washington: Frederick A. Praeger Publishers, 1966), 90.
2. About the impact of violence Job writes, "Behold I cry 'violence'! But I get no answer; I shout for help, but there is no justice. He has walled up my way so that I cannot pass; and he has put darkness on my paths. He has stripped my honor from me, and removed the crown from my head. He breaks me down on every side, and I am gone. And he has uprooted my hope like a tree" (Job 19:7).
3. Psalms 140:1–2.

240

The Impact of Ethnic, Political, and Religious Violence on
Northern Nigeria, and a Theological Reflection on Its Healing

engendering violence have developed. In this final chapter, I attempt to develop an ethical framework for a just or an egalitarian—religious, ethnic, and political—community in Northern Nigeria.

In order to do so I pay attention to the way of Jesus. This approach requires asking the questions:

(1) What kind of life together buoys hope, clears the eyes, and draws us out of our ethnic, political, and religious sentiments, which further divide and fragment our society?

(2) What structures of daily life and devotion lend grace to grimy souls, nudge them toward courage, enable sacrifice, and fire the imagination, while millions grieve over diminishing dreams and are inclined to clutch what little—or much—they have?

(3) How, in the end, do we learn, decide, and act prudently in the face of uncertainty and risk, within more limited parameters?

(4) What theology and ethics can engender the breaking in of the kingdom of God?

We cannot pretend we do not know about the in-breaking of God's kingdom, through which God is seeking to reconcile all things to Himself. Jesus Christ set the pace for all peace-lovers to follow. As Richard Bauckham correctly points out:

> Jesus' loving identification with people knew no limits. . . . Because he suffered out of love and loved in his suffering, the crucified Jesus was God's loving solidarity with all who suffer victimization. . . . The risen Jesus is our future. . . . In Jesus, God has given us the kingdom not only as hope for the final future but also to anticipate in the present. As the vision of God's perfect will for his creation it is the inspiration of all Christian efforts to change the world for the better.[4]

Undoubtedly, violence has crippled the Nigerian state.[5] Nigeria's violence is characterized by ethnic, political, and religious oppression

---

4. Richard Bauckham, *The Bible in Politics* (S.P.C.K., 1989), 150.
5. E.E. Osaghae, *Crippled Giant: Nigeria since Independence*, x.

and domination, which in any form are dangerous. As Glen Stassen aptly notes, "Oppression distorts power relationships and tempts the oppressed to either rebellion or collaboration."[6] This study demonstrates that ethnic, political, and religious-instigated violence are embedded in our societies. Violence is everywhere. Yet we are not without hope. Therefore, I propose the following measures for the remaking of Northern Nigeria. The forgoing chapters 1–5 have yielded the conclusions that birth this chapter. They have shown that for us to remake Northern Nigeria all over again we need certain shared understandings, which I delineate in the pages that follow.

1. Biblical Perspectives and Values

The shape of our perspectives and values formed over a lifetime by the images we have accepted and developed are intrinsically linked to our conception of God, of ourselves, and of one another. Biblical perspectives and values are constantly being eroded and challenged because of the manner in which human beings are viewed. Three views of humanity are prevalent in our contemporary world:

(1) Human beings are often seen as machines. This view is prevalent in the industrialized society where demand for the labor force is greater. In such situations the employer values only the employee's strength and energy. That is to say, one's value is based on one's production, skills, or capabilities. This approach reduces human beings to things; as means to an end rather than ends in and of themselves.[7] This leads to all kinds of strategies to induce the human being to perform his or her function. This conception of human beings is not limited to the workplace. Rather, today it has trickled down to other spheres of life. This view is defective because it leaves out the aspect of distribution and exchange. It eclipses the fact that human beings produce, distribute, and exchange social goods.[8]

---

6. Glen Stassen and David Gushee, *Kingdom Ethics*, 458.
7. Millard J. Erickson, *Introducing Christian Doctrine* (Grand Rapids: Baker Book House, 1992), 156.
8. Michael Walzer, *Spheres of Justice: A Defense of Pluralism and Equality* (Basic Books, 1983), Walzer correctly argues that "We come together to share, divide, and exchange"

(2) Humans are sometimes seen as animals; that is, as members of the animal kingdom and derived from some of its highest forms. In other words, just as you can train animals to behave in certain ways, so human beings can also be induced to behave in the ways the trainer wishes; that is, "Human beings can be conditioned" like animals to react in certain ways.[9] Albeit it is true that human beings are social animals, this view reduces human value to that of an animal. Once that happens it is very easy to kill, destroy, or maim other men and women without any moral sense of guilt.

(3) Human beings are seen as powerless and at the mercy of dangerous forces in the world. They are viewed as incapable of transforming their reality, they have no subjective political competence, no power over spiritual and economic forces. If one embraces this view, they become more likely to accept witchcraft accusation as a viable means of eliminating their problems and their fear allows them to either be party to violence or accept it passively.[10]

Of the three problems above, the latter is the most serious problem that Nigeria and much of Africa faces. Thus, studies show, in spite of the religiosity of Nigerians or Africans at large, the fear of evil forces really hinders confidence in God.

In fact, the three views of humanity above are symptoms of the collapse of confidence in God. Confidence in God is crucial because it gives us a moral compass that is able to deliver us from our masks: hiding behind the cloak of religious sanctity, political power and economic power impulses, religious fanaticism, unhealthy religious hatred, and deceptive or pretentious devotion to God.

From a Christian standpoint, biblical perspectives and values come from paying attention to the person and works of Jesus Christ who embodied confidence in God. Jesus exhibited confidence in the reign of God which, as Stassen noted, includes "salvation, peace, joy, justice, and God's presence" as well as healing and returning to God.[11] Biblical perspectives and

---

what we produce (*Spheres of Justice*, 3).
9. Erickson, *Introducing Christian Doctrine*, 156.
10. Erickson, *Introducing Christian Doctrine*, 156.
11. Stassen and Gushee, *Kingdom Ethics*, 28.

values give us a realistic posture and perspective. As James M. Gustafson also aptly argues, part of the facets of *posture* and *perspective* includes "confidence in God, in the goodness of the ultimate power and source of life, and in the power of goodness."[12] That is to say, in Christ, human beings can learn what it means to have confidence in the goodness of God, and in the ultimate power of life. "And surely this conviction evokes and commends a perspective, a posture toward the self, others, and the world."[13] This was the same spirit that influenced Martin Luther King Jr. He saw his oppressors as people who should be pitied not hated; that is, he saw others as brothers and sisters who deserve love not hatred. King was like the "Men of Issachar, who understood the times and knew what Israel should do."[14] Nigeria needs Christian men and women like King, who can discern the times and know what Nigeria should do.

One major difficulty is that people's perspectives and values are often shaped and formed by ideological dispositions that are deeply embedded in unfounded theological conclusions. That is why some religious groups emphasize individual sin to the detriment of other dimensions: For example, corporate sin, structural injustice, and so on. Put in another way, human life has horizontal and vertical dimensions. Failure to recognize the multidimensional nature of human life impairs our grasp of the existence of the multiplicity of social goods. As a result people tend to allow a single social good to gain dominance to the detriment of other equally important social goods. Hence, in order to avoid a one-dimensional conception of human life, there must be a strong emphasis on biblical perspectives and values. These help us to see the multidimensional nature of human life.[15] A one-dimensional perception of human life will obscure the full picture of the impact of violence on that life and experience.

The impact of violence is multidimensional. Violence affects the right to life, community, and participation in meaningful employment. As Klein has correctly pointed out, "African societies are seen as highly differentiated.

---

12. James Gustafson, *Jesus and the Moral Life*, 243, 239.
13. Gustafson, *Jesus and the Moral Life*, 248.
14. 1 Chronicles 12:32.
15. Jürgen Moltmann, *On Human Dignity: Political Theology and Ethics* (Philadelphia: Fortress Press, 1984), 110.

Conflict is constant, and where the oppressed have no legal channel to protest their oppression, violence inevitably results. It takes diverse forms and has diverse effects."[16] My comparative analysis of the impact of ethnic, political, and religious violence confirmed this assertion. It has shown that ethnic, political, and religious violence in Nigeria have shaped people's values and formed their convictions about socio-political, socioeconomic, and socioreligious issues. In other words, the experiences of violence have adversely affected our way of life (see chapter 4). As Willard Swartley observes, "Experience shapes perception and understanding."[17] In essence it shapes people's characters. Therefore, in order to reverse the damage done to people's moral sensibilities, one of the things required is the encouragement of ethnic cooperation and a clear sense of interdependency.

2. Ethnic Cooperation, Solidarity, Participation, and Recognition of Interdependency

Nigeria is host to diverse ethnic, religious, and political groups. In the Northern region, almost all the major ethnic groups in Nigeria are well represented. Therefore, the question is how do we turn our diversities into an advantage instead of a disadvantage? How do we avoid the mistake of the Hutus and the Tutsi in Rwanda where human beings were reduced and likened to *cockroaches and tall trees*, and were therefore mercilessly murdered in cold blood?

The answer to these and many other questions is within reach, because Africans generally place a premium on communal ethics; that is, social ethics. In this case, the emphasis is on communal values and interpersonal relationships. Ironically, this emphasis has not enabled us to eliminate violence because the social ethic has largely ignored toleration of difference.

---

16. J. Abbink, Mirjam de Bruijn, Klaas van Walraven, and NetLibrary Inc. *Rethinking Resistance, Revolt and Violence in African History* (Leiden, the Netherlands; Boston: Brill, 2003), 34.
17. Willard Swartley, *Slavery, Sabbath, War and Women: Case Issues in Biblical Interpretation* (Scottdale, PA: Herald Press, 1983), 62.

We should not let violence force us to abandon the communal sense of the common good. At the same time, we must also not let the one-dimensional pursuit of communal life and social goods overshadow the recognition of difference and the deliberate attempt to tolerate difference and, in fact, celebrate difference. As Hollenbach insists, sharing material goods is not enough.

The common good includes sharing relationships: "The relationships of concern or affection among siblings and friends go deeper than the sharing of such goods as a house and the income. . . . One of the key elements in the common good of a community or society, therefore, is the good of being a community or society. This shared good is immanent within the relationships that bring this community or society into being."[18]

Conflicts that result from difference are very costly. They cost human lives, and they destroy material resources that are desperately needed, those by those who survive the calamities. Thus they can be socio-politically and socio-economically devastating. Therefore I propose that ethnic differences should not be used to our disadvantage. Rather differences should be seen as part and parcel of what makes us human.

The ethnic-social problems of Northern Nigeria and the country at large are very complex. But the most complex problem—overshadowing the rest—is the politics of ethnic and political exclusion. The pursuit of economic power and political control by the aristocrats often leaves the poor masses in a situation of perpetual poverty—hunger and even starvation.

The masses are generally viewed not as full human beings but as second-class citizens—that is, as a means to an end rather than an end in and of themselves.[19] Bill Berkeley writes, "Their only offense is that they are not considered as part of the socioeconomic structure or sociopolitical system. This pathetic situation is almost the same all over Africa. For example, from

---

18. Hollenbach, *The Common Good*, 8, 9.
19. Yusufu Turaki has aptly argued that the problem with Northern Nigeria is the institutionalization of an inferior social status (see *The British Colonial Legacy in Northern Nigeria*, 1993).

1978–1989 a quarter of a million southern Sudanese starved to death."[20] The simple reason was they were not considered to be Sudanese.[21]

Without ethnic cooperation and the recognition of interdependency, this colossal problem will not be dislodged. Marginalization leads to a lack of full participation in the economic, social, political, and cultural development of our society, resulting in political and economic opportunists exacerbating traditional ethnic conflicts over land and cattle. Such unscrupulous opportunists specialize in waging proxy wars. They whip up ethnic conflicts by providing "ethnic militias with high-powered weapons, which give such groups an upper hand over their opponents who still use the traditional sticks and spears to fight." Berkeley further observes, "Ethnic conflicts that used to be fought with sticks, bows, arrows, and spears, and could be settled through negotiations by tribal elders, are now being waged with automatic assault rifles and hand grenades in an escalating spiral of attack and revenge."[22]

Thus I claim encouraging ethnic cooperation and participation in economic and political activities of the country will go a long way toward resolving the problem. Furthermore, as Joseph Luft points out, it must be recognized that "it is not easy to understand or appreciate the ways of other groups. Getting outside of one's group or one's culture is not a bad way to learn about one's own ways. In ordinary intergroup relations, however, opportunities to learn about how the others see your group are not easily created."[23] Thus what is needed is "the development of relations to a point that the processes of give and take, of impression and feedback, may be sustained."[24] That is, "developing acceptance and trust, and the ways of enlarging the view each group has of itself and of the other,"[25] will deliver us from our ethnic, political, and religious stalemates. It will engender

---

20. Billy Berkeley, *The Graves Are Not Yet Full: Race, Tribe and Power in the Heart of Africa* (New York: Basic Books, 2001), 215.
21. Berkeley, *The Graves Are Not Yet Full*, 215.
22. Berkeley, *The Graves Are Not Yet Full*, 216.
23. Joseph Luft, *Of Human Interaction* (Palo Alto: Mayfield Publishing Company, 1969), 83.
24. Luft, *Of Human Interaction*, 83.
25. Luft, *Of Human Interaction*, 82–83.

ethnic cooperation, participation, and recognition of interdependency in Northern Nigeria: It will promote religious freedom.

3. Religious Freedom

Religion has tended to divide us in Northern Nigeria. The enemies of social well-being, economic progress, and efforts toward a sustainable community seem bent on using religion as a scapegoat so that it will continue to mask their destructive activities in the region. Therefore, in order to escape their deception and to unmask their structural and institutional devices, people of faith must realize that genuine pursuit of religion is guarantor of "a robust civil society."[26] This is not to say that religion does not have problems. In the twenty-first century it is indisputably clear that religion has promoted intolerance and hatred. Yet this is not the whole story.

Religious freedom promotes shalom communities. Religion provides resources for toleration of difference and plurality, that is, "the willingness to live with, explore, and honor difference."[27] Northern Nigeria has the potential to encourage this willingness. This potentiality is nowhere clearer than in the common prayer of the region: "Allah ya bamu lafiya da zaman lafiya." That is, "May God give us good health (well being) and peaceful coexistence." However, today the prayer is rearranged thus, "Allah ya bamu zaman lafiya da lafiya." That is, "May God give us peaceful coexistence and good health (or well being)." Notice that the emphasis is on "peaceful coexistence" before "good health (or well being)." This is because whenever violence strikes, healthy men and women, adults and children alike are often murdered. The prayer reveals two things.

(1) It reveals that disease or other natural catastrophes are no more the only cause of death; but also it reveals the lack of peaceful coexistence. In fact, the lack of peaceful coexistence is a leading cause of death in the region. Whether or not you are healthy, once violence strikes, your life can

---

26. Harold Coward and Gordon S. Smith, eds., *Religion and Peacebuilding* (New York: State University of New York Press, 2004), 3.
27. Coward and Smith, *Religion and Peacebuilding*, 2.

248
The Impact of Ethnic, Political, and Religious Violence on
Northern Nigeria, and a Theological Reflection on Its Healing

be instantly taken away. In consequence, peaceful coexistence must become the priority of all religious communities in Northern Nigeria. Religious tolerance is not enough—there is the need for religious freedom. That is, the need to realize that every human being has a right to the religion of their choice; that religion is voluntary and therefore no one should be coerced.

(2) It reveals our mutual vulnerability. Some are more vulnerable than others. Nevertheless, recognition of our mutual vulnerability should enhance our vision for a peaceful society where religious pluralism and diversity are not a threat but a blessing; where "a generous social safety network provides multiple hedges against physical, social, and emotional harm."[28] When Northern Nigeria guarantees religious freedom, politicians will overcome the impasse to social integration, which Reinhold Niebuhr vividly describes. Niebuhr correctly points out that "One of the greatest problems of democratic civilization is how to integrate the life of its various subordinate, ethnic, religious, and economic groups in the community in such a way that the richness and harmony of the whole community will be enhanced and not destroyed by them."[29] Democracy in Nigeria needs the help of religious communities. Although, as Niebuhr further noted,

> Religious ideas and traditions may not be directly involved in the organization of community. But they are the ultimate sources of the moral standards from which political principles are derived. In any case both the foundation and the pinnacle of any cultural structure are religious; for any scheme of values is finally determined by the ultimate answer, which is given to the ultimate question about the meaning of life. . . . Religious-cultural diversity may prove the most potent source of communal discord because varying answers to the final question about the meaning of life produce conflicting answers on all proximate issues of moral order and political

---

28. Clive Calver and Gaten Carey, "Caring for the Vulnerable" in *Toward an Evangelical Public Policy*, edited by Ronald J. Sider and Diane Knippers (Grand Rapids: Baker Books, 2005), 229.
29. Reinhold Niebuhr, *Children of Light and Children of Darkness* (New York: Charles Scribner's Sons, 1960), 124.

organization. . . . Whenever religious and cultural diversity become geographically localized and so marked that interpenetration and mutual contact cease, the peril to the harmony of the community increases.[30]

Religion holds the solution to ethnic, political, and religious conflicts. But in order for religion to be the solution and not the problem it must avoid its one-dimensional disposition. Toleration must not only be rooted in the particular communities' religious insights, but also in the global desire for religious freedom. It is only religious freedom that can give us religious depth in Northern Nigeria and in Africa at large. As Niebuhr suggests,

There is a religious solution of the problem of religious diversity. This solution makes religious and cultural diversity possible within the presuppositions of a free society, without destroying the religious depth of culture. The solution requires a very high form of religious commitment. It demands that each religion, or each version of a single faith, seek to proclaim its highest insights while yet preserving a humble and contrite recognition of the fact that all actual expressions of religious faith are subject to historical contingency and relativity. Such recognition creates a spirit of tolerance and makes any religious or cultural movement hesitant to claim official validity for its form of religion.[31]

A profound religious commitment whose starting point is a high view of God and a humble participation in what God is doing in His creation can bring genuine religious freedom. Niebuhr calls this form of profundity "religious humility." Niebuhr aptly argues that "Religious humility is in perfect accord with the presuppositions of a democratic society. . . . Religious faith ought therefore to be a constant fount of humility."[32] Religious arrogance

---

30. Niebuhr, *Children of Light and Children of Darkness*, 125–6.
31. Niebuhr, *Children of Light and Children of Darkness*, 134–5.
32. Niebuhr, *Children of Light and Children of Darkness*, 135.

has proved destructive in Northern Nigeria. I therefore propose religious humility as a remedy to the present situation of intolerance, discrimination, and perpetual hatred.

It is religious humility that will lead all the religious communities in the region into a community of self-evaluation, self-repenting, self-forgiving, and mutual struggle for justice, love, peace and hope for the future: a community of deliverance. As this study has shown, through ethnic, social, economic, political, and religious control the elite of Northern Nigeria have kept the minorities and the poor under captivity for many centuries, drastically limiting their ability to participate in society as dignified human beings.[33] This reduced participation and muted voice in community life in Northern Nigeria act as both a cause and a result of perpetual poverty and violence. They work to the advantage of those with economic and political powers; and to the tragic disadvantage of the larger society. A high form of religious commitment and freedom will change this social structure to one in which there is justice—economic, political, and social.

4. Socioeconomic and Socio-political Justice

Social justice and political justice are high currencies in the twenty-first century. Yet in situations where socioreligious and sociopolitical structures have been violently broken down, social and political justice are not easy to come by. Much of Northern Nigeria is like most societies organized on what Walzer called "the golden standard":[34] a situation whereby "one good or one set of goods is dominant and determinative of value in all the spheres of distribution. And that good or set of goods is commonly monopolized, its value upheld by the strength and cohesion of its owners."[35] Walzer calls a good a dominant good when an individual who possesses it is able to use it to influence a wide range of other goods: "It is monopolized whenever a

---

33. Michelle Tooley, *Voices of the Voiceless: Women, Justice, and Human Rights in Guatemala* (Scottsdale, PA: Herald Press, 1997), 19.
34. Walzer, *Spheres of Justice*, 10.
35. Walzer, *Spheres of Justice*, 10.

single man or woman, oligarchs—successfully holds it against all rivals."[36] In Northern Nigeria economic wealth and political power have become the twin-dominant-social goods and those who possess their wherewithal to manipulate, exploit, and monopolize other social goods in the region have used them. This band of politicians claim that they are the stakeholders of their communities because of the dominating political and economic power they have acquired in the region.[37] Two things are critical here: dominance and monopoly. As Walzer explained,

> Dominance describes a way of using social goods that is not limited by their intrinsic meanings or that shapes those meanings in its own image. Monopoly describes a way of owning or controlling social goods in order to exploit their dominance.[38]

Walzer's graphic description is very helpful. It shows that the solution to our situation of violence lies in ensuring that we do not allow one single good to gain dominance; because the few who possess it will use it to determine the fate of the masses. Besides, it is important to recognize that underlying the assumption of dominance and monopoly is the belief that if one acquires the one best single social good it will enable one to have unhindered access to many others. Therefore the solution is to realize that there is no dominance that is not incomplete; and that there is no monopoly that is not imperfect.[39] It can therefore be challenged when a better alternative is found. As Walzer argues:

---

36. Walzer, *Spheres of Justice*, 10–11.
37. The reason is because of Nigeria's over dependency on oil as the key source of the Federation Account. In his chapter on "Oil: Maximizing our Opportunities," Alh. Ahmed Joda argued that the major cause of Nigeria's political and social instability is that "we have become totally dependent on oil." He explained that "There is what is called the Federation Account and the Federal Government is a mere Collecting Agent for the account" (see Omafume f. Onoge, ed., *Nigeria: The Way Forward: Proceeding and Policy Recommendations of the First Obafemi Awolowo Foundation Dialoque*).
38. Walzer, *Spheres of Justice*, 11.
39. Walzer, *Spheres of Justice*, 11.

Monopolistic control of a dominant good makes a ruling class, whose members stand atop the distributive system—much as philosophers, claiming to have the wisdom they love, might like to do. But since dominance is always incomplete and monopoly imperfect, the rule of every ruling class is unstable. Other groups in the name of alternative patterns of conversion continually challenge it.[40]

In fact, it is these continuous challenges that contribute to violence in Northern Nigeria. In every given society one finds men and women who try to conceal this truth—the incomplete nature of dominance and the imperfect nature of monopoly. They make claims that seek to legitimize their hold on power and control of the resources. What they are trying to avoid is the competitive, dynamic, and complex nature of social goods. Walzer exposes their underpinning ideology by pertinently observing that

The claim to monopolize a dominant good—when worked up for public purposes—constitutes an ideology. Its standard form is to connect legitimate possession with some set of personal qualities through the medium of a philosophical principle. So (1) aristocracy or the rule of the best, is the principle of those who lay claim to breeding and intelligence: they are commonly the monopolists of landed wealth and familial reputation. (2) Divine supremacy is the principle of those who claim to know the word of God: they are the monopolists of grace and office. (3) Meritocracy, or the career open to talents, is the principle of those who claim to be talented: they are most often the monopolists of education. (4) Free exchange is the principle of those who are ready, or who tell us they are ready, to put their money at risk: they are the monopolists of movable wealth.[41]

---

40. Walzer, *Spheres of Justice*, 11.
41. Walzer, *Spheres of Justice*, 12 (numbering mine).

It is a lack of understanding the underpinning ideology of dominant social goods that oftentimes leads to economic wealth becoming a problem that overshadows the centrality of the kingdom of God. For this reason the Apostle Paul reminded the saints about the need to pay attention to the centrality of the kingdom of God when it comes to the issue of economic concerns:

> For the kingdom of God is not a matter of eating and drinking, but of righteousness, peace, and joy in the Holy Spirit, because anyone who serves Christ in this way is pleasing to God and approved by men. Let us therefore make every effort to do what leads to peace and to mutual edification. Do not destroy the work of God for the sake of food. . . . And everything that does not come from faith is sin.[42]

The source of economic and political injustice is obsession with material possessions. It is the cause as well as the result of violence. Violence arises from a situation of economic and political insecurities, resulting in economic and political uncertainties. In other words, social and economic injustice creates an environment that impacts us enormously. It is under such conditions of social and economic uncertainties that fear and hate become commonplace. Uncertainty, of any kind, breeds fear. As King aptly points out,

> Hate is rooted in fear, and the only cure of fear-hate is love. Our deteriorating international situation is shot through with the lethal darts of fear. Russia fears America, and America fears Russia. Likewise China and India, and the Israelis and the Arabs. These fears include another's aggression, scientific and technological supremacy, and economic power, and our own loss of status and power. Is not fear one of the major causes of war? We say that war is a consequence of hate, but close

---

42. Romans 14:19–20, 23.

scrutiny reveals this sequence: first fear, then hate, then war, and finally deeper hatred.[43]

In Northern Nigeria fear takes different shapes: Selfish political and economic ambitions whip up and prompt striving for power and control over other people. The interactions of selfish political and economic ambitions generate a chain of reactions that play into the fear of losing one's status quo, and as King so eloquently describes, that fear drives us crazy, resulting in a violent disposition toward each other. Therefore, it is important that human beings realize that fear and hate often lead to more economic and political uncertainties and injustices. Wherever there is fear, treacherous people often erect a shelter of lies, deceit, and all kinds of wrongdoing—resulting in violence. But what does economic and political justice mean?

(1) It means just production, exchange, and distribution of the resources that make it possible for everyone in a particular region to participate meaningfully in the socioeconomic and sociopolitical activities of the region and the country at large.

(2) It means a comprehensive and holistic approach to humans' desperate, life-affecting needs. Biblically speaking, justice originates with the God and Father of all creation. As J. Milburn Thompson observes, "A Christian perspective is grounded in the conviction that God is sovereign and that God's rule is loving and just."[44]

This perspective pays attention to the fact that God created all human beings in God's own image and likeness. It recognizes that God has equally endowed every one of us with an intrinsic dignity and an infinite value. This human dignity is fostered and developed in community. Humanity is God's people—a family—called to love and care for one another and for the earth. As co-creators with God, human beings are responsible for creating a just or egalitarian community, which is advantageous to the actualization

---

43. Martin Luther King Jr. *Strength to Love* (New York: Harper & Row, 1963), 120.
44. J. Milburn Thompson, *Justice and Peace: A Christian Primer* (Maryknoll, New York: Orbis Books, 2003), 2.

of each person's potential.[45] It is against such understanding that Christians insist that politics, economics, and social policies are radically important.

In summary, I have shown that the meshing of political and economic power is a major key to the injustices in Nigeria. I have shown that a few in Nigeria grab as much power as they can, and that domination by these powerful elite is a key to the violence. Because of this, we need legally instituted checks and balances against the concentration of power in the hands of a few. We need that in the economic system, guarding against concentrating the economic power in the hands of a few, and in the political system, guarding against domination by any one elite group. And churches need to develop practices of listening to all members (1 Cor. 14:29–33) so churches themselves practice checks and balances against concentration of power in the hands of only a few.[46]

In other words, a realistic understanding of justice, with a realistic understanding of human nature, requires that justice be not only an ideal, but be built into the way power is distributed, and the way checks and balances are built into the system of governance, the system of the economy and the system of the churches. Justice fosters righteous relations.[47] Solid and just economic policies and structures encourage as well as guarantee right relationship.

5. Economic Justice

Nigeria—and Africa at large—needs to inculcate economic justice. That is one of the dimensions that will guarantee viable and sustainable economy.

---

45. Thompson, *Justice and Peace: A Christian Primer*, 2.

46. See John Howard Yoder, *Body Politics: Five Practices of the Christian Community before the Watching World* (Scottdale, PA: Herald Press, 2001).

47. Glen Stassen, *Living the Sermon on the Mount: A Practical Hope for Grace and Deliverance* (Jossey-Bass, 2006), 52. As Stassen rightly explains, "This is why the hungry and the thirsty hunger and thirst for righteousness; they yearn bodily for the kind of justice that restores them to community where they can eat and drink. It may be that only those readers who have experienced injustice, hunger, and exclusion from community can fully experience the significance of what the Bible means by justice. But they are the kind of people who especially flock to Jesus."

Sustainable economy encompasses the issue of ecological sustainability, equity (including gender equality), agricultural expansion, and democratization.

Nigerian government officials have to rediscover the workings of economic principles, which enable people to make decisions with some assurance despite factual uncertainty.[48] They must realize that economic issues are not beyond morality. Rather they require a fundamental ethical base to function adequately for the benefit of the citizenry. Wogaman writes, "Economic policies that do not encourage economic reforms have continued to breed grinding poverty. Such repressive policies are inevitable in a context of serious internal disorder, political corruption, and economic stagnation."[49] Such policies grounded in ulterior motives end up only granting opportunity for corrupt government officials to enrich themselves. But with social and political viability, our region will become a united enabling environment for political order and will foster adequate infrastructures, a calculable law and administration, and consistent, market-facilitating economic policies. This will transform the present situation of a bloated, overextended state of limited capacity that has been given to disorder, capricious management, and faulty policy.[50] Economic justice emerges from a high view of persons held by those who are in power and by those who are not.[51]

The church in Nigeria, and indeed Africa at large, is the hope of the poor. The church is the holistic voice of the masses. Therefore the Church, in the scheme of things, should pay attention to the economic policies of our nations because of the devastating effect they have on its lay members and clergy. The church should encourage government towards pro-pluralism, public accountability, respect for the rule of law, value for human rights, and market principles that take the plight of the poor and other most vulnerable members of our society seriously.[52] In this case, it is not enough to

48. J. Philip Wogaman, *The Great Economic Debate: An Ethical Analysis* (Philadelphia: The Westminster Press, 1977), 8.
49. Wogaman, *The Great Economic Debate: An Ethical Analysis*, 12.
50. See Douglas Hurd, the British Secretary of State for Foreign and Commonwealth Affairs' speech of June 1990 as cited by Richard Sandbrook, *The Politics of African's Economic Recovery* (Cambridge: Cambridge University Press, 1993), 3.
51. Wogaman, *The Great Economic Debate: An Ethical Analysis*, 11.
52. See Ronald Sider, *Rich Christians in an Age of Hunger: Moving from Affluence to*

preach about the political decadence but to exhort, rebuke and encourage politicians to do good to their poor communities. As Richard Sandbrook reminds us, "political and economic reform is expected not only to revive stagnant economies, but also to foster equity, satisfy basic needs, be environmentally sustainable, promote decentralization, and nurture popular sovereignty."[53] Yet without a high view of people, the lot of the poor will not be improved. Economic justice, as Sider defines it, is the realization that "God wants all people to have access to the productive resources so that they will be able to earn a living."[54] That is justice for everyone—for the privileged few and for the disadvantaged masses—in Northern Nigeria. It is the eradication of the barriers and structures that continue to create "economic stagnation, mass unemployment, mass poverty, marked inequalities, political oppression, and widespread corruption, resulting in local and foreign economic domination."[55]

The church has a vital role to play in the scheme of things. The church can only play its role well if it overcomes the temptation to align itself with the powerful. History, they say, always repeats itself. Perhaps this explains why today the church in Nigeria faces challenges more than ever before. In northern Nigeria, we are witnessing a terrible phenomenon. Consumerism is at its peak. We see churches collecting several offerings in a single church service. On December 25, 2005, I was reliably told that a church collected six offerings at the Christmas service. How can such a church escape the temptation or the challenge of consumerism in our society? How can such a church challenge its members who are obsessed with a desire to own more and more material possessions collectively as a church body, rather than facilitating the distribution of goods to the poor? The situation is so serious that most Churches pay little or no attention to Jesus' warning about possessions.[56] As Sider notes, "An abundance of possessions can easily lead us to

Generosity (Dallas: Word Publishers, 2000), 95.

53. Richard Sandbrook, *The Politics of African's Economic Recovery* (Cambridge; New York: Cambridge University Press, 1993), 121.

54. Sider, *Rich Christians in an Age of Hunger*, 94.

55. Sandbrook, *The Politics of African's Economic Recovery*, 121.

56. Sider, *Rich Christian in an Age of Hunger*, 96.

forget that God is the source of all good."[57] Several offerings at one service
unless taken for the benefit of the marginalized validate church greed. A
greedy Church will miss its focus. As Robert Webber and Rodney Clapp
write, "The focus is not on seeing the gospel proclaimed, seeing a community of God's people built, seeing the hungry and poor served. Instead,
the focus is on a self-fulfillment that supposedly will be attained apart from
other people."[58] This attitude trickles down to other spheres of church life.
It leads to a parochial and limited view of the Church's spheres of influence.
As Webber and Clapp further argue:

> A narrow, individualistic understanding of faith and a narrow
> view of politics make an unhappy combination. Their
> combination means that Christians concerned for the political
> and social health of the world bypass the church. They go
> directly to the only political bodies they can imagine—parties,
> lobbies, and governmental agencies. And in the process they
> put the gospel in the service of a particular political agenda.[59]

In order to escape a one-dimensional understanding of faith and economic life, it must be recognized that economic issues need communal
understanding. As Moltmann observed, "Persons can only be persons in
community; the community can only be free in its personal members."[60]
Economic principles without a good sense of community will not bring
the desired result of holistic transformation of society. Moltmann aptly
pointed out, "A person is a social being." Therefore, "Individualized people
can easily be dominated by political and economic forces. There is only resistance for the purpose of protecting personal human dignity if people join
together in communities and decide their lives socially for themselves."[61]
Generally, Christian economic theology in Northern Nigeria should have

---

57. Sider, *Rich Christians in an Age of Hunger*, 95.
58. Robert E. Webber and Rodney Clapp, *People of the Truth: The Power of the Worshiping Community in the Modern World* (San Francisco: Harper and Row, 1988), 8.
59. Webber and Clapp, *People of the Truth*, 9.
60. Moltmann, *On Human Dignity*, 332.
61. Moltmann, *On Human Dignity*, 333.

a sense of economically critical theology aiming at radical transformation of the political and social *status quo.* Yes, this is one of the keys that will unlock the windows of genuine ethnic, religious, and political engagement between Christians and non-Christians alike in Northern Nigeria.

The greatest weapon against religious, ethnic, and political violence is truth-telling. Religious, ethnic, and political violence create an environment whereby unfaithfulness increases and by extension a craving for violence as a way of cutting corners to disguise social, economic, and political injustice.[62] We need resources for action on behalf of truth, love, justice, and peace. Those resources include, among other things, a robust civil society, active and genuine non-governmental organizations (NGOs), and religious communities that are grounded in a sense of the Fatherhood of God to all God's creation. The sort of NGOs that will struggle for truth, love, justice, and peace are those that do not exclude, but whose work cuts across ethnic barriers, religious creeds, regional sentiment, and social barriers.[63] Emphasis on inclusion will go a long way in thwarting violence against each other in the region. What we need are people who respect the law; respect each other's religion; people who are ready to do whatever it takes to ensure that what they are doing is for the interest and well-being of humanity and the common good of all; people who do not slander anyone; people who are peaceable and considerate; people who show genuine interest in the affairs of their fellow men and women; people who do not live in malice and envy; people who are willing to repent, be forgiven as well as forgive themselves and others; people who reciprocate the kindness and love of God our Lord and Savior. In short, people who live as those who have been saved from the vicious cycle of "being hated and hating one another."[64]

In summary, it is extraordinarily important that Northern Nigeria elite see other human beings as an end in and of themselves rather than a means to an end! This approach will enable us to practice the way of Jesus Christ: inclusion. As the late Pope John Paul II once said, "All Nigerians must work

---

62. Proverbs 13:2.
63. Okwudiba NNoli, *Ethnic Politics in Nigeria* (Enugu, Nigeria: Fourth Dimension Publishers, 1980), 285.
64. Titus 3:1–4, 14.

to rid society of everything that offends the dignity of the human person
or violates human rights." Government must see NGOs as partners in the
effort to enhance the effectiveness of early warning. Early warning must
be listened to and must be converted into effective action, and preventive
diplomacy must be employed. Ethnic bigotry, gender hostility, religious
hatred, and political exclusion should be discouraged by markedly advanc-
ing the vision of an egalitarian society. Both Christians and non-Christians
should intensify efforts to boost religious and communal re-orientation and
to dislodge all forms of discrimination and intolerance in the twenty-first
century. Sider summarizes the following biblical norm that should guide
our political thinking:

(1) Protect the sanctity of life;

(2) Treasure religious and political freedom;

(3) Imitate God's special concern for the poor;

(4) Strengthen wholesome families;

(5) Work for peace in the world;

(6) Care for creation;

(7) Seek economic justice for everyone so that all people have access to
the productive resources they need to earn their own way and be
dignified participants in their community.[65]

President Olusegun Obasanjo of Nigeria made a point that is analogous
to the above summary in his 46th Independent Day speech, Sunday October
1, 2006,

> We must collectively resolve to fight political corruption and
> violence, election manipulation, the imposition of candidates,
> the culture of empty politicking, and the marginalization of
> women in the power and political process. We must fight those
> that continue to see our today and tomorrow with the lenses of
> our dark past; people with little to contribute to easing our pain
> and building a holistic and sustainable foundation for posterity.[66]

---

65. Ron Sider, "A Tough Call," *PRISM*, Vol. 7, No. 5 September/October 2000, 24.
66. President Olusegun Obasanjo: *"Time to Reject Pseudo Leaders,"* www.gamji.com

However, Obasanjo did not follow through what he said above. He and his political party used the nation's security agencies to harass, intimidate, and coerce the electorates into voting candidates that are not popular or the people choice. As a result, massive rigging, irregularities, violence, and killing marred the April 17, 2007 elections. The national newspapers reported that 52 persons were killed on the first day (April 14, 2007) of the elections. Violence has become the ethos of our nation. No wonder most people think that nonviolence is a simplistic approach to a very dicey social and political situation. In the next section, I argue that nonviolence works in different contexts of distressing and disturbing political and social conditions.

6. Redemptive Examples of the Way of Jesus: Practicing Nonviolent Direct Action in Various Contexts

> *Together we shall save our planet, or together we shall perish in its flames.*
>
> —John F. Kennedy

Violence is a disease of the heart; it is rooted in the fear that casts out love; it cannot be divorced from our selfishness and pride. That is why, as Storey says, "we cannot be Christ's peacemakers in this land unless our inward spirits begin to match our outward ideals. People must be able to look at how we live and say: *Perhaps it is possible for people to repent of their divisions, to come together and work and pray and struggle together, and to live a common life.*"[67] Christ's peacemakers must be signs of hope. Like Christ, their Savior and Lord, they must be what they proclaim and believe. This means, we need to model the way of Jesus—nonviolence—in our context. My point here is that nonviolence works and it is proliferating in our contemporary society. That is to say, while violence creates widespread fear and terror throughout the global community, nonviolence makes possible the creation

---

Sunday, October 1, 2006, 4.
67. Storey, *With Christ in the Crucible*, 13.

of widespread hope and peace in a world threatened by global violence in all its components.[68]

In a world where the rich acquire political power and it becomes a tool with which they destroy humanity and the ecosystem, nonviolence must be the path to take. Nonviolence, as illustrated in the life, ministry, death, and resurrection of Jesus, has been found to work in varying degrees and in different contexts of human experiences of evil, injustice, and suffering in the global community. Nonviolence is not an individualistic endeavor: Nonviolent engagement is communal. The movement for peace in the West has largely been necessitated by the threat of war.[69] It was in the midst of this threat that in 1961 John F. Kennedy said, "Together we shall save our planet, or together we shall perish in its flames."[70] Peace was believed to make possible reform, and the nineteenth century was an age of reform in Europe and America.

The struggle to abolish war was a significant aspect of the peace movement. This struggle led to the formation of peace societies in England, Germany, France, Scandinavia, Italy, Austria, Switzerland, the Netherlands, and the United States.[71] Since then, nonviolence has continued to unseat authoritarian and tyrannical regimes in different contexts.

In Northern Nigeria, Christians are wrestling with the question of turning the other cheek. What Prof. Ogbu Kalu calls, "The third slap."[72] The conclusion of some pastors and laities is that we have turned both cheeks and now we have no more cheek to turn. The basis of this argument lies in the belief that Jesus taught passivity. So they ask the "what if" questions that lead them to the conclusion just cited. But as Wink correctly argues, Jesus did not teach passivity. In fact, "Jesus did not forbid self-defense. He taught,

---

68. Glen H. Stassen, *Just Peacemaking: Transforming Initiatives for Justice and Peace* (Louisville, PA: Westminster/ John Knox Press, 1992), 137–145; see also Daniel Buttery, *Christian Peacemaking: From Heritage to Hope* (Valley Forge, PA: Judson Press, 1994).
69. Glen H. Stassen, et al., *Just Peacemaking: Ten Practices for Abolishing War* (Ohio: The Pilgrim Press, 1998), 3.
70. John F. Kennedy, Address to the General Assembly of the United Nations, September 25, 1961 in Cummings and Wise, *Democracy under Pressure*, 655.
71. Roland H. Bainton, *Christian Attitudes Toward War and Peace: A Historical Survey and Critical Re-evaluation* (Nashville: Abingdon 1960), 191.
72. Ogbu Kalu, "Dissertation evaluation report," to Center of Advanced Theological Studies (CATS) Office, March 27, 2007.

not nonresistance, but nonviolence."[73] Because of the complex nature of a violent situation, Wink suggests, "Christians are called to nonviolence, unequivocally. They are to engage evil nonviolently, in every circumstance, without exception. They must lean all their weight on divine grace, trusting that the Holy Spirit will reveal the third way not evident in the situation."[74] What many victims need to realize is "Nonviolence threatens the powerful because it would require relinquishing unjust advantage. But the powerless may fear it just as much, for it appears to nullify their hopes of assuming power by the very means used to keep them subjugated: violence."[75] This truth is nowhere exemplified as profoundly as in the life of Martin Luther King, Jr. However, Malcolm X did not follow in King's wake.

The past and present of nonviolence is best illustrated in the life of four people: Leo Tolstoy in his nonviolent direct action in Russia; Gandhi, in his struggle for independence in India (and justice in South Africa); King in his struggle for civil rights in the United States; and Desmond Tutu's role in the struggle against the infamous policies of apartheid in South Africa. Wink is right, "A people kept ignorant of the existence of the history of nonviolence will naturally believe that it is impractical and unrealistic."[76] Or as one of my respondents said, "Nonviolence is too simplistic to solve a complex problem." This is why I rehearse the redemptive examples of the workability of nonviolence in societies of unimaginable suffering and contradictions. The years of violence have resulted in the victims of centuries of injustice concluding that nonviolence is no longer feasible. But the examples that follow will demonstrate that nonviolence is alive and well!

6.1 Leo Tolstoy: Love as the Path beyond Violence: Russian Christian Context

In Russia and in much of the world, Leo Tolstoy is remembered as an ardent advocate of nonviolence. He was a member of the Russian Orthodox Church until the church excommunicated him.[77] Tolstoy had substantial

---

73. Wink, *Engaging the Powers*, 233.
74. Wink, *Engaging the Powers*, 237.
75. Wink, *Engaging the Powers*, 239.
76. Wink, *Engaging the Powers*, 243.
77. Lee Griffith, *The War on Terrorism and the Terror of God* (Grand Rapid: Wm. B.

influence on the thought and work of Gandhi and all those Gandhi has influenced, for example, King and Tutu.

Tolstoy's biography is full of incredible contradictions reflecting what he faced in his personal struggle with despair.[78] As Lee Griffith explains,

> It was only after Tolstoy had been born into nobility, joined the army, and realized considerable success as a novelist that he experienced a crisis that caused him to reflect anew on questions concerning God, love, community, and nonviolence. Tolstoy's crisis of despair did not come *despite* his success but *because* of success. As early as 1863, soon after his marriage to Sofya, there were hints that Tolstoy saw something illusory in the worldly standards of happiness and success. What started as terror at the thought of losing happiness turned into despair in the midst of success. Feeling his suicidal potential, Tolstoy gave up hunting trips so as not to be near guns. He wrote in his *Confession*, "All this was happening to me at a time when I was surrounded on all sides by what is considered complete happiness: I was not yet fifty, I had a kind, loving, and beloved wife, lovely children, and a large estate that was growing and expanding with no effort on my part."[79]

Violence is fostered by selfish ambition, envy, and the pursuit of happiness. Tolstoy's experiences help us to realize that this is true. Thus Tolstoy renounces the ethical dualism and demonizing of others that is itself a powerful contributor to violence. Self-criticism enables us to engage in nonviolence. Griffith observes that "even if one believes that some people are essentially evil (which Tolstoy did not), and even if one believes that the Gospel allows for violence in response to evil (which Tolstoy did not) . . .

Eerdmans Publishing Company, 2002), 253.

78. Henri Troyat, *Tolstoy*, trans. Nancy Amphious (Garden City, NY: Doubleday, 1967), 608.

79. Originally cited by David Edwards, *Burning All Illusions: A Guide to Personal and Political Freedom* (Boston: South End Press, 1996), 130 cited by Griffith, *The War on Terrorism and the Terror of God*, 2002), 253.

it is absolutely impossible to find that safe and indubitable sign by which a malefactor may be unerringly told from one who is not."[80] According to Griffith, "Tolstoy perceived the path of love as the one hope by which individuals and the human community could be freed from the violence associated with the self interested pursuit of happiness."[81]

While Tolstoy was fond of the word "non-resistance," it is clear that he did not view the concept as fostering passivity. Indeed, movement and engagement are central features of Tolstoy's ethic. Tolstoy believes "virtue cannot be accumulated and stored, but it is only realized in the movement toward love."[82]

Tolstoy described a certain fear that cripples its victims and makes them seek a way of escape. For example, Tolstoy says, "I think that I shall die and that my life will come to an end; I feel sorry for myself and this thought frightens and torments me."[83] The fear of the unknown, Tolstoy explains, forces people to be under foreign influence: "What most people want is not that their consciousness should work correctly; it is that their actions should appear to them to be just. It is for this end that they use substances which disturb the correct working of their consciousness."[84] In sum it is the lack of genuine love that keeps people in bondage, resulting in insecurity and frustration. Therefore for Tolstoy, love should be our watchword. For example, he argues, "The ideal is to love our enemies and those that hate us." According to him, this is a "precept indicating a level it is quite possible for us to keep to; it is to do no harm to our enemies, to speak well of them, not to make distinctions between them and our fellow citizens."[85] Tolstoy consistently argues that love is the basis of nonviolence.

Consequently, Tolstoy consistently condemned war both at home and abroad. In the chaotic Russian environment during and after the Russo-Japanese war, Tolstoy consistently denounced the methods of both the

---

80. Griffith, *The War on Terrorism and the Terror of God*, 255.
81. Griffith, *The War on Terrorism and the Terror of God*, 255.
82. Griffith, *The War on Terrorism and the Terror of God*, 256.
83. Leo Tolstoy, *The Lion and the Honeycomb: The Religious Writings of Tolstoy*, A.N. Wilson, ed., (San Francisco: Harper Row Publishers, 1987), 52.
84. Tolstoy, *The Lion and the Honeycomb*, 56.
85. Tolstoy, *The Lion and the Honeycomb*, 82.

terrorist revolutionaries and the counterterrorists set loose by the Tsar.[86] Griffith tells us,

> [T]he pursuit of success, power, and security only has the potential to divide humanity into opposing forces, nation states, terrorists and counterterrorists, and at the extreme, individuals segregated one from another, loudly proclaiming with gun in hand that they are free. Tolstoy taught the opposing forces are fated to be together, united not by some powerful emperor, but by the renunciation of power. It is the will of God, the will of love, that "we cannot be saved separately; we must be saved all together."[87]

This is the point John F. Kennedy made in his 1961 speech to the United Nations quoted above. Peace is better accomplished in community with others. But peace is also accomplished in self-criticism and being able to say that the violence must stop with me. Tolstoy's vision defied and broke away from Eastern beliefs in pantheism (all is God) to panentheism (all in God).[88]

6.2 Mohandas K. Gandhi's Path beyond Violence: Indian Context

The well-known leaders who have emphasized the concept of nonviolent direct action—Jesus, Mohandas K. Gandhi, Martin Luther King Jr., and a host of others—started with an understanding of (to borrow Stassen's terms), God's *compassionate love* and *delivering justice*. Gandhi writes,

> Satyagraha differs from Passive Resistance as the North Pole from the South. The latter has been conceived as a weapon of the weak and does not exclude the use of physical force

---

86. Griffith, *The War on Terrorism and the Terror of God*, 257.
87. Griffith, *The War on Terrorism and the Terror of God*, 258.
88. Richard F. Gustafson, *Leo Tolstoy, Resident and Stranger: A Study in Fiction and Theology* (Princeton University Press, 1986), 100–101.

or violence for the purpose of gaining one's end, whereas the former has been conceived as a weapon of the strongest and excludes the use of violence in any shape or form. The term *Satyagraha* was coined by me in South Africa to express the force that the Indians there used for full eight years and it was coined in order to distinguish it from the movement then going on in the United Kingdom and South Africa under the name of Passive Resistance.[89]

Gandhi believed that "A meek submission when one is chafing under a disability or a grievance which one would gladly see removed, not only does not make for unity, but makes the weak party acid, angry, and prepares him for an opportunity to explode. By allying myself with the weak party, by teaching him direct, firm, but harmless action, I make him feel strong and capable of defying the physical might. He feels braced for the struggle, regains confidence in himself and knowing that the remedy lies with himself, ceases to harbor the spirit of revenge, and learns to be satisfied with a redress of the wrong he is seeking to remedy."[90]

Like Tolstoy, Gandhi emphasized the principle of love. In 1930 Gandhi wrote his speech entitled "My Faith in Nonviolence" in which he said,

I have found that life persists in the midst of destruction and, therefore, there must be a higher law than that of destruction. Only under that law would a well-ordered society be intelligible and life worth living. And if that is the law of life, we have to work it out in daily life. . . . I have found, however, that this law of love has answered as the law of destruction has never done.[91]

---

89. Mohnadas Karamchand Gandhi, *Non-violent Resistance (Satyagraha)* (New York: Schocken Books, 1951), 6.
90. Gandhi, *Non-violent Resistance*, 110.
91. For the full text of this quote see Howard Zinn, editor, *The Power of Nonviolence: Writings by an Advocate of Peace* (Boston: Beacon Press, 2002), 45–46.

The Impact of Ethnic, Political, and Religious Violence on
Northern Nigeria, and a Theological Reflection on Its Healing

268

It is this law of love that shows that Gandhi built his nonviolence stance on the character of God. Gandhi showed that those who think nonviolence is simplistic are expressing their ignorance of the depth of nonviolence. He points out that

> It takes a strenuous course of training to attain to a mental state of nonviolence. In daily life it has to be a course of discipline, though one may not like it—like, for instance, the life of a soldier. But I agree that, unless there is a hearty cooperation of the mind, the mere outward observance will be simply a mark, harmful both to the man himself and to others. . . . Nonviolence is a weapon of the strong. With the weak it might easily be hypocrisy. Fear and love are contradictory terms. Love wrestles with the world as with the self and ultimately gains a mastery over all other feelings.[92]

Gandhi's conclusion is that "The law of love will work, just as the law of gravitation will work, whether we accept it or not. Just as a scientist will work wonders out of various applications of the law of nature, even so a man who applies the law of love with scientific precision can work greater wonders."[93] So Gandhi's starting point was the character of God: justice and love. That is the communicable attribute of God, which includes, among other things, love, peace, compassion, and justice. Some authors have suggested that Gandhi learned the principle of love through comparing the life of Jesus and that of the Buddha. Gandhi found a symbiosis between Jesus and the Buddha. He seeks to know the teaching of Jesus and the Buddha by asking this important question:

> What was the larger symbioses that Buddha and Christ preached? Buddha fearlessly carried the war into the enemy's camp and brought down on its knees an arrogant priesthood. Christ drove out the moneychangers from the temple of

---

92. Zinn, *The Power of Nonviolence*, 46.
93. Zinn, *The Power of Nonviolence*, 46.

Jerusalem and drew down curses from Heaven upon the hypocrites and the Pharisees. Both were for intensely direct action. But even as Buddha and Christ chastised they showed unmistakable gentleness and love behind every action of theirs. They would not raise a finger against their enemies, but would gladly surrender themselves rather than the truth for which they lived. Buddha would have died resisting the priesthood, if the majesty of his love had not proved to be equal to the task of bending the priesthood. Christ died on the cross with a crown of thorns on his head defying the might of a whole empire. And if I raise resistances of a non-violent character I simply and humbly follow in the footsteps of the great teachers named by my critic.[94]

Despite the fact that Gandhi has shown the world that nonviolence works (nonviolent direct action brought colonialism down in India), we still find people in Northern Nigeria who think that nonviolence is very irrational and simplistic approach to a complex situation.[95] As a matter of fact, we find people who claim faith in a loving God using this faith as a launch pad for intolerance and war. Those who argue that nonviolence is a simplistic approach to a complex problem reveal certain truths:

(1) This argument indicates a lack of seeing nonviolence from the proper perspective. I believe that if nonviolence is understood from the standpoint of God's character, power, and justice, nonviolence will be welcomed not only by Christians but also by non-Christians because it supports democracy and religious ideals.[96]

(2) Nonviolence needs grounding in a faith community. Gandhi learned how to control his anger from the Hindu tradition. For the Church, the advice of Saint Jude is a profound proposal for a nonviolent direct action:

---

94. Mohnadas Karamchand Gandhi, *Non-violent Resistance (Satyagraha)* (New York: Schocken Books, 1951), 111–112.
95. Some of my respondents say that nonviolence will not work in our situation.
96. P.R. Râegamey, *Nonviolence and the Christian Conscience* (New York, Herder and Herder, 1966), 12.

> But you, beloved, building yourselves up on your most holy
> faith; praying in the Holy Spirit; keep yourselves in the love of
> God, waiting anxiously for the mercy of our Lord Jesus Christ
> to eternal life. And mercy on some who doubt; save others,
> snatching them out of the fire; and on some have mercy with
> fear, hating even the garment polluted by the flesh.[97]

In order to be effective in peacemaking, the Church has to build itself
up in the most holy faith and constantly pray in the Holy Spirit. It must
keep itself in God's love and consistently wait for the mercy of our Lord
Jesus Christ as well as being merciful to those who doubt the workability of
nonviolent direct action in our Northern Nigerian context.

(3) Nonviolence is not something that happens on the spur of the
moment. It takes training, time, and persistence. As Gandhi shows, it is
holistic; our whole being is involved in this effort: mind, body, and soul.
Hence there has to be a mental acceptance of the reliability of nonviolence
and emotional commitment to its principles.

6.3 Dorothy Day and the Path of Nonviolence: Roman Catholic Feminist Context

Dorothy Day is of the Roman Catholic background. Day understood
nonviolence not only as an expression of her discipleship to Christ but also
as her commitment to a hurting world. Put simply, Day's approach to nonviolence was simultaneously a refusal to do injury to any other person while
actively resisting all the violence engendered by the powers and authorities
by what Day calls, "this filthy, rotten system." Day did not view herself as
naturally predisposed to acts of resistance. Roberts Coles writes, "She never
gave Satan the mighty authority some writers have, but she knew there was
an unavoidable struggle between good and evil even in those who have
come to believe in the saving of Jesus. At times, as she talked about her
life, she seemed engrossed with *His life,* so that a listener felt her passion

---

97. Jude vs. 20–23.

responding to the Gospels."[98] Jesus' life of compassion captivated Day's life. Day explains:

> I don't only think of the Passion as the Crucifixion. I think of His whole life as "the Passion." I don't mean to become a theologian now; I have never been good at theology. My mind isn't abstract enough. But when I think of Jesus I think of someone who was constantly passionate; I think of all His experiences as part of the Passion: the stories He told, the miracles He performed, the sermons He delivered, the suffering He endured, the death He experienced. His whole life was a Passion—the energy, the love, the attention He gave to so many people, to friends and enemies alike.[99]

As a virtuous ethicist Day construed her ethic within Jesus' love and compassion toward the victims of circumstances. Thus June O'Connor writes, "Dorothy Day's ethic is an ethic of personal care and social criticism grounded in the values of justice and the will to love."[100] In her chapter on "The Radical: On Power, Poverty, and Pacifism" O'Connor writes,

> Dorothy Day's self-understanding as a radical endured throughout her life. Although the revolutionary consciousness she found compelling in her twenties was modified, due to her conversion, with a shift from a community world view to a Catholic Christian world view, an underlying continuity between these two historical periods and competing world views can be seen in her ethical concerns and social change. In both contexts, Dorothy was drawn to work for radical social change. As a Catholic Worker she considered herself one a "new social order" (HH, 239) marked by anarchism, pacifism,

---

98. Robert Coles, *Dorothy Day: Radical Devotion* (New York: A Merloyd Lawrence Book, 2987), 117.
99. Coles, *Dorothy Day*, 117.
100. June O'Connor, *The Moral Vision of Dorothy Day: A Feminist Perspective* (New York: Crossroad, 1991), 66.

and the works of mercy. This ambitious goal brought her into conflict with the giant power of the state, with here chosen church, and even with her Catholic Worker associates.[101]

The underpinning stance Day adopted is based on the Sermon on the Mount. On that count she reasoned that the "evildoer" who must not be resisted in Matthew 5 is another human being. Do not strike back. Do not seek retribution. Do not rely on the tools of the "evildoer." On the contrary, the "devil" that must be resisted is not a human being but a power that represents the malignant spirit of the age.[102] Day realized that "the mode of resistance includes the willingness to bear suffering rather than to inflict it." In nonviolence one must be willing to go out of one's comfort zone. This is because we live in a world where things will not be normal, a world of contradictions. Day's realization of this fact helped her to face social injustice nonviolently.[103]

Day was influenced by the work of Peter Maurin, an itinerant philosopher of peasant background from France. As Griffith notes, Day and Maurin saw mercy and justice as the two crucial components not only of their discipleship but also to their service to humanity. As a result, with the support of a small community, they started hospitality houses and free kitchens in response to the needs of the homeless and the hungry.[104] Griffith aptly points out:

> The principles of nonviolent resistance maintain that evil and terror can never be defeated once and for all in "a war to end all wars" or in a decisive "war on terrorism." What are required instead are daily acts of resistance, beginning first with resistance to the terror and lack of love within oneself.[105]

---

101. O'Connor, *The Moral Vision of Dorothy Day*, 88.
102. Griffith, *The War on Terrorism and the Terror of God*, 259.
103. Griffith, *The War on Terrorism and the Terror of God*, 259.
104. Griffith, *The War on Terrorism and the Terror of God*, 261.
105. Griffith, *The War on Terrorism and the Terror of God*, 261.

This violence and lack of love within oneself are often overshadowed by our focus on the violence of others. Self-criticism is a significant instrument in the hand of the nonviolence advocator! Like Tolstoy, Gandhi, and others, Day embodied nonviolent direct action. Like the prophet Ezekiel, she believed that if one does not hate violence, violence will pursue one. "Since you do not hate bloodshed, bloodshed will pursue you."[106]

In summary, Day's life of nonviolence provides an extraordinary insight into the fact that the "violence without" is consequence of the "violence within," as Jesus showed in the Gospels. Saint James grasped that fact: "What causes fights and quarrels among you? Don't they come from your desires that battle within you?"[107] Day conquered her own violence; that was why she was able to follow Jesus' way in her. Day's life and ministry are an extraordinary reminder that advocates of nonviolence must realize their own vulnerability to violence and be willing to get help through partnership with other advocates or through grassroots communities.

6.3 Martin Luther King Jr.'s Path to Nonviolence: African American Perspective

The nonviolent protest ministry of Martin Luther King Jr. is a striking example of how nonviolence, if properly perceived, can undermine structural and institutional injustice. Cheryl A. Kirk-Duggan relates how the backdrop of World War II necessitated a change in perspective. Kirk-Duggan notes that "the Black soldiers who had proven themselves on the 'stage' of war, returned to the United States, where they were not allowed 'standing room.' These veterans' children heard their parents' rage, cynicism, and despair and, like King, wrestled with civil and political life. They sought to respond through protest for equality and social justice and not march to a drumbeat of a deterred dream. Those concerns birthed Civil Rights Movements of various kinds. The Movement, from King's perspective, was a response to immoral white supremacist uncivilized behavior toward Blacks."[108]

---

106. Ezekiel 35:6.
107. James 4:1.
108. Cheryl A. Kirk-Duggan, *Refiner's Fire: A Religious Engagement with Violence*

274

The Impact of Ethnic, Political, and Religious Violence on
Northern Nigeria, and a Theological Reflection on Its Healing

King realized that violence is the way of the world, while nonviolence is the way of Jesus. In other words, King believed that anyone who chooses to be a friend of violence becomes an enemy of God. As such he condemned violence in all its facets. King's speech of 1963, "Declaration of Independence from the War in Vietnam," is a case in point. King wrote, "Here is the true meaning and value of compassion and non-violence, when it helps us to see the enemy's point of view, to hear his questions, to know of his assessment of ourselves." More importantly, in his 1967 address to the anti-war group Clergy and Laity concerned, King maintains;

> When I speak of love I am not speaking of some sentimental and weak response. I am speaking of that force which all of the great religions have seen as the supreme unifying principle of life. Love is somehow the key that unlocks the door, which leads to ultimate reality. This Hindu-Moslem-Christian-Jewish-Buddhist belief about ultimate reality is beautifully summed up in the first epistle of Saint John: "Let us love one another; for love is God and everyone that loveth is born of God and knoweth God."[109]

King had learned how to apply Christ's message of love in all spheres of life from Gandhi. The connection between love and nonviolence is not in doubt. Like Tolstoy, Gandhi, and Day, King's ethical stance is love. King recognizes that love is the eternal religious principle while nonviolence is its external concrete expression. For King, "It logically followed that if love is the eternal religious principle . . . nonviolence is its external expression and worldly counterpart." Thus he wrote,

> At the center of nonviolence stands the principle of love. The nonviolent resister would contend that in the struggle for human dignity, the oppressed people of the world must not succumb to the temptation of becoming bitter or indulging

---

(Minneapolis: Fortress Press, 2001), 74.
109. Martin Luther King Jr., *Strength to Love* (Philadelphia: Fortress Press, 1981), 8.

in hate campaigns. To retaliate in kind would do nothing but intensify the existence of hate in the universe. Along the way of life, someone must have sense enough and morality enough to cut off the chain of hate. This can only be done by projecting the ethic of love to the center of our lives.[110]

King's starting and finishing point is love in all its truth. King, Day, Gandhi, Tolstoy, Tutu, and Jesus have taught the world that nonviolence is legit and realistic. It is not some high ideal, which is only good for a selected few. Yet it is striking to realize that despite Jesus, Tolstoy, Gandhi, Day, Tutu, and King epitomizing nonviolence, people's faith does dwindle when there is violence. King realized that when hope dwindles, hate usually turns most harshly on those who first fostered hope.[111] Above all, however, King's personal and social-ethics strategy, which sought to put people in harmony with God, gave impetus to his efforts for the realization of civil rights, human rights, and economic justice. King had a deontological concept of responsibility. Thus while "many of King's contemporaries saw nonviolence as a tactic, not an ideal, King saw nonviolence as the absolute modus operandi and rejected violence as either a tool or ethic for social change."[112] King enhanced his ethic by using his theology of a personal God, amid a faith of justice, love, and power, which supported his belief in nonviolence and aimed him toward preserving human life and redeeming human personality.[113] In summary, King's theology was based in God's *Agape*—love. King writes, "*Agape* is understanding, creative, redemptive good will for all men."[114] According to King, "*Agape* says you must go on with wise restraint and calm reasonableness but you must keep moving."[115] Finally, King believed that love is fundamentally the source of nonviolence. However, he argued, "Nonviolent resistance does call for love, but it is not

110. King, *Strength to Love*, 8–9.
111. Martin Luther King Jr., *I Have a Dream: Writings and Speeches that Change the World*, James Washington, ed., (New York: HarperSanfrancisco, 1992), 44.
112. Kirk-Duggan, *Refiner's Fire*, 77.
113. Kirk-Duggan, *Refiner's Fire*, 77–78.
114. King, *I Have a Dream*, 31.
115. King, *I Have a Dream*, 32.

a sentimental love. It is a very stern love that would organize itself into collective action to right a wrong by taking on itself suffering."[116] King's overarching desire was to dislodge "the unjust system, rather than individuals who were caught in that system."[117]

6.4 Desmond Tutu: Reconciliation as the Path Beyond Violence: South African Context

Desmond Tutu served as the Anglican Bishop of several South African cities throughout and after the apartheid period. Tutu was one of the greatest threats to apartheid in South Africa because it was simply impossible for the regime to dismiss him as a "terrorist."[118] Like Jesus, Tolstoy, Gandhi, Day, King, and a host of other proponents of nonviolence, Tutu saw the need for total consistency between means and ends. When the U.S. policy toward apartheid was "being neglected" during the Reagan administration, Tutu writes,

> Our People are rapidly despairing of a peaceful resolution in South Africa. Those of us who still speak "peace" and "reconciliation" belong to a rapidly diminishing minority. . . . Freedom is coming. We will be free whatever anybody does or does not do about it. We are concerned only about *how* and *when*. It should be soon, and we want it to be reasonably peaceful.[119]

The *how* and the *when* developed in nonviolent direct action. Tutu reasoned that if the goal is an end to violence, then violence cannot be the means by which one arrives there. If the goal is the "beloved community," as Martin Luther King Jr. called it, then the path leading towards the goal must somehow embody that community as already present. Such a view of

---

116. King, *I Have a Dream*, 44.
117. James Melvin Washington, ed., *A Testament of Hope: The Essential Writings and Speeches of Martin Luther King, Jr.* (New York: HarperSanfrancisco, 1986), 47.
118. Griffith, *The War on Terrorism and the Terror of God*, 265.
119. Desmond Tutu, *Hope and Suffering* (Grand Rapids: Wm. B. Eerdmans Publishing Company, 1985), 117.

the consonance of means and ends is fully in accord with Jesus' proclamation of the presence of the Kingdom of God. For Tutu, faith has never been a facet of life that is sometimes separable from politics or the struggle for freedom.[120] Tutu's consistency birthed freedom from apartheid in South Africa and thereafter launched the unprecedented Truth and Reconciliation process in South Africa. These clouds of witnesses provide rebuttal to any excuse based on assumed unique context.

7. Doing Political and Theological Reflection: Assessing Ideologies

In the context of ethnic, political, and religious violence, political and theological reflections are crucial. There is the need for critical assessment of the ideologies that shape people's perception of the larger picture of the context of political and theological actions. That means that we cannot look at the impact of religious, political, and ethnic violence as givens. The impact of violence must be seen within the confines of other global events. Therefore it is important to know the workings of global events. Hertz's work shows this crucial need. In his chapter on "The Problem of Political Involvement," Hertz asks and answers a rhetorical question:

> Why should Christians have anything to do with politics? The simple truth seems to be that we have no choice. Our common humanity includes entanglement in all kinds of relationships with other persons. . . . Most of those who answer the question negatively will not deny that they live in the same world with the rest of us.[121]

I believe that to say that the Christian has no business dealing with politics is tantamount to saying religious organizations should not involve

---

120. Griffith, *The War on Terrorism and the Terror of God*, 265.
121. Karl H. Hertz, *Politics Is a Way of Helping People: A Christian Perspective for Times of Crisis* (Minneapolis, MN: Augsburg, 1974), 9.

themselves in programs of social innovation. If we truly claim that Jesus is Lord of all of life, there is no way we cannot see the Christian calling as involving all spheres of life. Christian political and theological reflection will lead to asking the question, "Has the church in Nigeria organized a campaign against issues like corruption, tribalism, the neglect of the poor, the misdistribution of health care services, and the inhumanity of elements of our correctional system and so on?" If not, what is the matter?

Something is wrong with our theology. Our Protestant theology has generally been structurally inadequate to deal with the problems of socioeconomic issues and institutionalized injustice. Our theological institutions have to reorient their students to do more political and theological reflection. Only such an approach will give the Church the basic foundation for social and ethical action in society. Theological students must be shown how to "hold evangelism and social action in perfect balance."[122] This reorientation is necessary because compartmentalizing Christianity is not the best for our situation in the Northern region. As Hertz noted, most of the Euro-American missionaries that came to Nigeria came out of a culture where:

> [T]he emphasis in the churches, both middle class and working class, was fundamentally on personal ethics, personal development, whether this took the more moderate form of the undergirding of the virtues of Protestant respectability (for which the Prohibition campaign could serve as a prime example) or more emotionally intense insistence on 'holiness.' The stirring evangelistic campaigns of the nineteenth century, the national dominance of a Protestant morality which resulted in the Prohibition amendment, the ways in which an individual-centered code of conduct fit into the patterns of American public life during the decades from the Civil War to

---

122. See Ronald Sider, *Evangelism and Social Action: Uniting the Church to Heal a Lost and Broken World* (London: Hodder & Stoughton, 1993).

the Great Depression, have left a remarkable and determinative residue of attitudes and beliefs among many Americans.[123]

Christians in Northern Nigeria need to trace the remote context of Nigerian Protestant theologies back to the missionary movement of the nineteenth century; and ask what was going on in the lands from which the missionaries emerged and how that whole context impacted the theologies they passed to Nigerians clergies and their laities.[124] For example, it will be important to remember, as Stassen notes, "In the nineteenth century, many Americans were defending slavery, racism, segregation, and discrimination, and were working to keep Jesus silenced about these gross injustices. It lives on in Jerry Falwell, Pat Robertson, James Kennedy, and Franklin Graham. Thus without theological and political reflection our harsh experiences will not be turned to a blessing to humanity."[125] As Hertz also remarks,

> Reflection and experience belong together; too often the tools furnished in theological study did not fit the tasks, which experience set. Pastors did not get a conceptual framework that enabled them to see the need for social policy as Christian witness within the contexts of their ministries: only a handful caught in a situation where oppression was blatant found themselves able to develop a theology that undergirded a social ethic.[126]

On the one hand, some conservative Christians tend to think that politics is a dirty game because the politicians are self-serving and they have an ethically wrong approach to politics. Hence they have little or no interest in political affairs. On the other hand, some committed Christians feel that

---

123. Hertz, *Politics Is a Way of Helping People*, 93–94.
124. Hertz, *Politics Is a Way of Helping People*, 94.
125. Stassen's comment on my draft, Feb. 7, 2007. As Paul says, "Blessed be the God and Father of our Lord Jesus Christ, the Father of mercies and God of all comfort; who comforts us in all our affliction so that we may be able to comfort those who are in any affliction with the comfort with which we ourselves are comforted by God" (2 Cor. 1:3–4).
126. Hertz, *Politics Is a Way of Helping People*, 104.

the pursuit of self-interest in politics in itself is not morally wrong. All these postures indicate a lack of concrete theological reflection on the nature of politics in our nation and elsewhere. Thus I contend that getting involved in politics requires deep reflection on political issues. The politicians need the tools to do the right thing. Without deep theological and ethical reflection, I argue, Tolstoy, Gandhi, Day, King, and Tutu could not have been able to do what they did.

Doing theological reflection helps the political process. Doing theological reflection is an activity in which we seek to trace out what it means to live as Christians in particular places, involved in concrete sets of rights and duties, opportunities and privileges. As Karl Hertz aptly noted,

> Doing theology means probing for the implicit credos by which persons run their secular enterprises and testing the adequacy of those credos as bases for life-commitments. Doing theology means constantly exploring how the particular commitments one has made relate to one's ultimate faith-commitments. Doing theology in this way means uncovering what beliefs one is really willing to own, to live by and for, what beliefs really serve as the foundation for meaning, trust, and hope.[127]

The outcome of both political and theological reflection is moral criticism. Deep reflection leads to the constant reminder that power can corrupt anyone, which means only constant critical scrutiny can hold power in check. Christians, as Hertz suggests, need to know that "our generation has been called upon to make a particular witness about war; it may also be called upon to make a particular witness about human equality and about the care of the earth."[128] That means that Christians need to be taught how to encourage discussion within "the political community" in their ward levels and local government areas. The crucial goal of political and theological reflection is the well being of persons in our given society. The nature of

---

127. Hertz, *Politics Is a Way of Helping People*, 104–105.
128. Hertz, *Politics Is a Way of Helping People*, 88.

Christian political and theological reflection includes, among other things, the following:

(1) Christian political and theological ethics grow out of Christian dynamic commitment to seek the neighbor's welfare. It is a commitment to an alternative community of deliverance and hope. That is, it comes from a spirit of reciprocating God's liberating events in our lives.

(2) Christian political and theological reflection begins with the concept of God's image and likeness in every human being. Thus it is a genuine recognition of the equal standing and moral worth of all persons. This is illustrated in the concrete style with which the other is encountered.[129]

(3) Christian political and theological reflection involves seeking identity and meaning for all humanity in Kingdom ethics: the reign of God. It is a realization of the tragic history of human search for identity and meaning outside the parameter of the reign of God. That is why much of humanity's history reveals the sad story of the elusive nature of this quest. Identity and meaning have evaded human beings. For instance, at first it was thought to find identity and meaning in life, "what we needed was imagination. We have to find a new view of the world." But today the search for identity and meaning has demonstrated that this question is beyond imagination; it has actually been responsible for much of the world's violence. When it comes to identity and meaning most people are "in error" because they "do not know the scriptures or the power of God."[130] Hence political and theological reflection is necessary to enable us to redirect our search for identity and meaning back to the God who gives us identity and meaning, resulting in economic justice.

Serious ethical deficiencies exist in Northern Nigeria's polity because the infrastructure needed to support honest politics is—depending on the issue—either partly built, neglected, or nonexistent. I therefore propose that a deliberate attempt must be made to create ethical standards that will guide the political class in Northern Nigeria and the country at large. Such standards must go beyond what we presently have. At present there are counselors at the local level and political advisors at the state and federal

---

129. Hertz, *Politics Is a Way of Helping People*, 99.
130. Mark 12:24.

levels. Their communities elect the counselors while the advisors are appointed by the governor in the case of state and by the president in the case of the federal government.

Given that Nigeria has serious political and economic problems it is not enough to talk about checks and balances without concretely proposing the safest way to ensure the workability of that agenda. Generally, Nigeria needs an alternative approach to the present political arrangement. Therefore, I propose the following reform measures:

(1) Political accountability and responsibility: It is an understatement to say that politicians in Northern Nigeria need help. They need constant reminders that in a democratic society public officials are expected to first and foremost be accountable and responsible to those who elected them to their various positions. In other words, they need to continuously acknowledge the fact that their first duty post is the electorate. Thus the Nigerian constitution should include a legal penalty for any public servant who misappropriates or siphons public money for private profits.

(2) Ethics audits: One way to promote accountability in public office is to use periodic ethics audits. Thus, the ethics-audit committee's terms of reference should include, among other things, a periodic survey of public officials to assess their awareness of ethics-related rules. Government should plan periodic ethics training seminars for elected officials. In that case, the ethics-audit committee will also need to review periodically the extent and effectiveness of the ethics training program(s) in the different tiers of governance.

(3) Ethics commissioners: the role of an ethics commissioner includes, but is not limited to, providing one-on-one counseling to elected political members. The commissioners' terms of reference should include holding consultative meetings with an elected official to ascertain or to advise him or her about the need to avoid the potential conflicts of interests that might arise from their personal financial situations or in the course of executing their political duty. This will not only provide such an official the moral wherewithal, which he or she needs, but it will also give them a dose of preventive medicine. Therefore, persons who are to be appointed to the position of an ethics commissioner must be individuals who are not only the

best and the brightest but also are well known as people of high principle, moral integrity, and financial transparency. They are to be a model to the politicians, especially, to young and inexperienced politicians.

(4) Ethics legislation: one of the reasons why some politicians are politically ineffective is due to their response to the activities of special interest groups or lobbyists. Because of what these groups contribute during campaign period politicians become susceptible to their improper influence. Thus the terms of reference of ethics legislation committee should include, but not be limited to, the regulation of special interests groups and lobbyists so that they do not sidetrack elected officials from the real job of serving the interests of their immediate communities. In other words, the ethics legislation committee should be required to make sure that special interests groups and lobbyists do not stand in the way of socioeconomic development of the poor communities.

Conclusion

I have argued that violence is whipped up by a brood of corrupt elite who stand in the place of their colonial masters and take advantage of the poor and frustrated youths for their individual interests. In retrospect, our elite used to struggle for the interest of one Northern region. But now for the sake of economic greed and obsession with political power the elite and the rich tend to pit the poor against one another because violence gives them the opportunity to achieve their goal of holding unto power unchallenged. Thus in Northern Nigeria violence has become not only one of the useful weapons that the elite and the rich use against their political rivals but also as a tool to divide and rule the poor. In so doing they limit the poor's ability to resist their injustice. They neglect the causes of both Muslim and Christian orphans, widows, poor, as well as the rights of all those who are marginalized.

Given that the Muslim and non-Muslim poor in Northern Nigeria are the most impacted by violence, they need each other. The Christians should not give up on the poor Muslims in Northern Nigeria. Both non-Christian and Christian poor should make every effort to work with their poor friends in the North. That is, those who are also suffering the same oppression, exploitation and domination by their elite and the rich. This realization has helped GAWON Foundation to model a new approach to the question of poverty and its resultant consequences: violence. The GAWON Foundation focuses on reversing the social, economic, and spiritual conditions of the people of Northern Nigeria by creating communities of sound economic and spiritual vision—a community where both Christians and Muslim can live together as brothers and sisters; a community where religious freedom and economic justice are guaranteed. GAWON Foundation is a non-governmental organization that is based in Southern Kaduna, Nigeria. One of the objectives of GAWON Foundation is building bridges between Muslims and Christians. Thus GAWON Foundation seeks to eradicate poverty and illiteracy among Christian and Muslim widows, orphans, and the less privileged people in Northern Nigeria.

Because of violence the Northern region is polarized. GAWON Foundation realizes that in order to heal and mend broken relationships and the fragmentation of our society, we need to move out of our comfort zones to meet and embrace the different other. Thus the Foundation gives revolving loans to the widows in groups that tend to metamorphose into a community. This grouping is based on the economic and business interests of each member. The members of each group comprise Muslim and Christian widows and orphans. In such an arrangement, the Muslim and the Christian widows work together. Consequently, they are not only economically empowered but also spirituality invigorated. The Christian widows learn to forgive their Muslim counterparts through working with them and getting to see them not only as victims of the same structure of injustice but also as human beings created in the image of a good and compassionate God.

Finally, I propose that they should have a declaration of religious freedom and equality. The Declaration, adopted by Muslim and non-Muslim

Poor in Northern Nigeria should include the following statements adopted from the *Lusaka Declaration*[131] but paraphrased:

> United in our desire to rid North Nigeria of the evils of religious hatred, exclusion, and violence, we the poor of Northern Nigeria proclaim our faith in the inherent dignity and worth of the human person and declare that:

> The people of Northern Nigeria have the right to live freely in dignity and equality, without any distinction or exclusion based on religion or ethnic origin;

> While everyone is free to retain diversity in his or her culture and lifestyle this diversity does not justify the perpetuation of religious prejudice, hatred and exclusion, and ethnic or religious discriminatory practices;

> Everyone has the right to equality before the law and equal justice under the law; and

> Everyone has the right to effective remedies and protection against any form of discrimination based on the grounds of religious persuasion or ethnic origin.

> We reject Northern-Nigeria elite who try to corner policies in order to maintain the status quo. We reaffirm that it is the duty of all the people of Northern Nigeria to work together for the transformation of the infamous policies that give our political leaders the opportunity to perpetuate poverty in the region.

---

131. The original idea of this declaration is drawn from the Lusaka declaration on racism and racial prejudice as found in Donald L. Sparks, "The Commonwealth" *Africa South of the Sahara 1998*, 27th Edition, Regional Surveys of the World, edited by Gavin Williams and Donald L. Sparks (London: European Publications Ltd, 1997), 113. But I have paraphrased and modified it to fit the intention of this research.

286

The Impact of Ethnic, Political, and Religious Violence on
Northern Nigeria, and a Theological Reflection on Its Healing

We agree that everyone has the right to protection against acts
of incitement to religious hatred and discrimination, whether
committed by individuals, groups, or other organizations.

Inspired by the principles of religious freedom and equality,
which is stipulate in the Nigerian constitution, we accept
the solemn duty of working together to eliminate religious
exclusion and violence.

Being aware that legislation alone cannot eliminate religious
hatred, exclusion, and violence, we endorse the need to
initiative public information and education policies designed
to promote understanding, tolerance, respect, and friendship
among the peoples and ethnic groups in Northern Nigeria.

We note that religious hatred, exclusion, and violence, wherever
they occur, are significant factors contributing to lack of shared
understandings and thus inhibit peaceful economic progress
and social development. We encourage government officials,
religious leaders, and political elite in Northern Nigeria to
make the goal of eradicating religious hatred, exclusion, and
violence a critical priority. This will facilitate the promotion of
justice, peace, and transformation in the region.

These principles are not exhaustive. But they do give a picture of how
justice and peace could be achieved in Northern Nigeria.[132] I encourage
both Christians and Muslims to recognize that "Nonviolence is a way of
thinking, a way of life—not a tactic, but a way of putting love to work in
resolving problems, healing relationships, and generally raising the quality
of our lives."[133]

---

132. Ian Greene and David P. Shugarman, *Honest Politics: Seeking Integrity in Canadian
Public Life* (Toronto: James Lorimer & Company, Publishers, 1997), 198–209.
133. Mahatma Gandhi, *The Essential Gandhi: An Anthology of His Writings on His Life, Work,
and Ideas*, ed., by Louis Fischer (New York: Vintage Books, 2002), xxv.

Bibliography

Abashia, Chris, and Ulea, Ayuba. *Christian and Islam: A Plea for Understanding and Tolerance.* Jos, Nigeria: Midland Press, 1991.

Abbink, J., de Bruijn, Mirjam, van Walraven, Klaas and NetLibrary Inc. *Rethinking Resistance, Revolt and Violence in African History.* Leiden the Netherlands; Boston: Brill, 2003.

Abramovitz, Janet N. Vital Signs 2002: The Trends to Democracy in Post-Transition Nigeria: *Research Report 127.* W. W. Norton & Company, 2002.

Achebe, Chinua. *Things Fall Apart.* Ibadan, Nigeria: Heinemann, 1958.

Achtemeier, P. J. "Newborn Babes and Living Stones: Literal & Figurative in 1 Peter" in *To Touch the Text: Biblical and Related Studies in Honor of Joseph A. Fitzmyer, S.J.* New York: Crossroad, 1989.

Aquinas, Thomas. *Commentary on the Four Gospels, Collected Out of the Works of the Fathers*, Vol. 4. London: Oxford, John Henry Parker, 1940.

Agu, Osita. *Ethnic Militias and the Threat to Democracy in Post-transition Nigeria: Research Report 127.* Nordic Africa Institute, 2004.

Akinyemi, A.B., P.D. Cole, Walter, I. "Ofonagoro and Nigerian Institute of International Affairs." *Readings on Federalism.* Lagos: Nigerian Institute of International Affairs, 1979.

Alexander, Archibald. *The Ethics of St. Paul.* Glasgow: James Maclehose and Sons Publishers to the University, 1910.

Alias, Norbert. *The Civilizing Process: The Development of Manners: Changes in the Code of Conduct and Feeling in Early Modern Times.* (New York: Urizen Books, 1978.

Appleby R. Scott. *The Ambivalence of the Sacred*. INC. New York: Rowman & Littlefield Publishers, 2000.

Appiah-Kubi, Kofi and Torres, Sergio, eds. *African Theology En Route*. New York: Orbis Books, 1979.

Arbesmann, Rudolph, Daly, Emily Joseph, and Quinoa, A. Edwin, trans. *The Fathers of the Church: Tertullian Apologetical Works and Minuscius Felix Octavius*. New York: Fathers of the Church, 1950.

Arbuckle, Geral. *Violence, Society, and the Church: A Cultural Approach*. Minnesota: Liturgical Press, 2004.

Arthur, George Buttrick, ed. *The Interpreter's Dictionary of the Bible*, Vol. 4. New York: Abingdon Press, 1962.

Assefa, Hizkias. *Peace and Reconciliation as a Paradigm*. Nairo: Peace Initiative, 1993.

Augsberger, David. *Caring Enough to Confront*. Regal Books, 1984.

Augustine, Aurelius. *The City of God*, Vol. 1. Edinburgh: John Grant, 1909.

Azevedo, Mario. *Roots of Violence: A History of War in Chad*. U.K.: Routledge, 1998.

Azikiwe, Nnamdi. *My Odyssey*. New York: Praeger, 1970.

Azumah, J. A. *The Legacy of Arab-Islam in Africa: A Quest for Inter-religious Dialogue*. Oxford: Oneworld, 2001.

Bainton, Roland. *Christian Attitudes Toward War and Peace*. Nashville: Abingdon Press, 1991.

Banseka, Cage. *Development for Peace: In Search for Solutions for Conflict in Sub-Sahara Africa*. Universal Publishers, 2005.

Barber, Benjamin R. *Jihad vs. McWorld*. New York and Canada: Times Books, 1995.

Berkow, H. Jerome. "Hausa" in *Muslim Peoples: A World Ethnographic Survey*, Richard V. Weeks, ed. Westport, Connecticut, London: Greenwood Press, 1978.

Barret B. David and Johnson, M. Todd. *World Christian Trends, AD30–AD 2200: Interpreting the Annual Christian Megacensus*. Pasadena, California: William Carey Library, 2001.

Barnett, Richard J. and Cavanaugh, John. *Global Dreams: Imperial Corporations and the New World Order*. New York, London, Toronto, Sydney, Tokyo and Singapore, 1994.

Barton, H. Allen. *Communities in Disaster: A Sociological Analysis of Collective Stress Situation*. New York: Doubleday & Company, 1970.

Bauckham, Richard. *The Bible in Politics: How to Read the Bible Politically*. Louisville, Kentucky: Westminster John Knox Press, 1989.

_____. *God Will Be All in All: The Eschatology of Jürgen Moltmann*. Edinburgh: T&T Clark, 1999.

_____, ed. *The Theology of Jürgen Moltmann*. Edinburgh: T&T Clark, 1995.

_____. *The Theology of Jürgen Moltmann*. Edinburgh: T & T Clark, 1995.

Beck, Robert R. *Nonviolent Story: Narrative Conflict Resolution in the Gospel of Mark*. Maryknoll N Y: Orbis Books, 1996.

Bediako, Kwame. *Jesus in Africa: The Christian Gospel in African History and Experience*. Malaysia: Regnum Africa, 2000.

Beinart, Peter. *The New Republic*, July 6, 1998.

Bellah, Robert, Madsen, Richard, Sullivan, William, Swidler, Ann, and Tipton, M. Steven. *Habits of the Heart: Individualism and Commitment in America Life*. Berkeley, Los Angeles and London: University of California Press, 1985.

Benavides, Gustavo, M. W. Daly. *Religion and Political Power*. Albany: State University of New York Press, 1989.

Berkeley, Bill. *The Graves are not Yet Full: Race, Tribe and Power in the Heart of Africa*. New York: Basics Books, 2001.

Berman, Eric. *Peacemaking in Africa: Capabilities and Culpabilities*. United Nations Publications UNIDIR, 2000.

Bloch, M. *The Historian's Craft*. New York, 1953.

Blumenfeld, Bruno. *The Politics of Paul: Justice, Democracy and Kingship in a Hellenistic Framework*. London and New York: Sheffield Academic Press, 2001.

Bobboyi, H. Yakubu, A.M., ed. *Peace-Building and Conflict Resolution in Northern Nigeria*, Kaduna. Nigeria: Arewa House, 2005.

Boer, H. Jan. *Muslims: Why the Violence? Studies in Christian-Muslim Relations*, Vol. 2. Belleville, Ontario, Canada: Essence Publishing, 2004.

Bond, I. Gilbert. *Paul and the Religious Experiences of Reconciliation: Diasporic Community and Creole Consciousness.* Louisville, Ky.: John Knox Press, 2005.

Borg, J. Marcus. *Conflict, Holiness, and Politics in the Teaching of Jesus.* Harrisburg, Pennsylvania: Trinity Press International, 1984.

Brandon, S. G.F. *A Dictionary of Comparative Religion.* New York: Scribner, 1970.

Bromley, David G. and Melton, J. Mordon. *Cults, Religion, and Violence.* Cambridge: Cambridge University Press, 2002.

Brown, Colin. *Jesus in European Protestant Thoughts, 1778–1860: Studies in Historical Theology 1.* Durham, N.C.: The Labyrinth Press, 1985.

Brown, Michael Barratt. *Africa's Choices: After Thirty Years of the World Bank.* Westview Press, 1997.

Brown, W. Dale. *Biblical Pacifism: A Peace Church Perspective.* Illinois: Brethren Press, 1986.

Bujo, Bénézet. *The Ethical Dimension of Community: The African Model and the Dialogue Between North and South.* Nairo, Kenya: Pualines Publications Africa, 1998.

Burkholder, R. and Benders. *Children of Peace.* Elgin, Illinois: The Brethren Press.

CAN. *Kano Religious Disturbance Memorandum.* Kano: Church of the Lord, 1982.

Chapman, G. C. *Facing the Nuclear Heresy: A Call to Reformation.* Ellingwork Illinois: Brethren Press, 1986.

Cashman, Greg. *What Causes War?: An Introduction to Theories of International Conflict.* New York: Lexington Books, 1993.

Chai, Sun-Ki. *Choosing and Identity: A General Model of Preference and Belief Formation.* Michigan: University of Michigan Press, 2001.

Clark, T. Mary, tran. and intro. *Augustine of Hippo: Selected Writings.* New Jersey, 1984.

Coleman, S. James. *Nigeria: Background of Nationalism.* Berkeley and Los Angeles: University of California Press, 1963.

Cooney, Mark. *Warriors and Peacemakers: How Third Parties Shape Violence.* NYU Press, 2002.

Cone, H. James. *Speaking the Truth: Ecumenism, Liberation, and Black Theology.* Grand Rapids: Wm. B. Eerdmans Publishing Company, 1986.

_____. *God of the Oppressed.* New York: Orbis Books, 1975.

_____. *Risks of Faith: The Emergence of a Black Theology of Liberation, 1968–1998.* Boston: Beacon Press 1999.

_____. *A Black Theology of Liberation.* Philadelphia and New York: J.B. Lippincot Company, 1970.

Corner, M and Rowland, C. *Liberation Exegesis: The Challenge of Liberation Theology to Biblical Studies.* Westminster John Knox Press, 1989.

Coward, Harold G. and Smith, Gordon S. *Religion and Peacebuilding.* New York, Bristol: State University of New York; University Presses Marketing, 2004.

Crampon, Edmund Patrick Thurman. "Christianity in Northern Nigeria" in *Christianity in West Africa: The Nigerian Story*, Ogbu Kalu, ed. Ibadan: Daystar Press, 1978.

Crowder, Michael. *A Short History of Nigeria.* New York: Fredrick a Praeger, Publishers, 1966.

Cummings, Milton C., and Wise, David. *Democracy under Pressure: An Introduction to the American Political System*, 8th Edition. Philadelphia, New York, London: Harcourt Brace College Publishers, 1997.

Curtin, Deanw and Litke, Robert. *Institutional Violence.* Rodopi, 1999.

Daume, Daphne. *Britannica World Data.* Chicago: Encyclopaedia Britannica, Inc., 1991.

Demy, J. Timothy and Steward, P. Gary, eds. *Politics and Public Policy: A Christian Response: Crucial Considerations for Governing Life.* Grand Rapids: Kregel Publications, 2000.

Diamond, Jared. *Guns, Germs, and Steel: The Fates of Human Societies.* New York, London: W. W. Norton & Company, 1999.

Dickson, K. A. and P. Ellingwork, et al. *Biblical Revelation and African Beliefs.* New York: Orbis Books, 1969.

Doi, I. Rahman. *The Cardinal Principles of Islam.* Zaria: Hudahuda Publishing Company, 1982.

Dunn, James D. G. *The New Perspective on Paul: Collected Essay.* Germany: Mohr Siebeck, 2005.

Dretke, P. James. *A Christian Approach to Muslims: Reflections from West Africa.* California: William Carey Library, 1979.

Dyer, Wayne W. *The Power of Intention: Learning to Co-Create Your World Your Way.* Carlsbad, California: Hay House, Inc., 2004.

Dyrness, William. *Learning about Theology from the Third World*. Grand Rapids Michigan: Academic Books, 1990.

Earhart, Bryon H. *Religious Traditions of the World: A Journey through Africa, Mesoamerica, North America, Judaism, Christianity, Islam, Hinduism, Buddhism, China, and Japan*. San Francisco: HarperCollins Publishers, 1993.

Elias, Norbert, and Edmund Jephcott. *The Civilizing Process: The Development of Manners: Changes in the Code of Conduct and Feeling in Early Modern Times*. New York: Urizen Books, 1978.

Enahoro, Peter. "The African Perspective" *African Now*, July 1983 as cited in Matthew Hassan Kukah, *The Mustard Seed*, Vol. 1. Ibadan: Umbrella Books, 1988.

Enayat, Hamid. *Modern Islamic Political Thought*. Austin: University of Texas Press, 1982.

Enwerem, M. Iheanyi. *A Dangerous Awakening: The Politicization of Religion in Nigeria*. Ibadan: Ifra-Ibadan, 1995.

_____. *The Politicization of Religion in Modern Nigeria: The Emergence and Politics of the Christian Association of Nigeria (CAN)*, Thesis. Ontario: York University North York, 1992.

Erickson, J. Millard. *Introducing Christian Doctrine*. Grand Rapids: Baker Book House, 1992.

European Center for Conflict Prevention. *People Building Peace: 35 Inspiring Stories from Around the World*. The Netherlands, 1999.

Fabella, Virginia and Torres, Sergio, eds. *Doing Theology in a Divided World*. Maryknoll, New York: Orbis Books, 1985.

Falola, Toyin. *Violence in Northern Nigeria*. Rochester New York: University of Rochester Press, 1998.

Falola, Toyin and Kukah, Matthew Hassan. *Religious Militancy and Self-Assertion*. Aldershot, Brookfield USA; Hong Kong, Singapore, and Sydney: Avebury, Athenaeum Press Ltd, Gateshead, Tyne & Wear, 1996.

Francis, Paul. *State, Community, and Local Development in Nigeria*. World Bank Publication, 1996.

Friesen, K. Duane. *Christian Peace Making and International Conflict*. Scottsdale: Harold Press, 1985.

Ferguson, John. *The Politics of Love*. New York: Fellowship Publications, 1979.

Ford, F. David, ed. *The Modern Theologians: An Introduction to Christian Theology in the Twentieth Century*, 2nd Edition. Berlin, Germany: Blackwell Publishing, 2002.

Furnish, Victor Paul. *The Moral Teaching of Paul*. Nashville: Abingdon, 1979.

Gaebelein, E. Frank and Douglas, J. D. *The Expositor's Bible Commentary*, Vol. 12. Grand Rapid: Zondervan Publishing House, 1981.

Gandhi, Mahatma. *The Essential Gandhi: An Anthology of His Writings on His Life, Work, and Ideas*, ed., by Louis Fischer. New York: Vintage Books, 2002.

Gantzel, Klaus Jurgen and Schwinghammer, Torsten. *Warfare since the Second World War*. Transaction Publishers, 1999.

Germond, A. Paul. "Liberation Theology: Theology in the Service of Justice" in Charles Villa-Vicencio, ed. *Theology & Violence: The South African Debate*. Grand Rapids: Wm. B. Eerdmans Publishing Company, 1987.

Griffith, Lee. *The War on Terrorism and the Terror of God*. Grand Rapids: Wm. B. Eerdmans Publishing Company, 2002.

Gifford, P. *African Christianity: Its Public Role*. Bloomington: Indiana University Press, 1998.

Gilligan, J. *Violence*. New York: Vintage Books, 1996.

Gonlur, Paul, L. "An Investigation into the Problem of Culture in COCIN Churches In Kabwir RCC." Thesis, Jos, Nigeria: ECWA Theological Seminary, 1999.

Gopin, Marc. *Between Eden and Armageddon: The Future of World Religions, Violence, and Peacemaking*. Oxford University Press, 2000.

Grossman, D. *On Killing: The Psychological Cost of Learning to Kill in War and Society*. Boston, New York: Brown Company, 1996.

Guinness, O.S. *Violence. A Study of Contemporary Attitudes*. Illinois: InterVarsity Press, 1974.

Gushee, P. David, ed. *Christians & Politics Beyond the Culture Wars: An Agenda for Engagement*. Grand Rapids: Bakers Books, 2000.

_____. *Righteous Gentiles of the Holocaust: Genocide and Moral Obligation*, 2nd edition. Minnesota: Paragon House, 2003.

Gustafson, M. James. *Christ and the Moral Life*. Chicago and London: The University of Chicago Press, 1968.

Gwyn, Douglas. *A Declaration on Peace.* Scottsdale, Waterloo: Herald Press, 1991.

Haas, Richard N. *Transatlantic Tensions: The United States, Europe, and Problem Countries.* Brookings Institutions Press, 1999, 201.

Haines, Byron and Cooley, Frank. *Christians and Muslims Together.* Philadelphia: The Geneva Press, 1987.

Hauerwas, Stanley. *A Community of Character: Toward a Constructive Christian Social Ethic.* Notre Dame, University of Notre Dame Press, 1981.

_____. *A Better Hope: Resources for a Church Confronting Capitalism, Democracy, and Postmodernity.* Grand Rapids: Brazos Press, 2000.

Hays, Richard B. *The Moral Vision of the New Testament: A Contemporary Introduction to New Testament Ethics.* San Francisco: HarperSanFrancisco, 1996.

Hein, Mark, S. *Grounds for Understanding: Ecumenical Resources for Responses to Religious Pluralism.* Grand Rapids, Michigan: Wm. B. Eerdmans Publishing Company, 1998.

Helf, James L., ed. *Beyond Violence: Religious Sources for Social Transformation in Judaism, Christianity and Islam.* Fordham University Press, 2004.

Hertz, Karl H. *Politics Is a Way of Helping People: A Christian Perspective for Times of Crisis.* Minneapolis, Minn.: Augsburg Pub. House, 1974.

Hiskett, M. *The Development of Islam in West Africa.* London, New York: Longman, 1984.

Hodge, Charles. *Ephesians; Crossway Classic Commentaries.* Wheaton, Illinois, England: Crossway Books, 1994.

Hodgkin, Thomas. *Nigerian Perspectives.* London: Oxford University Press, 1960.

Hoge, James F., and Zakaria, Fareed, ed. *The America Encounter: The United States and the Making of the Modern World.* Basic Books, 1998.

Hollenbach, David. *The Common Good and Christian Ethics.* Cambridge: Cambridge University Press, 2002.

Homer-Dixon, Thomas F. *Environment, Scarcity, and Violence.* Princeton University Press, 2001.

Horowitz, Donald L. *The Deadly Riot.* California: University of California Press, 2003.

Horsley, Richard A. *Jesus and the Spiral of Violence: Popular Jewish Resistance in Roman Palestine*. Minneapolis: Fortress Press, 1993.

Hostetler, Mariam. *They Loved Their Enemies*. Scottdale, Kitchener: Herald Press, 1988.

Homburg, David A., and Hamburg, Beatrix, A. *Learning to Live Together: Preventing Hatred and Violence in Children and Adolescent Development*. Oxford University Press, 2004.

Huntington, P. Samuel. *The Clash of Civilizations and the Remarking of World Order*. London: Cox & Wyman, 1997.

Hunter, Ian. *Catholic Insight*, December 1, 2000.

Isichei, Elizabeth Allo. *A History of Nigeria*. London and New York: Longman, 1983.

James, Ibrahim, ed. *Settler Phenomenon in the Middle Belt and the Problem of National Integration in Nigeria*. Jos, Nigeria: Midland Press Limited, 1998.

Jansen, H.G. *Militant Islam*. London: Pan Books, 1979.

Jenkins, Philips. *The Next Christendom: The Coming of Global Christianity*. Oxford: Oxford University Press, 2002.

Jenness, Valerie and Broad, Kendal. *Hate Crime: New Social Movements and the Politics of Violence*. Aldine Transaction, 1997.

Johnston, Douglas and Sampson, Cynthia. *Religion, the Missing Dimension of Statecraft*. New York: Oxford University Press, 1994.

Johnstone, Patrick, Mandryk, Jason and Johnstone Robyn. *Operation World*, 21st Century Edition. Waynesboro, Georgia: Gabriel Resources, 2005.

Jones, Thomas David. *Human Rights: Group Defamation, Freedom of Expression and the Law of Nations*. Martinus Nijhoff Publishers, 1997.

Kacowicz, Arie Marcelo. *Zones of Peace in the Third World: South America and West Africa in Comparative Perspective*. Suny Press, 1998.

Kane, Ousmane. "Izala: The Rise of Muslim Reformism in Northern Nigeria" *Accounting for Fundamentalisms: The Dynamic Character of Movements*. Martin E. Marty and R. Scott Appleby, eds. Chicago and London: University of Chicago Press, 1994.

Kärkkainen, Veli-Matti. *Toward Pneumatological Theology: Pentecostal and Ecumenical Perspectives on Ecclesiology, Soteriology, and Theology of Mission*. Lanham, Maryland: University Press of America, 2002.

Kässmann, Margot. "Overcoming Violence: The Challenge to the Churches in All Places." no. pub. comp., 1998.

Käe, Mana. *Christian and Churches of Africa Envisioning the Future: Salvation in Jesus Christ and the building of a new African society*. Yaoundae; Great Britain: Editions Clâe, 2002.

Kannengiersser, Charles and Petersen, L. William. *Origen of Alexandria: His World and His Legacy*. Indiana: University of Notre Dame Press, 1988.

Kegley, W. Charles and Bretall, W. Robert, eds. *Reinhold Niebuhr: His Religious, Social, and Political Thought*. New York: The Macmillan Company, 1956.

Kelsey, John. *Islam and War: The Gulf War and Beyond: A Study in Comparative Ethics*. Louisville, Kentucky: Westminster John Knox Press, 1993.

Keylor, William R. *The Twentieth-Century World: An International History*. Oxford University Press, 2000, 419.

Kimball, Charles. *When Religion Becomes Evil*. New York: HarperCollins Publishers, 2002.

King, M. L. Jr. *Strength to Love*. New York: Harper & Row, 1963.

Kirk-Greene, Anthony and Rimmer, Douglas. *Nigeria Since 1970*. New York: African Publishing Company, 1981.

_____. *Crisis and Conflict in Nigeria: A Documentary Sourcebook 1966–1970* Vol. 2. New York and Ibadan, Nigeria: Oxford University Press, 1970.

Kirk-Duggan, Cheryl A. *Refiner's Fire: A Religious Engagement with Violence*. Minneapolis: Fortress Press, 2001.

Korten, C. David. *Globalizing Civil Society: Reclaiming our Right to Power*. New York: Seven Stories Press, 1998.

Kraft, K. *Inner Peace, World Peace*. State University Press, 1992.

Kraybill, R. *An Anabaptist Paradigm for Conflict Transformation*. Thesis Dissertation, University of Cape Town, 1996.

Krieg, Carmen, Kuchaz, Thomas and Volf, Miroslav, eds. *The Future of Theology: Essays in Honor of Jürgen Moltmann*. Grand Rapids: Wm. B. Eerdmans Publishing Company, 1996.

Kukah, H. Matthew. *Religion Politics and Power in Northern Nigeria*. Ibadan, Nigeria: Spectrum Books Limited, 1993.

Küng, Hans. *The Church*. New York: Sheed and Ward, 1967.

_____. *On Being a Christian*, trans. by Edward Quinn. New York: Doubleday & Company, 1976.

Kurt, Paul. *Free Inquiry*: "Agenda for the Humanist Movement in the Twenty-first Century" in *High Beam Research* www.highbeam.com (Editorial), June 22, 1995.

Laremont, Ricardo Renâe, ed. *The Causes of Warfare and the Implications of Peacekeeping in Africa*. Portsmouth, New Hampshire: Heinemann, 2002.

Lass Erie, Jean. *War and the Gospel*. Scottdale: Herald Press, 1962.

Lear, V. Marie. *Neighbors: Christians and Muslims*. Ibadan: Bezekos Printing Press. 1989.

Lederach, J.P. *Building Peace*. *United States Institute of Peace Press*. Washington, D.C., 1997.

Lederach, John Paul. *The Journey Toward Reconciliation*. Scottdale, Pennsylvania: Herald Press, 1999.

Lederach J. P. and Cynthia S. *From the Ground Up*. Oxford University Press, 2000.

Levtzion, N. *Conversion to Islam*. New York: Holmes & Meier, 1979.

Lewis, Bernard. *The Crisis of Islam: Holy War and Unholy Terror*. London: Clays Ltd, 2003.

Lifton, Jay Robert. *Death in Life: Survivors of Hiroshima*. New York: Random House, 1967.

Lind, C. Millard. *Yahweh is a Warrior*. Scottsdale: Herald Press, 1980.

Little, E. Paul. *Know What You be Believe*. Suffolk: The Chaucer Press, 1975.

Lohse, Eduard, ed. *Theological Ethics of the New Testament*. Trans. M. Eugene Boring. Minneapolis: Fortress Press, 1991.

Loimeier, R. *Islamic Reform and Political Change in Northern Nigeria*. Evanston Ill: Northwestern University Press, 1997.

Longley, C. *Chosen People: The Big Idea that Shaped England and America*. London: Hodder & Stoughton, 2002.

Lonergan, Bernard. *Method in Theology*. Toronto: University of Toronto Press, 1999.

Lovatt, F.W. Mark. *Confronting the Will-to-Power: A Reconsideration of the Theology of Reinhold Niebuhr*. Cambria, UK and Waynesboro, Georgia, 2001.

Lovejoy, P. E. *Slavery on the Frontiers of Islam*. Princeton: Markus Wiener Publishers, 2004.

Lovejoy, P. E. and P. A. T. Williams. *Displacement and the Politics of Violence in Nigeria*. Leiden; New York: Brill, 1997.

Lynch, Monica. *Facing the Enemy*. Ontario: Waterloo, Graphic Services, 1991.

Lyons, David. *Ethics and the Rule of Law*. London, New York, Cambridge: Cambridge University Press, 1984.

MacIntyre, Alasdair. *After Virtue*. Notre Dame, Indiana: University of Notre Dame Press, 1981.

Maddy, Monique. *Learning to Love Africa*. New York: HarperCollins Publishers, 2004.

Magesa, Laurent. *African Religion: The Moral Traditions of Abundant Life*. Paulis Publications Africa, 1998.

Magura, Daniel. *Sacred Energies: When the World's Religions Sit Down to Talk About the Future of Human Life and the Plight of the Planet*. Minneapolis: Fortress Press, 2000.

Maier, Karl. *This House has Fallen*. Colorado: Westview Press, 2000.

Makarfi, Ja'afaru. "The Role of Religious Leaders in the Establishment of Durable Peace in Northern States," *Peace-Building and Conflict Resolution in Northern Nigeria: Proceedings of the Northern Peace Conference*. Kaduna: Baraka Press and Publishers, 2005.

Malan, Jannie. *Conflict Resolution Wisdom from Africa*. African Center for the Constructive Resolution of Disputes (ACCORD), 1997.

Marshall, Laurence Henry. *The Challenge of New Testament Ethics*. London: Macmillan, 1947.

Martin, Gus and Martin, Clarence Augustus. *Understanding Terrorism: Challenges, Perspective, and Issues*. Sage Publications Inc, 2003.

Matâe, Gabor and Roberts, Harold. *When the Body Says No: The Cost of Hidden Stress*. Burnaby B.C.: Public Library Interlink, 2003.

Maybury, J. Richard. *World War I: The Rest of the Story and How it Affects You Today*. Placerville: Bluestocking Press, 2003.

_____ *World War II: The Rest of the Story and How it Affects You Today*. Placerville: Bluestocking Press, 2003.

_____. *The Thousand-Year War in the Middle East*. Placerville: Bluestocking Press, 2003.

Mbiti, John S. *Concepts of God in Africa*. London: S.P.C.K, 1979.

Meeks, M. Douglas. *Origins of the Theology of Hope*. Philadelphia: Fortress Press, 1974.

Michelle, Jules, and Allison, A. R. (trans.). *Satanism and Witchcraft: A Study in Medieval Superstition*. New York: Kessinger Publishing, 2005.

Miller, M. William. *A Christian's Response to Islam*. Wheaton: Tyndale House Publishers, 1980.

Moe-Lobeda, Cynthia D. *Healing a Broken World: Globalization and God*. Minneapolis, Minnesota: Fortress Press, 2002.

Moltmann, Jürgen. *The Theology of Hope: On the Ground and the Implications of Christian Eschatology*. London: SCM Press, 1967.

_____. *Religion, Revolution, and the Future*. New York: Scribner, 1969.

_____. *Man: Christian Anthropology in the Conflicts of the Present*. Philadelphia: Fortress Press, 1974.

_____. *Experiences of God*. Philadelphia: Fortress Press, 1980.

_____. *On Human Dignity: Political Theology and Ethics*. Philadelphia: Fortress Press, 1984.

_____. *Justice Creates Peace*. Louisville, Kentucky: Baptist Peacemakers International Spirituality, 1988.

_____. *Creating a Just Future: The Political Peace and the Ethics of Creation in a Threatened World*. London and Philadelphia: SCM Press; Trinity Press International, 1989.

_____. *God in Creation: A New Theology of Creation and the Spirit of God*. Minneapolis, Fortress Press, 1993.

_____. *The Way of Jesus Christ: Christology in Messianic Dimensions*. Minneapolis: Fortress Press, 1993.

_____. *The Church in the Power of the Spirit: A Contribution to Messianic Ecclesiology*. Minneapolis: Fortress Press, 1993.

_____. *Jesus for Today's World*. Minneapolis: Fortress Press, 1994.

_____. *Experiences in Theology: Ways and Forms of Christian Theology*. Minneapolis MN: Fortress Press, 2000.

_____. *The Crucified God. Theology Yesterday and Today.* Vanderbilt: Vanderbilt University Divinity School, 2002.

_____. *In the End—The Beginning: The Life of Hope.* Minneapolis: Fortress Press, 2004.

Montgomery, Dan. *Courage to Love.* Glendale California: GL Regal Books, 1980.

Mounce, H. Robert. *A Living Hope: A Commentary on 1 and 2 Peter.* Grand Rapids: Wm. B. Eerdmans Publishing Company, 1982.

Müller-Fahrenholz, Geiko, ed. *The Kingdom and the Power: The Theology of Jürgen Moltmann.* London: SCM Press, 2001.

Musa, Balarabe. *Struggle for Social and Economic Change.* Zaria, Nigeria: Northern Nigeria Publishing Company Ltd, 1982.

Musk, Bill. *Holy War: Why Do Some Muslims Become Fundamentalist?* Mill Hill, London and Grand Rapids: Monarch Books, 1984.

Musser, Donald W. and Joseph L. Price. *Handbook for Christian Theologians.* Nashville: Abingdon Press, 1996.

Muzorewa, G. H. *The Origins and Development of African Theology.* Eugene, Oregon: Wipf and Stock Publishers, 2000.

Myers, B. L. *Walking with the Poor: Principles and Practices of Transformational Development.* Maryknoll New York: Orbis Books, 1999.

Myers, Ched. *Binding the Strong Man: A Political Reading of Mark's Story of Jesus.* Maryknoll, New York: Orbis Books, 1988.

Neiers, M. *The Peoples of the Jos, Plateau Nigeria.* Frankfurt/main: Peter Lang Ltd, 1979.

Nelson, Harold D. *Area Handbook for Nigeria.* Washington: American University Foreign Area Studies, 1972.

Nelson-Pallmeyer, J. *Is Religion Killing Us?: Violence in the Bible and the Quran.* Harrisburg, Pennsylvania: Trinity Press International, 2003.

Ngewa, S. M. Shaw, et al. *Issues in African Christian Theology.* Nairobi: East African Educational Publishers, 1998.

Niebuhr, Reinhold. *The Nature and Destiny of Man: Human Nature*, Vol. 1. New Jersey: Prentice Hall, 1964.

_____ *An Interpretation of Christian Ethics.* New York: The Seabury Press, 1935.

_____. *The World Crisis and American Responsibility*. New York: Association Press, 1958.

_____. *Faith and Politics: A Commentary on Religious, Social and Political Thought in a Technological Age*. New York: George Braziller, 1968.

_____. *Moral Man in an Immoral Society*. Louisville: Westminster John Knox Press, 1960.

_____. *The Children of Light and the Children of Darkness: A Vindication of Democracy and a Critique of Its Traditional Defense*. New York: Charles Scribner's Sons, 1960.

_____. *Love & Justice: Selections from the Shorter Writings of Reinhold Niebuhr*. Cleveland and New York: Meridian Books, 1967.

Niebuhr, H. Richard. *Christ and Culture*. New York: Harper & Row, 1951.

_____. *The Purpose of the Church and Its Ministry*. New York: Harper & Row, 1956.

Nirenberg, David. *Communities of Violence: Perspective of Minorities in the Middle Ages*. New Jersey: Princeton University Press, 1996.

Nickel, Gordon. *Peaceable Witness among Muslims*. Scottsdale, Pennsylvania: Herald Press, 1999.

Nnoli, Okwudiba. *Ethnic Politics in Nigeria*. Enugu, Nigeria: Fourth Dimension Publishers, 1980.

Nyamiti, Charles. *African Tradition and the Christian God*. Kenya: Gaba Publications, 1975.

_____. *Christ as Our Ancestor: Christology from an African Perspective*. Gweru, Zimbabwe: Mambo Press, 1984.

_____. *African Theology: Its Problems and Methods*. Uganda: Gaba Publications, 1977.

Obi, Cyril I. *The Changing Forms of Identity Politics in Nigeria Under Economic Adjustment*: Nordic Africa Institute, 2000.

Oduyoye, Mercy Amba. "Commonalities: An African Perspective" K.C. Abraham, ed. *Third World Theologies: Commonalities & Divergences*. New York: Orbis Books, 1986.

O'Donovan, Jr. W. *Biblical Christianity in African Perspective*. Carslile, UK: Paternoster Press, 1996.

Olupona, K. Jacob. *Religion and Peace in Multi-Faith Nigeria*. Ibadan: Awolowo University Press, 1992.

Osaghae, E. Eghosa. *The Cripple Giant: Nigeria since Independence*. Bloomington: Indiana University Press, 1998.

Ottenberg, Simon and Phoebe, Ottenberg. *Cultures and Societies of Africa*. New York: Random House, 1960.

Otto, Whitney. *How to Make an American Quilt*. New York: Villard Books, 1991.

Owusu, Maxwell. *Uses and Abuses of Political Power: A Case Study of Continuity and Change in the Politics of Ghana*. Chicago: University of Chicago Press, 1970.

Oyinbo, John. *Nigeria: Crisis and Beyond*. London: C. Knight, 1971.

Paden, John N. Ahmadu Bello. *Sarduna of Sokoto: Values and Leadership in Nigeria*. London, Portsmouth N.H: Hodder and Stoughton, 1986.

Paden, E. William. "Religion" in *Religious Worlds: The Comparative Study and Interpreting the Sacred: Ways of Viewing Religion*. 2006.

Page, H. T. Sydney. *Powers of Evil: A Biblical Study of Satan & Demons*. Grand Rapids: Baker House Company, 1996.

Peachey, T. and Peachey, L. *Seeking Peace*. Pennsylvania: Good Books, Intercourse, 1991.

_____. *Reconciliation International "Non-violence" the African Way*. Netherlands, 1988.

Peters, Ralph. *Beyond Terror: Strategy in Changing World*. Stackpole Books, 2002.

Petersen, Roger D. *Understanding Ethnic Violence: Fear, Hatred, and Resentment in Twentieth-Century Eastern Europe*. Cambridge: Cambridge University Press, 2002.

Pile, Steve. *Geographies of Resistance*. UK: Routledge, 1997.

Pipes, Daniel. *The Long Shadow: Culture and Politics in the Middle East*. Transaction Publishers, 1989.

Polsby, Nelson W. *Community Power and Political Theory*, Yale Studies in Political Science, 7. New Haven: Yale University Press, 1963.

Prunier, Gerard. *The Rwanda Crisis: History of Genocide*. New York: Columbia University Press, 1995.

Qurshin, Emran Sells and Michael A. *The New Crusades: Constructing the Muslim Enemy*. Columbia: Columbia University Press, 2000.

Râegamey, P. R. *Nonviolence and the Christian Conscience.* New York: Herder and Herder, 1966.

Rapport, Anatol. *The Origins of Violence: Approaches to the Study of Conflict.* Transaction Publishers, 1995.

Rasmussen, Larry L. *Earth Community Earth Ethics.* New York: Orbis Books, 2003.

Reienner, Lynne. *Exploring Sub-regional Conflict: Opportunities for Conflict Prevention.* Lynne Reinner Publishers, 2004.

Riddlell, Jean Shackelford, Tom and Stamos, Steve. *Economics: A Tool for Understanding Society,* 2nd ed. California: Addison-Wesley Publishing Company, 1982.

Richards, O. Lawrence. *Expository Dictionary of Bible Words.* Grand Rapids: Zondervan Publishing House, 1985.

Rhoads, David. *The Challenge of Diversity: The Witness of Paul and the Gospels.* Minneapolis: Fortress Press, 1996.

Rohr, Richard. "Fear Itself" in *Sojourners* magazine, October 2004.

Rolston, Holmes. *1 Peter: The Apostle Peter Speaks to Us Today.* Atlanta: John Knox Press, 1977.

Rotherg, Robert I. *Peacekeeping and Peace Enforcement in Africa: Methods of Conflict Prevention.* Brookings Institution Press, 2000.

Rupersinghe, Kumar. *The Culture of Violence.* United Nations University Press, 1994.

Ryrie, Caldwell Charles. *A Survey of Bible Doctrine.* Chicago: Moody Press, 1972.

Sachedina, Abdulaziz. *The Islamic Roots of Democracy Pluralism.* Oxford: Oxford University Press, 2001.

Sandbrook, Richard. *The Politics of African's Economic Recovery.* Cambridge: Cambridge University Press, 1993.

Sanneh, Lamin. *West African Christianity: The Religious Impact.* Maryknoll, New York: Orbis Books, 1994.

Schildgen, Brenda Deen. "Crisis and Continuity: Time in the Gospel of Mark." *Journal for the Study of the New Testament.* Supplement Series 159. Sheffield England: Sheffield Academic Press, 1998.

Schultz, A. Emily, and Lavenda, H. Robert. *Cultural Anthropology: A Perspective on the Human Condition.* St. Paul, New York, Los Angeles and San Francisco: West Publishing Company, 1987.

Scott, Ernest Findlay. *The Ethical Teaching of Jesus.* New York: Macmillan, 1944.

Sharp, Gene. *The Politics of Non-Violent Action: The Power and Struggle.* Boston: Porter S. Publishers, 1984.

Shedd, G. T. William. *A Critical and Doctrinal Commentary upon the Epistle of St. Paul to the Romans.* New York: Charles Scribner's Sons, 1893.

Shenk, Calvin. *Who Do You Say That I Am?: Christians Encounter Other Religions.* Scottsdale Pennsylvania: Herald Press, 1997.

Shenk, David. *Surprises of the Christian Way.* Scottsdale, Pennsylvania: Herald Press, 2000.

Shenk, D. and Kateregga B. *A Muslim and a Christian in Dialogue.* Scottsdale, Pennsylvania: Herald Press, 1997.

Shittu, A. Raheem. *Islam and Christianity: Why the Conflicts.* Shaki, Oyo State: Arowojeka Press, 1979.

Sider, J. Ronald. *Christ and Violence.* Scottsdale, Kitchener: Harold Press, 1970.

_____. "A Tough Call" *PRISM*, Vol. 7, No. 5 September/October 2000.

_____. *Rich Christians in an Age of Hunger: Moving from Affluence to Generosity.* Dallas: Word Publishers, 2000.

_____. *Evangelism and Social Action: Uniting the Church to Heal a Lost and Broken World.* London: Hodder & Stoughton, 1993.

Sider, Ronald J and Knippers, Diane, eds. *Toward An Evangelical Public Policy.* Grand Rapids: Baker Books, 2005.

Sindima, Harvey J. *Religious and Political Ethics in Africa: A Moral Inquiry. Contributions in Afro-American and African Studies*, No. 188. Westport Conn: Greenwood Press, 1998.

Singer, Peter. *The President of Good and Evil: Questioning the Ethics of George W. Bush.* New York: A Plume Book, 2004.

Sklar, Richard L. *Nigerian Political Parties: Power in an Emergent African Nation.* New Jersey: Princeton University Press, 1963.

Smedes, B. Lewis. *Shame and Grace: Healing the Shame We Don't Deserve.* New York: Zondervan Publishing House, 1993.

Smith, Z. Jonathan and Green, Scott William, eds. *The HarperCollins Dictionary of Religion*. San Francisco: HarperCollins Publishers, 1995.

Smith-Christopher, D. *Subverting Hatred: The Challenge of Nonviolence in Religious Traditions*. Boston: Research Center for the 21st Century, 1998.

Sorokin, A. Pitirim. *Man and Society in Calamity: The Effect of War, Revolution, Famine, Pestilence upon Human Mind, Behavior, Social Organization and Cultural Life*. New York: E.P. Dutton and Company, 1942.

Soyinka, Wole. *The Open Sore of a Continent: A Personal Narrative of the Nigerian Crisis*. New York: Oxford University Press, 1996.

Sparks, L. Donald and Williams, Gavin, eds. "The Commonwealth" *Africa South of the Sahara 1998*, 27th Edition, Regional Surveys of the World. London: European Publications Ltd, 1997,

Spohn, C. William. *Go and Do Likewise: Jesus and Ethics*. New York: Continuum, 2000.

Stassen, G. *Just Peacemaking*. Cleveland, Ohio: The Pilgrim Press, 1998.

_____, et al. *Just Peacemaking: Ten Practices for Abolishing War*. Cleveland, Ohio: The Pilgrim Press, 1998.

_____, et al. *Kingdom Ethics: Following Jesus in Contemporary Context*. Downers Grove, Illinois: InterVarsity Press, 2003.

_____. *Journey into Peacemaking*. Memphis, Tennessee: Brotherhood Commission, SBC, 1983, 1987.

_____. *Living the Sermon on the Mount: A Practical Hope for Grace and Deliverance*. Jossey-Bass, 2006.

Stegger, M. and Lind N. *Violence and Its Alternatives*. New York: St. Martin's Press, 1999.

Steinbeck, J. and J. Holder. *Travels with Charley: In Search of America*. London, Folio Society, 2004.

Stilwell, Sean. "Power, Honor and Shame: The Ideology of Royal Slavery in the Sokoto Caliphate" in *Africa* magazine, June 22, 2000.

Stinton, Diane B. *Jesus of Africa: Voices of Contemporary African Christology*. Nairobi: Paulines Publications Africa, 2004.

Storey, Peter. *With God in the Crucible: Preaching Costly Discipleship*. Nashville: Abingdon Press, 2002.

Suberu, Rotimi T. *Federalism and Ethnic Conflict in Nigeria.* Washington D C: United States Institute of Peace Press, 2001.

Swartley, Willard M. *Slavery Sabbath War and Women: Case Issues in Biblical Interpretation.* Scottsdale, Pennsylvania: Herald Press, 1983

Tapkida, G. *Religious Conflict in Jos North Local Government Council.* Thesis, Jos, Nigeria: ECWA Theological Seminary, 1998.

Thatcher, Paul. *Students' Notes on the History of Africa in the 19th and 20th Centuries.* Harlow Essex: Longman, 1981.

Thielman, Frank. *The NIV Application Commentary: Philippians.* Grand Rapids: Zondervan Publishing House, 1995.

Thistlethwaite, Susan. *A Just Peace Church.* New York: United Church Press, 1986.

Thompson, J. Milburn. *Justice and Peace: A Christian Primer.* Maryknoll, New York: Orbis Books, 2003.

Thompson, Henry O. *World Religions in War and Peace.* Jefferson, North Carolina, and London: McFarland & Co., Inc., Publishers, 1988.

Tilly, Charles. *The Politics of Collective Violence.* Cambridge: Cambridge University Press, 2003.

Tisdall, W. Clair. *Christian Reply to Muslim Objective.* Austria: Light of Life, 1980.

Tooley, Michelle. *Voices of the Voiceless: Women, Justice, and Human Rights in Guatemala.* Scottsdale, Pennsylvania: Herald Press, 1997.

Trochne, Andre. *Jesus and the Non-Violent Revolution.* Scottsdale, Kitchener: Harold Press, 1973.

Trull, E. Joe. *Walking in the Way: An Introduction to Christian Ethics.* Nashville, Tennessee: Broadman & Holman Publishers, 1997.

Tucker, A. Ruth. *Another Gospel: Alternative Religions and the New Age Movement.* Grand Rapids: Academie Books, 1989.

Turaki, Yusufu. *The Colonial Legacy in Northern Nigeria.* Jos, Nigeria: Challenge Press, 1993.

_____. "Socio-Political Role and Status of Non-Muslim Groups of Northern Nigeria: Analysis of a Colonial Legacy" (PhD thesis). Boston University 1982.

Tutu, Desmond. *Hope and Suffering*. Grand Rapids: Wm. B. Eerdmans
Publishing Company, 1983.

_____. "The Theology of Liberation in Africa" Kofi Appiah-Kubi and Sergio
Torres, eds. *African Theology En Route*. New York: Orbis Books, 1979.

Twain, Mark, and Warner, Dudley Charles. *The Gilded Age a Tale of to-Day*.
Hartford Chicago, Illinois: American Pub. Co.; F.G. Gilman, 1873.

Twyman, James F. *Praying Peace*. Scotland and Florida: Findhorn Press, 2000.

Umar, F. *Islamic Sects History*. al-Tawzåi: Karmathians, 1999.

Uzokwe, Alfred Obiora. *Surviving in Biafra: The Story of the Nigerian Civil War*.
New York: Writers Advantage, 2003.

Vella, J. *Training Through Dialogue*. San Francisco. California: Jassey-Bass
Inc, 1995.

Viorst, Judith. *Necessary Losses*. New York: A Fireside Book, Published &
Schuster, 1986.

Volf, Miroslav. *Exclusion & Embrace: A Theological Exploration of Identity,
Otherness, and Reconciliation*. Nashville: Abingdon Press, 1996.

_____. and Katerberg, William, eds. *The Future of Hope: Christian Tradition
amid Modernity and Postmodernity*. Grand Rapids: Wm. B. Eerdmans
Publishing Company, 2004.

Wallerstein, Immanuel. *Africa: The Politics of Independence: An Interpretation
of Modern African History*. Vintage Books Vol. 206. New York: Random
House, 1961.

Walter, James. *Ethnic Issues in Paul's Letter to the Romans: Changing Self-
Definitions in Earliest Roman Christianity*. Pennsylvania: Trinity Press
International, 1993.

Walzer, Michael. *Thick and Thin: Moral Argument at Home and Abroad*. Notre
Dame: University of Notre Dame Press, 1994.

_____. *Just and Unjust War: A Moral Argument with Historical Illustrations*.
BasicBooks, HarperCollins Publishers, 1977.

_____. *Interpretation and Social Criticism*. Cambridge, Massachusetts, and
London: Harvard University Press, 1987.

Washington, James Melvin. *A Testament of Hope: The Essential Writings and
Speeches of Martin Luther King, Jr*. New York: HarperSanFrancisco, 1986.

Watts, Michael. *Silent Violence: Food, Famine and Peasantry in Northern Nigeria.*
Berkeley, Los Angeles and London: University of California Press, 1983.

Webber, E. Robert and Clapp, Rodney. *People of the Truth: The Power of the
Worshiping Community in the Modern World.* San Francisco: Harper and
Row, 1988.

West, Cornel. *Race Matters.* New York: Vintage Books, 2001.

Wevers, J. W. "War, the Idea of" *The Interpreter's Dictionary of the Bible*, Vol. 4.
New York: Abingdon Press, 1962.

Wheatcroft, Andrew. *Infidel: A History of the Conflict between Christendom and
Islam.* New York: Random House, 2004.

Whitman, Andrew. *1 Peter: Free to Hope.* Grand Rapids: Baker Books, 1994.

Wink, Walter. *Engaging the Powers: Discernment, and Resistance in a World of
Domination.* Minneapolis: Fortress Press, 1992.

_____. *Naming the Powers: The Language of Power in the New Testament.*
Philadelphia: Fortress Press, 1984.

_____. *Unmasking the Powers: The Invisible Forces that Determine Human
Existence.* Philadelphia: Fortress Press, 1986.

_____. *Peace Is the Way: Writings on Nonviolence from the Fellowship of
Reconciliation.* Maryknoll New York: Orbis Books, 2000.

_____. *The System Belongs to God.* Nashville Tenn: EcuFilm, 1996.

_____. *Cracking the Gnostic Code: The Powers in Gnosticism.* The Society of
Biblical Literature Monograph Series No. 46. Atlanta, Georgia: Scholars
Press, 1993.

Wogaman, Philip. *Christian Moral Judgment.* Westminster John Knox
Press, 1989.

_____. *The Great Economic Debate: An Ethical Analysis.* Philadelphia: The
Westminster Press, 1977.

Wright, N. T. *Jesus and the Victory of God.* Minneapolis: Fortress Press, 1996.

_____. "The Letter to the Romans: Introduction, Commentary, and
Reflection" in *The New Interpreter's Bible*, Vol. 10. Edited by Leander E. Keck
and associates. Nashville: Abingdon Press, 2002.

Wuye, James & Ashafa Muhammad. *The Pastor and the Imam: Responding to
Conflict.* Lagos, Nigeria: Ibrash Press, 1999.

Yoder, John Howard. *The Politics of Jesus:* 2nd Edition. Grand Rapids. Michigan: Publishing Company, 1994.

_____. *Body Politics: Five Practices of the Christian Community before the Watching World.* Scottdale, Pennsylvania: Herald Press, 2001.

Zartman, William. *Traditional Cures for Modern Conflicts: African Conflict "Medicine."* Lynne Reinner Publishers, 2000.

Zehr, Howard. *Changing Lenses.* Scottsdale, Pennsylvania: Herald Press, 1995.

Zoaka, Emmanuel. *Selected New Testament Principles of Conflict Management in the Church.* Nigeria. Kano Publishers, 1989.

No Author. "Faith Based Facilitative Mediation Training for Religious/ Community Leaders of Shendam Local Government Area, Plateau State" organized by Interfaith Mediation Center Kaduna Nigeria supported by United States Institute of Peace (USIP) Washington D. C. July 3–6, 2005.

B.B.C. News Africa: *Country Profile*: Nigeria www.bbc.africannews/nigeria.com.